COLLINS GUIDE TO
MOUNTAINS
AND MOUNTAINEERING

COLLINS GUIDE TO
MOUNTAINS
AND MOUNTAINEERING

JOHN CLEARE

To AAR who first took me to the mountains.
And to my Mother who encouraged me to go.

A *Webb&Bower* book

Edited, designed and produced by
Webb & Bower Limited, Exeter, England
Designed by Vic Giolitto
Maps by Jennifer Johnson
Picture Research by Anne-Marie Ehrlich
© 1979 Webb & Bower Limited

First published by
William Collins Sons & Co. Ltd.,
London. Glasgow. Sydney. Auckland.
        Toronto. Johannesburg

ISBN 0 00 211371 6

Typeset and originated by
C. E. Dawkins Ltd, London.

Printed in Great Britain by
William Clowes and Sons Ltd., Beccles, Suffolk.

Bound by Webb Son & Company,
London and Wales.

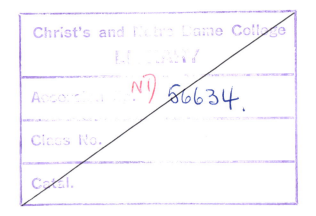
Endpapers: **Pennine Alps from North Face of
Aigulle du Chardonnet**

Half-title **Mount Athabasca,
Canadian Rockies**

Title page: **From left to right
Garwhal, Alexandra—Ruwenzori,
Cathedral Peak—Sierra Nevada, Loch
Coruisk—Skye, Mt Eisenhower—Canadian
Rockies, Half Dome—Yosemite**

Contents

Introduction

'In a hundred ages of the Gods I could not tell thee of the glories of Himachal. As the dew is dried by the morning sun so are the sins of man by the sight of Himachal.'*

(from the Skanda Purana, an ancient Hindu text)

Since first he descended from the trees man has drawn inspiration from the mountains which were always on his horizon. But for thousands of years he kept them at arms length, mindful perhaps that his own evolution had involved climbing down, prefering to gaze at them rather than climb upon them. Only comparatively recently did man overcome this inhibition to invent the 'sport' of mountaineering.

In many countries mountaineering is now a mass sport with all the commercialism and brou-haha that that entails. Uniquely it is a sport that has no rules and, in theory at any rate, no competitors but oneself. (Here I dismiss Soviet competition climbing as mere gymnastics—an isolated phenomena with precious little connection to the adventure in which we indulge.) Mountaineering is a selfish and anarchistic sport and long may it remain so! The competent all-round mountaineer must master a wide range of skills. Besides being a proficient performer on steep rock, ice and mixed ground he must be a useful off-piste skier, an expert back-packer and something of a navigator and survival specialist. He may, of course, pursue one or more of these disciplines as an end in itself. What is important however—and here I quote John Ruskin—is that '. . . these threatening ranges of dark mountains . . . are, in reality, sources of life and happiness far fuller and more beneficient than the bright fruitfulness of the plain.'

Mountains are truly all things to all men and each can find among them that for which he seeks. Thus it is perhaps no surprise that mountaineering boasts the most prolific literature of any sport or pastime. What then of this present book?

In original concept it was to be a practical gazetteer, a guide-book in fact not to individual climbs, not to individual peaks but to the mountain ranges of the world themselves. Personally I consider the present surfeit of guide-books—along with helicopters, huts and cable-cars—to be one of the less desirable manifestations of modern mountaineering, but this book was to be couched on a higher plane and by its very nature it would, I hoped, inform and enthuse rather than direct and specify.

I drew up a list of one hundred 'great' ranges only to realise that, in the context of world mountaineering, many were irrelevant while others were unapproachable, usually for political reasons. Paring the list by over a third I was left with a more practical catalogue containing only ranges worthy of a visit and which can all be reached by the simple expedient of buying an airline ticket.

While I have tried to be reasonably objective, my selections and treatment are bound to reflect something of my own tastes and experiences. For those who would disagree with me, or who would object to the space I have—or have not—allocated to their own favourite mountains, I have no apologies. Mountaineering is all about 'doing one's own thing', a freedom that mountaineering authors also enjoy!

In a book of this nature certain omissions are unavoidable; unfortunately I have had to pass over British Columbia's superb Interior and Coast Ranges, the Chilean and Argentine Andes which include mighty Aconcagua (22,835′/6960m)—the Western Hemisphere's highest summit, the interesting Taurus, Pontine and Elburz ranges of Turkey and Iran and—home ground of a major mountaineering nation—the Japanese Alps, besides several lesser but still significant groups.

Every expedition to a major peak ascends on its predecessor's shoulders and similarly this book owes much to a host of previous publications. Particularly useful sources have been the *Alpine, American Alpine* and *Himalayan* Journals and the many volumes of *Mountain World* besides *Mountain, Summit* and *Ascent* magazines. Among many other invaluable books those by my old friends Ian MacMorrin and Chris Jones—*World*

*Himachal is a Brahman rendering of Himalaya—a Sanscrit word meaning 'Abode of Snow'. An approximate translation would be 'The Snows cradled in a Mother's Arms'.

Atlas of Mountaineering and *Climbing in North America* respectively—have proved indispensible. Useful too have been D. Mordecai's Himalayan tables which have provided the height order numbers prefixing the lists of important Himalayan peaks: while not always accurate—there are, for instance, far more than 568 Himalayan summits topping 20,000 feet—the number does give some indication of a mountain's status. I owe a great debt to all these editors and authors.

I have also lent heavily on many friends, both in Britain and abroad, who have encouraged me and fed me information. Especially must I thank Monty Alfold, Stuart Allan, Rusty Baillie, Arthur Battagel, Hamish Brown, Noel Dilly, Derek Fordham, John Grindley, Ian Howell, Tim Jepson, Joe Kelsey, Leo LeBon, Hamish MacInnes, Bill March, Bill O'Connor, Janusz Onyszkiewicz, Bob Pettigrew, Al Read, Galen Rowell, Doug Scott, Peter Steele, Jim Stuart, Lance Tickell, John Tyson and Derek Walker. All have spent valuable time reading, criticizing, correcting and suggesting improvements to the manuscripts covering the areas in which they are local experts. To them my special gratitude.

Others too have made crucial contributions: Anne-Marie Ehrlich—my ever-patient picture researcher, 'Goldie Johnson'—my hard-pressed cartographer, Pat Johnson—the ever-helpful Alpine Club librarian and Audrey Salkeld, who besides tying up the loose ends contributed so much to the research. And last but by no means least the photographers—they are individually acknowledged elsewhere. Without any of these the project would have been impossible.

Finally I would like to hope that this book, besides informing and enthusing—and perhaps even entertaining—both the active and the arm-chair mountaineer, might encourage climbers in their search for pastures new. The days of the great virgin peaks are unfortunately over but in an age of cheap air-travel and high wages the world is more an oyster than it has ever been. Personally I have discovered more enjoyment on small Himalayan summits than I have ever found on over-populated Alpine classics and as much excitement locating uncrossed passes between unknown valleys (they still exist!) as I have on any summit. But such adventures are best kept to oneself or shared only among close friends: only thus can every ascent be a 'first' and every valley remain 'unexplored'. Meanwhile this book may suggest where such adventure might be found, and if it does so then it will have succeeded. I am particularly fond of a quote from Albert Mummery, the greatest mountaineer of his day, who disappeared high on Nanga Parbat in 1895:

'The true mountaineer is a wanderer' he wrote '. . . a man who loves to be where no human being has been before, who delights in gripping rocks that have previously never felt the touch of human fingers, or in hewing his way up ice-filled gullies whose grim shadows have been sacred to the mists and avalanches since earth rose out of chaos . . . whether he succeeds or fails he delights in the fun and jollity of the struggle. The gaunt bare slabs, the square precipitous steps in the ridge and the black bulging ice in the gully are the very breath of life to his being . . .'

Himalchuli Base Camp. November 1978.

AUTHOR'S NOTE: Throughout the text I have noted heights and distances in both Imperial and Metric renderings. Obviously a mountain's height is a pretty exact measurement, and the feet have been converted exactly to metres—and vice versa. The height of a crag or a climb however is always an approximation and is thus expressed—in feet—as a round number. This has usually been translated exactly into metres, although such exactness is, strictly speaking, incorrect in its very accuracy.

▲ Peaks in data list

▲ Other important peaks

⊔ Passes

○ Cities Towns Village Hamlet

■ Huts Bivouacs

⌒ Cave Rock shelter

Ⓐ Airstrip Airfield

▰ Motorways Freeways

═ Roads

▬ Railways

---- Well frequented trails

Key to symbols used on maps

7

Mountain Structure

To move easily among mountains it is useful to understand something of their structure and foundation.

This is a hypothetical mountainscape: it illustrates many of the features common to mountains the world over – most of which are, or have been at one time, glaciated to a greater or lesser extent.

In the foreground is a cwm or corrie, typical of so many found in the British Isles. The words are, in fact, Welsh and Gaelic respectively. The ice has long since disappeared and the cwm contains many of the features familiar to the rock-climber which are also found, of course, on larger snowy mountains.

Beyond, to the right, is a glacial *cirque*. The word is French, as are so many of the terms used for features among icy mountains. A *cirque* is another name for a cwm but the term is more often used in alpine areas and the typical features are those well known to the alpinist.

Further left are large snow and ice peaks whose features tend to be more Himalayan but are, of course, only accentuated examples of those found on smaller mountains.

cornice
glacier terrace
summit ice-field
rockstep
ice-plateau
rockband
rognon
col
head wall
bergschrund
névé
ice-fall
crevasses
tor
crackline
pinnacle
buttress
gully
Buttress
roof
pillar
rake
niche
slab
wall
diédre
ledge
overhang
scree shoot
crag
glacis
talus or scree
perche
tarn
cho

summit ridge
summit
shoulder
rock tower
gendarme
flutings
rock peaks
aiguille
gendarme
breche
rib
rock arête
couloir
serac
cornices
serac band
ice-wall
ice arête
snow arête
avalanche runnels
spur
couloir
avalanche cone
cirque
crevasses
névé basin
ice-fall
snow-field
ice-fall
seracs
penitentes
medial moraine
truncated spur
nney
amphitheatre
erratic block
crevasses
glacier tables
dry glacier
moulin
moraine lake
lateral moraine
snout

9

European Alps

The peaks of the Pennine Alps,
seen from the Aiguille du Chardonnet
(Mont Blanc Range)

Opposite: **Above Verbier, Switzerland, looking
across the clouds to the Gran
Paradiso group in Italy**

South West Alps

The great chain of the Alps rises from the Mediterranean behind Monaco and wriggles northwards for 150 miles (241km) until it reaches the Mont Blanc Massif at the Col de la Seigne and swings eastwards. From the frontier crest the mountains fall steeply on the one hand to the flat Piedmont plains and the Po, but on the other they continue as a series of high massifs deep into France before falling away slowly to the Rhône some 90 miles (145km) distant. Only in the far north do the mountains—the Eastern Graians—intrude far into Italy.

The southernmost massif is the Maritime Alps whose highest summit is only 30 miles (48km) from the sea: indeed the climate, and some of the valley vegetation, is sub-tropical and the weather is known as the most stable in the Alps. Small and rugged rock-peaks, usually of gneiss, rise from boulder-filled cwms, great scree-fields and rock-strewn pastures noted for their spring flowers. In summer, snow lingers only in the higher and most sheltered recesses and there are several tiny dry glaciers on the northern flanks.

The region is known for its rock-climbing and the best is concentrated in the relatively small area around the highest peaks: the Argentera itself gives an excellent traverse along its several spiky tops and has a splendid 2,000ft (609m) South Ridge. Its tremendous West Face gives several climbs of up to 3,500ft (1,067m)! There are other fine routes on the curious Corno Sella—a difficult peak even by its easiest way—and on the adjoining jagged ridge of the Guides Chain. A famous classic is the long West Ridge of Mont Ponset (9,268ft/2,825m) with its four big gendarmes.

Northward the Cottian Alps are little-known to other than local climbers and, although there are several small glaciers, the scenery is generally unexciting. Monte Viso, however, is famous for its isolated pyramid which is a feature of the view from the Pennine Alps far to the north. On its East Face is an interesting route by Guido Rey. It is the Cottian's only 12,000ft (3,657m) summit, although there are a further eight above 11,000ft (3,353m).

The Dauphiné is also known as the Massif du Pelvoux or des Écrins and is one of the more important groups in the Alps. Entirely within France, it is a compact yet complex region of large upstanding peaks, often characterized by long summit ridges and well covered by glaciers, ice and snow. Below the peaks are barren hillsides and long stony val-

leys and the whole area has a desolate wilderness flavour. The valleys radiate from Les Bans (12,037ft/3,669m) at the hub of the range and no less than twenty-three peaks rise above 12,000ft (3,657m).

The Dauphiné is noted for its fine rock-climbs on large peaks with a real 'high-mountain' atmosphere, and it does lack the commercialisation of the higher Western Alps. The most interesting

peak is the Meije: Coolidge attempted it in 1870, but was unable to reach the Grand Pic, the highest top. Its comb-like summit crest, first traversed by the brothers Zsigmondy with Purtscheller in 1891, was further complicated in 1964 by the collapse of the Brèche Zsigmondy and is still not easy. It is a major alpine classic. Pierre Allain made a fine route up the 2,500ft (762m) summit buttress of

the South Face in 1934. A feature of the great Ailefroide, too, is a long summit ridge—a fine traverse made by Graham Brown in 1933—but the mountain is known for its huge rectangular North-West Face, a maze of gullies and ribs up which Gervasutti and Devies forced a

Since the war the great North Wall of the Ailefroide and the adjoining Pic Sans Nom (12,841/3,914) has seen much development. It has been compared in size and grandeur to the Argentière Wall but it is largely rock and holds hard modern routes both on rock and mixed ground besides some ice climbs in the couloirs. Especially notable is the George/Russenberger Route, 3,300ft (1,000m) of sustained grade V rock. Elsewhere the Olan North Face is also highly sought after. The Dauphiné is a popular region with British parties.

There are many subsidiary ranges to the west, the Grandes Rousses, the Aiguilles d'Arves, the Belledonne, the Chartreuse and others. Several small glaciers adorn the peaks and there is a wealth of good rock-climbing on steep limestone walls. Best known is the Vercors massif (7,697ft/2,346m) which includes the incredible mesa of Mont Aiguille (6,880ft/2,097m) whose ascent —using aid—by Antoine de Ville in 1942 is held to be the first alpine rock climb!

The Tarentaise is an area of outstanding beauty: it is entirely within France and most of it is now part of the Vanoise National Park. The principal peaks hold heavy glaciation and rise from lower ground in isolated groups offering a variety of splendid easy snow-climbs. The best ice-route is the straightforward 2,700ft (823m) North Face Direct on the

Col de la Seigne

Alberville

Petit St. Bernard

AOSTE

Cogne

Grivola

Herbetet

Apostoli

Gran Paradiso

Torre del Gran San Pedro

Mont Pourri

Ciarfon

Val d'Isere

Tribolazione

Massif du Grand Paradis

Col de l'Iseran

EASTERN GRAIANS

Grande Casse

Pralognan la Vanoise

Aiguille de la Vanoise

Chasseforêt

Ciamarella

Besanese

WESTERN and CENTRAL GRAIANS

Pointe de Charbonnel

Col. du Mt Cenis

Rochemelon

GRENOBLE

Chain de Belledonne

Massif des Grandes Rousses

SUZE

L'Assiette

TURIN

Chain de

Col du Galibier

La Grave

Col du Lautaret

La Meije

Glacier Blanc

Barre des Écrins

La Bérade

Ailefroide

Mont Pelvoux

Glacier Noir

Les Bans

VERCORS

DAUPHINÉ

Briançon

Col de Montgenèvre

ALPS

Crissolo

Monte Viso

COTTIAN

ITALY

Massif de Champsaur

GAP

FRANCE

CUNEO

Col de Larche

Barcelonnette

MARITIME

St Etienne de Tinée

Corno Sella

Punta del'Argentera

Col de Tende

Mont Ponset

0   15   30
Kilometres
0   10   20
Miles

Saint Martin de Vésubie

ALPS

Grande Casse. Many of the smaller peaks give excellent rock-routes among which the two superb and very difficult lines on the North Face of the Aiguille de la Vanoise—a great rock-blade—are classic.

There is good easy climbing also in the relatively unfrequented Central Graians. The main frontier chain is well glaciated and the area is attractive. The most interesting mountains are the aloof Uia di Ciamarella (12,000ft/3,676m) with its lovely 1,300ft (396m) northern ice-face and the 'Matterhorn of Maurienee'—the 11,801ft (3,597m) Bessanese which boasts a fine rock-traverse. Nearby Rochemelon (11,608ft/3,538m) is an easy climb, but has the distinction of a first ascent in 1358 by the knight Rotario d'Asti!

The Eastern Graians, lying entirely in Italy—of which country the Paradiso is the highest complete mountain—are still fairly unspoilt. The peaks are a series of impressive shark-fins, heavily glaciated and looking out across the deep Val d'Aosta straight towards the Pennine Alps and Mont Blanc. Twenty of them rise above 11,500ft (3,505m). The region is a National Park, a former hunting preserve of Italian kings, and a particular charm is its wealth of flora and fauna: large numbers of chamois, steinbock and other creatures roam freely throughout the mountains.

The speciality of the massif is its snow-and-ice-climbing, although there is some good climbing on fair gneiss or schist also. The popular West Flank of the Gran Paradiso itself is a very easy climb but the sweeping ice of the North-West Face gives several superb 2,000ft (609m) lines as fine as any of their kind in the Alps. The best 'expedition' in the massif is the traverse from the Gran over the Piccolo Paradiso to the huge rock pyramid of the Herbetet, an extremely long, and not easy, mixed route pioneered by Captain Farrar in 1898. Seamed with huge parallel *dièdres*, the great eastern rock-face of the Grivola appears most formidable, but it is not steep and holds an easy climb: a better route is the elegant North Ridge, a fairly straightforward ice-*arête*. The northern ice-face of the Ciarforon (11,949ft/3,642m) has a good reputation and is quite hard, and there are several good rock-climbs on the sawtooth ridge of the Apostoli to the eastern end of the massif. The area is often visited as a bad-weather alternative to the Mont Blanc Range close, by, but its beautiful peaks and fine climbs are worthy in their own right.

Maritime Alps
Situation: France Basses—Alpes and Alpes—Maritimes Départements
1 Punta del'Argentera (10,817/3,297) 1879: W. Coolidge with C. Almer and Son
7 Corno Sella (10,007/3,050) 1903: V. de Cessole and party
Huts and Bivouacs Some twenty-six CAF and CAI
Convenient Centre St Martin Vesubie—small resort town
Guide-book: *Maritime Alps*, West Col (UK)

Cottian Alps
Situation: France Hautes-Alpes Département; Italy—Piedmont Province
1 Monte Viso (12,602/3,841) 1861: W. Mathews, W. Jacomb with M and J Croz
Huts and Bivouacs Some nine, CAF and CAI
Convenient Centre Crissolo—small village

Dauphiné
Situation: France Isere and Hautes-Alpes Départements
1 Barre des Écrins (13,455/4,101) 1864: E. Whymper, A. Moore and H. Walker with C. Almer and M. Groz
2 La Meije (13,068/3,983) 1877: E. B. de Castelnan with P. Gaspard and son
3 Ailefroide (12,972/3,954) 1870: W. Coolidge, C. Almer and party
4 Mont Pelvoux (12,946/3,946) 1848: V. Puiseux with P-A Barnéoud
L'Olan (11,690/3,563) 1875:

Major Glaciers
Glacier Blanc system—4.6 miles (7½km)
Glacier Noir system—3.7 miles (6km)
Huts and Bivouacs Some thirty-seven mostly owned by CAF and some private
Convenient Centres: La Grave—a small resort but with all facilities
La Berade—an unspoilt hamlet catering for climbers
Ailefroide—a small unspoilt hamlet with basic facilities
Guide-books *Selected Climbs in the Dauphiné and Vercors*, Alpine Club (London)

Western and Central Graians
(Tarentaise and Maurienne)
Situation: France Savoie Département; Italy Piedmont Province
1 Grande Casse (12,638/3,852) 1860: W. Mathews with M. Croz and E. Fvre
2 Mont Pourri (12,398/3,779) 1861: M. Croz—solo
3 Pointe de Charbonnel (12,303/3,750) 1862: M. Boniface and party
4 Aiguille de la Vanoise (9,154/2,790)

Major Glacier
Chasseforet snow-fields system—7 × 3 miles (11 × 5km)
Huts and Bivouacs Some twenty-six mostly CAF
Convenient Centres Pralognan la Vanoise, Val d'Isère—both are resort villages
Guide-book *Graians West*, West Col (UK)

Eastern Graians (Cogne Massif)
Situation: Italy Val d'Aosta Region
1 Gran Paradiso (13,323/4,061) 1860: J. Cowell and W. Dundas with J. Tairraz and M. Payot
2 Grivola (13,022/3,969) 1859: J. Ormsby and R. Bruce with J. Tairraz, etc

3 Herbetet (12,395/3,778) 1873: L. Barale with A. and G. Castagneri

Major Glacier
Tribolazione ice-fields—2 × 1.5 miles (3 × 2km)
Huts and Bivouacs More than eleven, mostly CAI or National Park
Convenient Centre Cogne—small resort
Guide-book *Graians East*, West Col (UK)

Major Passes
Petit St Bernard (7,178/2,188) historic international main road-pass over watershed
Col due Mt Cenis (6,834/2,083) international arterial road-pass across watershed
Col de Montgenèvre (6,083/1,854) international road-pass across watershed
Col de Larche (6,555/1,998) international main road-pass over watershed
Col de Tende (6,135/1,870) international road- and rail-pass with tunnelled summit over watershed
Col de l'Iseran★(9,085/2,769) north to south—highest road-pass in Alps
Col du Lautaret★ (6,752/2,058) east to west
Col du Galibier★ (8,678/2,645) north to south
★ minor road passes within France but between mountain groups

Access
The western flanks of the South-West Alps are easily reached by road (bus services to all resorts) via Nice, (international airport), Gap (railway to Briançon) or Grenoble (rail to Mondane and on to Turin);
The eastern (Italian) flank can be reached via Turin (major airport) to Cuneo (railway) or Susa (on the Grenoble line) and the East Graians by rail to Aosta. By road there are good approaches via the Mont Blanc tunnel

Maps
For most of the South-West Alps the French IGN 1:50,000 and 1:100,000 maps are available. IGN publish a good 1:25,000 series of the Maritimes of which there is also a good 1:50,000 *Kammkarte* by Paschetta (Nice). Of the Eastern Graians there is the Austrian *Kompass* series at 1:50,000 and the Italian Military Survey 1:100,000 maps

Guide-books
A comprehensive series of guide-books, other than those published in English detailed above, are published by the CAF, the FFM, the CAI and by Rudolf Rother (Munich) in their respective languages

15

Mont Blanc

To the mountaineer the massif of Mont Blanc is the most important single range in the Alps. The great snow dome of Mont Blanc itself, the highest point in Europe west of the Caucasus, is surrounded by avenues of spectacular and jagged lesser peaks, some high and some small, but all claiming the attention of alpinists the world over.

The range runs south-west to north-east along the main watershed of the Western Alps—that between the Rhône and Po—and thus forms the frontier between France and Italy although the north-east corner lies in Switzerland: the three countries meet on Mont Dolent. It is surprisingly compact for an area containing so many fine peaks and it is encompassed by the famous 'seven valleys'—the two most important of which, that of the Arve to the north west and the Doire to the south east, are deep trenches a mere 8 miles (13km) apart. Between them rises Mont Blanc presenting a steep and mighty face of rock and ice—an 11,000ft (3,352m) flank of Himalayan scale and grandeur—to Italy and a less steep but even higher 12,500ft; (3,810m) ice-draped flank to France. Elsewhere in the range the frontier peaks tend to rise from Italy as steep and rocky walls holding small hanging glaciers, while on the French side longer valley glaciers descend, separating lengthy ridges of extraordinary aiguilles. The most famous of these glaciers—indeed the most famous in the Alps—is the Mer de Glace–Géant system whose upper basin forms the strategic hub of the range.

Politically Mont Blanc lay in Savoy until 1860 when the present frontiers were drawn, and French is spoken throughout the area, though as patois on the Italian side. Chamonix, a bustling and vulgar town, and the most important mountain resort in France, is now linked by a 6-mile (9½km) road tunnel to Courmayeur on the Italian side, which draws the two valleys even closer together: it has certainly made life easier for the alpinist. Superb mountains and easy access have confirmed the range as the tourist mecca of the Alps both in summer and winter and the resulting development, with its commercial manifestations, has changed the whole character of the area for the worse. The excellent high-altitude cable-car facilities, while fine for skiing, have unfortunately made public the inner recesses of the mountains and many consider that the *téléphérique* link from the Aiguille du Midi in France to the Col du Géant in Italy—

technical marvel though it is—has ruined the remote inner sanctum of the Géant Glacier, perhaps the finest glacier *cirque* in Europe, over which it passes. Such is progress!

Because technical standards in the range have always been as high or higher than elsewhere, and because it has been here that nearly every great alpinist has earned his title, it must suffice to mention only a few of the important achievements in the complex and prolific climbing history of the massif.

Appropriately Mont Blanc, probably because its icy summit is tantilizingly visible from Geneva, was the first major alpine peak to be ascended. The story of that climb, in 1786, by Dr Paccard and Jacques Balmat, to claim the reward offered by the Geneva scientist, de Saussure, is well documented. Soon a

The Aiguille Verte is seen from the Géant Ice-Fall to the south west. On the left are the Petit and Grand Dru, on which the standard routes ascend the southern flanks, seen here above the little hanging Charpoua Glacier. The prominent gendarme is the Pic Sans Nom. At the centre is the black pyramid of the Aiguille du Moine, noted for its rock-climbing. On the right Les Droites rises above the snowy expanse of the Taléfre Glacier

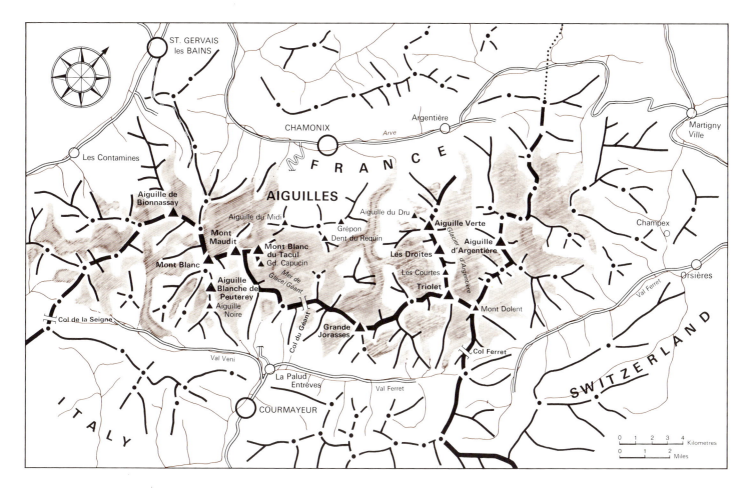

steady stream of adventurers were climbing the mountain, but only one other summit in the range, and that a minor one, was ascended before the dawn of the 'Golden Age' in 1855, when Kennedy, Hudson and their party reached the summit of Mont Blanc du Tacul. It was to be another thirty-three years before the last of the thirty-two separate peaks above 12,000ft (3,657m) had been climbed—twenty-five of them claimed by British parties. Especially active during the Golden Age was Edward Whymper who—with various combinations of his guides, the great Croz, Payot, Charlet, Almer or Biner— ascended the Aiguille d'Argentière in 1864 and Mont Dolent, the Aiguille Verte and the second summit—the Point Whymper—of the formidable Grandes Jorrases in 1865. That year too, Mathews, Moore and the Walker brothers discovered the 'Old Brenva', the first route on the Italian side of Mont Blanc, still a popular yet fairly serious *grande course* and well ahead of its time.

The proliferation of secondary summits and difficult rock-spires was to give scope for the ascent of virgin summits for almost another century and great rock-climbs soon became an important characteristic of the range. Clinton Dent's

ascent of the Grand Dru in 1878, that of the Grépon by Mummery's party in 1881 and the innovative guideless ascent of the Requin by Mummery, Collie, Hastings and Slingsby in 1893, were milestones.

The greatest achievements, however, prior to 1914, were on Mont Blanc itself. In 1877 Eccles, with the Payots, made a remarkable journey over the South Face of the mountain, across the Brouillard and Freney glaciers, finally reaching the summit by way of the Peuterey Arête; Klucker's party added the approach over the Aiguille Blanche in 1893 to produce one of the classic routes of the Alps. Finally with the addition, in 1935, of the traverse of the Aiguille Noire the 'Peuterey Integrale' has become the longest and arguably the finest route in the Alps. It is rarely completed. Mention should also be made of the fine climbs pioneered by the Gugliermina brothers in 1901 and Geoffrey Winthrop Young's party in 1911 on the great Brouillard Ridge.

Since 1918 there has been a never-ending succession of 'last great problems'—initially obvious ones, but of recent years more and more devious. First there was the tangled ice of Mont Blanc's huge Brenva Face, a problem solved by Graham Brown and Frank

Smythe with their Red Sentinel route in 1927 and their Route Major in 1928. Graham Brown went on to discover the still formidable Pear route in 1933. Then, in 1935, Pierre Allain forced the difficult rock of the Dru North Face and the same year Peters and Meier cracked the intimidating North Face of the Grandes Jorasses by the Croz Spur. Cassin added the classic Walker Spur route, direct to the highest point of the Jorasses in 1938. The Dru and the Walker have become two of the 'great six' north faces but, on a good day, there may be as many as thirty parties on the latter climb. Such is modern alpinism!

After 1945 alpinism became really competitive and nowhere more so than in the Mont Blanc Range. Hitherto inviolate rock-walls such as the East Face of the Grand Capucin and the Dru's 2,000ft (609m) West Face fell to determined attacks using full aid techniques, the former to Bonatti and Ghigo over four days in 1951 and the latter to the seige tactics of Magnone's team over eight days the following year. Bonatti went on to solo the South-West Pillar of the Dru, now a largely free climb, in a six-day epic in 1955. Modern technical standards are so high that these climbs are now repeated many dozens of times each year!

The same determination, applied to high and 'mixed' ground, led to the 1957 ascent of the Eckpfeiler—a formidable buttress high on the South-East Face of Mont Blanc—by Bonatti and Gobbi and to the ascent, amid fierce competition, of the remote and beautiful Central Pillar of Freney, again high on Mont Blanc, by Whillans, Bonington, Clough and Dlugosz in 1961. New developments in ice-climbing equipment and techniques paved the way for new lines on steep ice and routes proliferate today on such intimidating walls as the Shroud of the Grandes Jorasses, the northern faces of Droites, Courtes and Triolet, on the Eckpfeiler and in the ice-hung recesses of such places as the North Couloir of the Dru. Aggressive climbing, the spur of competition, and the possibility of a helicopter rescue from literally anywhere should things go wrong, have ensured that new climbs, first solo ascents and first winter ascents still happen with monotonous frequency. Climbing in the Mont Blanc Range is unlike that anywhere else in the Alps!

Nevertheless, the range holds enormous attraction for the ordinary alpinist in the quantity, quality, character and choice of its more than 2,000 climbs, particularly those on rock, even if it is a little overcrowded in season. The rock is an excellent and firm granite, usually seamed with crack lines, giving climbing that is often strenuous, or as the French say *athlétique*. Certainly the best climbs in the Mont Blanc Massif are among the best—and the most famous—in the world.

Seen from high on the East Ridge of the Aiguille du Plan, the North Face of the Grandes Jorasses rises over the gendarmes of Les Périades. Between the Jorasses and the Dent du Géant, on the far right, lies the classic Rochefort Ridge

Seen from the Aiguille du Moine, Mont Blanc dominates the Géant Glacier. On the left is the Dent du Géant and on the right the Chamonix Aiguilles, culminating in the Aiguille du Plan

Situation: France—Département de Haute-Savoie; Italy—Val d'Aosta Autonomous region; Switzerland— Canton Valais

Most Important Peaks
1 Mont Blanc (15,771/4,807) 1786; Dr M. G. Paccard with Jacques Balmat
2 Mont Maudit (14,649/4,465) 1878: W. Davidson, H. Seymour Hoare with J. Jaun and J. von Bergen
3 Mont Blanc du Tacul (13,937/4,248) 1855: T. Kennedy, C. Hudson and party
4 Grandes Jorasses (13,806/4,208) 1868: H. Walker with M. Anderegg, J. Jaun, etc
5 Aiguille Verte (13,524/4,122) 1865: E. Whymper with C. Almer and F. Biner
6 Aiguille Blanche de Peuterey (13,474/4,107) 1885: H. Seymour King with Emile Ray, etc
7 Aiguille de Bionnassay (13,294/4,052) 1865: E. Buxton, F. Grove, R. Macdonald with J.-P. Cachet and M. Payot
11 Les Droites (13,123/4,000) 1876: W. Coolidge with C. Almer *père et fils*
13 Aiguille d'Argentière (12,795/3,900) 1864: E. Whymper, A. Adams Reilly with M. Croz, M. Payot and H. Charlet
14 Aiguille de Triolet (12,697/3,870) 1874: J. Marshall with U. Almer and J. Fischer

Major Passes
(East to west in order)
Col Ferret (8,323/2,537) a mule-track and theoretically the eastern extremity of the Mont Blanc Massif

Fenêtre de Saleina (10,705/3,263) an easy glacier-pass
Col du Géant (11,040/3,365) one of the most famous glacier-passes in the Alps, easy on foot. Although there are ice-fall problems lower down in France, it can now be crossed by *téléphérique*
Col de la Seigne (8,241/2,512) a mule-track and the theoretical southern extremity of the range

Longest Glacier
Mer de Glace—Géant system—7½ miles (12km)

Major Centres
French
Chamonix—also a ski resort
Argentière—terminus of Grands Montets *téléphérique*
St Gervais les Bains—terminus of Mont Blanc tramway
Les Contamines

Italian
Courmayeur—also a ski resort

Swiss
Champex—small lakeside resort

Huts and Bivouacs
More than forty, mostly belonging to the French and Italian Alpine Clubs

Access
By air
There are international airports at Geneva and Turin and a helicopter base in Chamonix. Light aircraft and helicopters can be chartered from the Aerodrome de Passy to Mont Blanc near St Gervais

By rail
Regular express service from Paris to Chamonix. Local service from Geneva via La Roche and from Lausanne via Martigny and the little Col des Montets line
Express service from Turin to Pré St Didier near Courmayeur

By road
Good roads virtually encircle the range and there is a direct toll tunnel under Mont Blanc linking Chamonix to Courmayeur

Maps
The best maps are the official French IGN *Carte Touristique* at 1:25,000 scale in two sheets, available in France or at specialist stores in Britain

Guide-books
Every climb is well documented. The French *Guide Vallot*, published by Arthaud for the Groupe de Haute Montagne, in 3 volumes, is the definitive work
Selected Climbs in the Mont Blanc Range, in 3 volumes, published by the Alpine Club (London)
Numerous magazines, notably *Mountain* (UK) and *Alpinisme* (France) publish details of new developments
Chamonix Mont Blanc—a general guide, Constable (London)

Pennine Alps

The Pennines contain the greatest concentration of high mountains in Europe, west of the Don, among them no less than ten of the twelve highest summits in the Alps. Generally the peaks are aloof and alone, and often classical in shape: indeed the silhouette of the famous Matterhorn is familiar everywhere. Perhaps it is fitting that the greatest wall in the Alps is the ice-hung East Face of Monte Rosa and it is no surprise that Zermatt, the village at the foot of the Matterhorn, is the most famous mountain resort in the world.

The range is a frontier, not only between Switzerland and Italy, but also between central and southern Europe—hence the unsettled local weather on the frontier peaks. Its crest, a main watershed between the Rhône and the Po, is consistently high and, except near both extremities, is crossed by only a few high glacier passes. Most of the high peaks cluster around the Zermatt valley, while to the west the peaks are lower and more remote, except for the final icy bastion—the huge massif of the Grand Combin.

A feature of the Pennines is the long narrow valleys, running right up to the frontier ridge from north and south, between which the mountain barrier has never prevented intercourse. In medieval times cattle were traded across the glaciers of the Col Collon (10,226ft/3,116m), between the Val D'Herens and the Val Pelline, and Roman coins have been found on the Theodule (10,883ft/3,317m).

Ethnically the area is complex: French is spoken on the northern side, westward from the Val d'Anniviers, and Swiss-German from the Visptal eastwards. In the southern valleys the native tongue is Valdotain—a French-based patois, while, in the south-eastern valleys of Monte Rosa, an Italianized form of Swiss-German is spoken. Some years ago the author was surprised to hear a local woman in a village store using French, German and Italian in one and the same sentence! Each valley has its own folk customs and it is still possible to tell apart the inhabitants of each by their distinctive Sunday costumes.

The main industry today is tourism: thanks to altitude, excellent communications and superb facilities, several of the ski resorts are of world class. But the rock beneath the peaks is riddled by tunnels of the Grand Dixence hydroelectric scheme, a complex of catchments and dams completed in the mid-sixties and harnessing the waters of almost every glacier on the Swiss side.

The 1855 ascent of the Dufourspitze, at the dawn of the so-called 'Golden Age', was the start of serious mountaineering in the range, although several of Monte Rosa's other ten summits had been reached during the previous fifty years. In the ensuing decade every important Pennine peak was climbed, no less than twenty-four of the thirty-three over 12,000ft (3,600m) by British parties. The last great virgin peak in the

A winter view from the Plateau Rosa above the Theodul Pass. Left to right: the Matterhorn, with the Italian Ridge on the left skyline; the Dent Blanche, Obergabelhorn, Zinal Rothorn and Weisshorn, with the East Ridge – the standard route – on the far right

Alps was the Matterhorn and the epic story of its final conquest in 1865—and the tragic accident on the descent—is well known.

The next fifty years have been called the 'High Summer' of alpinism. No longer were climbers searching for the easiest way to the top. Notable milestones were the ascents of the Matterhorn's Zmutt Ridge and the Taschhorn's Teufelsgrat by A. F. Mummery—the greatest mountaineer of his era—in 1879 and 1887; J. Stafford Anderson's climb on the 'Four Asses Ridge'—the Viereeselgrat of the Dent Blanche in 1882, and Broome's Weisshorn ascent via the lovely Shaligrat in 1895. Two teams dominated the opening of the new century: Captain V. J. Ryan with his guides, the Lochmatter brothers, and Geoffrey Winthrop Young, climbing usually with Josef Knubel. In 1906 Ryan climbed the superb East Arête of the Dent d'Hérens—one of the longest ridges in the Alps—and the mysterious Santa Caterinagrat on Nordend—unrepeated for seventeen years. The same year he joined forces with Young to tackle the extremely formidable and still rarely climbed Taschhorn South Face—a climb many years ahead of its time. Young went on to discover the Breithorn's classic Younggrat and later to ascend all three faces of the beautiful Weisshorn. By 1914 only the most intimidating lines were left.

Five great achievements stand out over the next thirty years. One is Willo Welzenbach's ascent of the North Face of the Dent d'Hérens—a long and difficult ice-wall. Another was the climbing of the last great ridge—the North Ridge of the Dent Blanche—pioneered by Mr and Mrs I. A. Richards with their guides, the Georges, in 1928. Finest of all was the forcing of the Matterhorn North Face—loose, dangerous and spectacular—by the young Schmid brothers from Munich in 1931. That same year Lagarde and Devies found their superb line up the North East Face of Monte Rosa's Signalkuppe. Finally, in 1945, André Roch climbed the Pennine's only great rock-wall—the East Face of the Zinal Rothorn.

With the questionable exception of certain fine, but 'alternative' lines, it would be fair to say that there have been no important new climbs among the great Pennine peaks since 1945. There are no 'last great problems'—unlike the Mont Blanc range—and the emphasis now is on winter ascents and new lines on minor or outlying peaks.

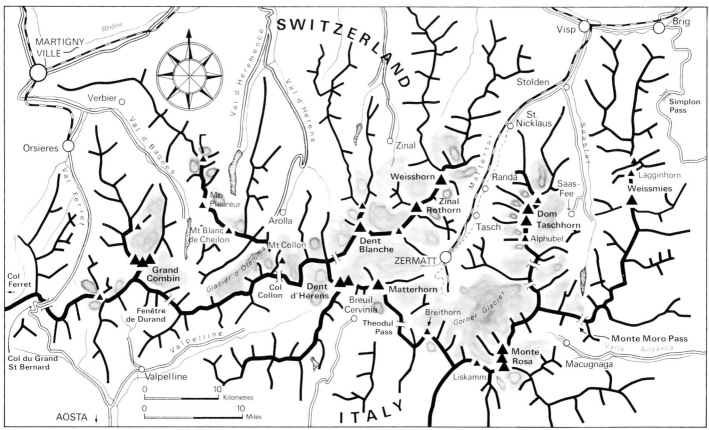

In winter the geography of the range favours ski-mountaineering and ski-touring. The Haute Route—the 80 mile (128km) ski-traverse from Chamonix which zigzags from pass to pass and hut to hut along the Pennine crest to Zermatt and Saas-Fee—is probably the finest ski-tour in Europe. Even in summer skiing is popular on the glaciers near the Theodule Pass.

Today the Pennines are the mecca of the classic-style mountaineer. Typically the climbs are old and on mixed ground: they are still long and tough and serious, if rarely technically difficult by modern standards. The quality of the rock is often dubious and there are few important rock-climbs. It is easy to understand why competitive climbing and the scramble for new routes plays no part in the Pennine scene. Repeat ascents of the great ice and mixed faces—those climbed between the wars—do attract top alpinists, however. Such routes have lost none of their aura and belong to any list of the Alps' top climbs—as indeed the great Pennine ridges belong to any list of the best alpine climbs.

Situation: Switzerland—Canton Valais; Italy—Val d'Aosta Autonomous Region and Piemonte

Most Important Peaks
1 Monte Rosa—Dufourspitze (15,203/4,633) 1855: J. and C. Smyth and E. Stephenson with J. and M. Zumtaugwald, etc

2 Dom (14,911/4,544) 1858: J. Davies with J. Zumtaugwald, etc
4 Weisshorn (14,780/4,504) 1861: J. Tyndall with J. Bennen, etc
5 Taschhorn (14,734/4,490) 1862: J. Davies and J. Hayward with J. and S. Zumtaugwald, etc
6 Matterhorn (14,688/4,476) 1865: E. Whymper, C. Hudson, D. Hadow, F. Douglas with M. Croz and P. Taugwalder *père* and *fils*
7 Dent Blanche (14,295/4,357) 1862: T. Kennedy and W. Wigram with J. Croz and J. Konig
9 Grand Combin (14,154/4,314) 1859: C. Deville with the Balleys and B. Dorsaz
12 Zinal Rothorn (13,848/4,220) 1864: L. Stephen and F. Grove with M. and J. Andregg
17 Dent d'Hérens (13,684/4,170) 1863: W. Hall, F. Grove, R. Macdonald, M. Woodmass with M. Andregg, P. Perren and J. Cachet
24 Weissmies (13,199/4,023) 1855: J. Heusser with P. Zurbriggen

Major Passes
(East to west in order)
Simplon Pass (6,578/2,004) major transalpine road-pass
Monte Moro (9,409/2,867) a mule-track, often snow-free in summer
Theodul Pass (10,833/3,300) a series of *téléphériques* make crossing easy today
Col Collon (10,226/3,116)
Fenêtre de Durand (9,203/2,805)
Col du Grand St Bernard (8,100/2,468) a major transalpine road-pass, crowned by the famous hospice of dog and brandy fame. The crest is now bypassed by a tunnel
Col Ferret (8,323/2,536) theoretically the western extremity of the Pennine Alps

Longest Glacier
Gorner-Grenz system of Monte Rosa—8½ miles (15½km)

Major Centres
Swiss
Zermatt—also a ski resort
Saas-Fee—also a ski resort
Arolla
Zinal

Verbier—primarily a ski resort

Italian
Breuil/Cervinia—also a ski resort
Macunagna—also a ski resort

Huts and Bivouacs
Seventy-five plus, mostly belonging to the Swiss and Italian Alpine Clubs

Access
By air
There are international airports at Geneva, Zurich and Milan and a local airport at Sion.
  There is a helicopter base at Zermatt
  Light planes and helicopters can be chartered from Sion or Zermatt for flights onto the high glaciers—a popular start to a ski expedition

By rail
Trans-European expresses run on the Simplon line, Berne–Brig–Domodossola–Milan
  Main lines are: Geneva–Martigny–Sion–Brig; Turin–Chivasso–Aosta
  Local lines: Andermatt–Brig; Visp–Zermatt; Aosta–Pré St Didier

By road
Road access to most valleys *except* Zermatt which can only be reached by rack-railway from Visp

Maps
The best maps are the excellent Swiss National *Landeskarte* published by the Service Topographique Federal in Bern and available everywhere in Switzerland and also at specialist stores in Britain. Available in 1:100,000, 1:50,000 and 1:25,000 scales

Guide-books
Climbing in the Pennines is well documented. The most useful guide-books are: *Pennine Alps,* 3 vols (east, central and west) published by the Alpine Club (London); *High Level Route—ski touring in the Pennines,* published by Westcol (UK); *Zermatt and District—a general guide,* Constable (London)
  The Swiss Alpine Club publishes *Alpes Valaisannes* in 4 vols in the French language

Bernese Alps

The Bernese Alps are the third of the great mountain groups of the Western Alps. With a length of some 70 miles (112km) from the Grimsel Pass to the highlands close above Lake Geneva, they form the longest continuous major range in the Alps, their crest marking the watershed between the Rhône and the Rhine via its tributary, the Aar. The western 30 miles (48km) are a narrow chain of little importance compared to the wide knot of great peaks, no less than thirty-seven of them above 12,000ft (3,657m), that lies to the east of the Gemmi Pass.

The western chain contains three major summits, Les Diablerets (10,531ft/3,210m), a complex massif above the Rhône's right-angle bend at Martigny, the massive Wildhorn (10,655ft/3,247m) and the Wildstrubel (10,641ft/3,243m) with its remarkable 'Plaine Morte' Glacier plateau. The rock is generally poor but there are some interesting and straightforward snow-climbs. Rock-climbing in outlying areas, however, can be excellent: the limestone slabs of L'Argentine above Bex and the 'Leysin Dolomites' around the Tour d'Ai (7,675ft/2,339m) in Canton Vaud are noteworthy.

Massive glaciation is the prime feature of the eastern knot. Ten glaciers are over three miles long and there is virtually continuous ice-cover over an area some 13 miles by 3 miles (21 × 5km). The hub of the area is the Concordia ice-plateau and long valley glaciers radiate in all directions. Fine snow-peaks of individual and distinctive form rise in rows from the ice, and east of Concordia the crestlines become angular and intricate. To the north the mountains present a well defined wall overlooking the Swiss lowlands and the plains of north-west Europe. This is the 'North Face of the Alps' in fact—with all that entails—and one reason why the weather in the range is probably the worst in the Alps. Several of the peaks of this northern wall, the Eiger, the Mönch and the Jungfrau in particular, are world famous, as much for their impressive visage as for their mountaineering. This northern aspect of the group is the true 'Bernese Oberland', a title often applied to the whole range.

Tourism is important and tends to be concentrated along the northern flank in a string of well known summer and winter resorts. Besides good piste-skiing, the range is an ideal one for long and high ski-tours which are among the best in the Alps. Among the facilities that attract tourists, and make life easier

for alpinists too, is the remarkable railway which tunnels 5 miles (8km) through the Eiger and the Mönch to emerge on the Jungfraujoch. Completed in 1912, it gives easy if expensive access to the heart of the mountains. German is the language of the region, although some French is spoken on the western and southern flanks.

To the mountaineer the Bernese Alps offer an unusual variety of climbs and the largest concentration of major ice-routes in the Alps. Best known of the peaks is the dark, brooding Eiger (the Ogre) whose north face, the 'Eigerwand'

The northern flank of the beautiful Jungfrau forms part of the 'northern wall' of the Alps. Seen from above Kleine Scheidegg, the Jungraujoch is the col on the left from which the long North-East Ridge leads to the summit. On the right stands the little Silberhorn

often known as the 'Mortwand'!— 4,600ft (1,402m) of steep or vertical limestone hung with ice-fields—is, both figuratively and literally, very much in the public eye. Objective dangers and great length make all of its several routes very serious undertakings, although the original or '1938' route is not desperately

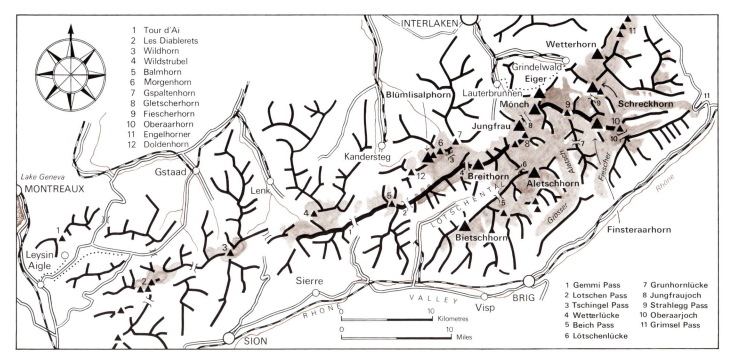

difficult under rare perfect conditions. Among great climbs, the Eigerwand is unique in its situation: it seems incongruous to look down from the stone-swept ice-fields to the smiling green meadows below, or from the 'Death Bivouac' out to the twinkling neon lights of the Grindelwald hotels! Also on the Eiger are two Oberland classics: Lauper's 1932 route on the North-East Face, a superb ice and mixed route of great style, and the North-East or Mittelegi Ridge, first climbed by the Japanese alpinist, Yuko Maki, and his Swiss guides in 1921.

The Mönch (the Monk) has a fine North Face, mostly of ice, with several routes, the classic being the Nollen Buttress, a fairly straightforward ice-climb. The ice-hung northern flank of the beautiful Jungfrau (the Maiden) is a complex of twisted *séracs*, pointed peaklets and fluted ribs. Both the North-West Ridge via the Silberhorn (Reverend J. J. Hornby's party in 1865) and the Guggi Route (Reverend George's party in 1865) are long, interesting and varied ice-climbs, neither very hard but both classic. The two mountains are very popular and are easily climbed on their southern flanks via the Jungfraujoch.

The north faces of the Breithorn, the Grosshorn, the Ebnefluh and the Gletscherhorn, block the head of the Lauterbrunnental. This 5 miles (8km) of hanging ice is known as the Lauterbrunnen Wall and holds an impressive series of great ice-climbs of up to 2,500ft (762m). Notable figures in their exploration during the early 1930s were Willo Welzenbach and Alfred Drexel, both of whom died later on Nanga Parbat. Other great ice-faces include the north faces of the massive Aletschhorn towards the centre of the range, the shapely Nesthorn to the south, the Schreckhorn—whose ice-curtain gives an extremely difficult and rarely completed climb—and the pretty little Studerhorn. Above Kandersteg the Doldenhorn North Face and the easier face of the Blumlisalphorn are popular and the narrow snowy crest of the latter peak, combined with those of its neighbours, the Weissefrau and the Morgenhorn, is a beautiful ridge-traverse of some reputation.

Pre-eminent among the great mixed faces—apart from the Eiger—is perhaps the North-East Face of the noble Finsteraarhorn, whose sharp pointed fin so dominates the ice-fields east of Concordia. The face is 3,500ft (1,067m) high and was first climbed in 1904 by Gustav Hasler and Fritz Amatter via the North-East Rib, a remarkable climb for the period and still considered difficult and dangerous. The second and third ascents were by Americans, V. A. Fynn in 1906 and Miriam O'Brien in 1931, with their guides. The East Rib is shorter, rather easier, on perfect granite and a superb expedition.

Another of the great mixed north walls is the huge and remote Kilchbalm Face of the magnificent Gspaltenhorn (11,277ft/3,437m). As long as the Eigerwand, but only rarely climbed, the face contains several lines and is known among connoisseurs as one of the finest limestone faces in the Alps. Once again it was originally pioneered by Welzenbach. On the same mountain is the famous South-West, or Rote Zahne, Ridge, a long climb bristling with huge pinnacled gendarmes and right worthy of its authors, the great Winthrop Young and Siegfried Herford who, with Joseph Knubel, climbed it in 1914.

Young, with George Mallory who later died on Everest, also pioneered the 2 mile (3km) long South-East Ridge of the Nesthorn in 1909. A real mountaineering expedition on excellent gneiss and granite, it is one of the best routes of its kind in the Alps. Of similar length is the ascent of the elegant Bietschhorn, a modern classic climbed by Erich Friedli in 1964. Other rock-climbing areas are in the Baltschiedertal close by, on the Fusshorner Ridge above the Oberaletsch Glacier and especially in the Engelhörner group at the far north-east corner of the Oberland above Meiringen. This is a maze of fine limestone peaks and pinnacles giving steep and airy climbs of all grades of difficulty and up to 1,500ft (457m) in length, but at low altitude.

The Bernese Alps are a fine range with easy climbs and desperate ones but, in recent years, it has not been popular with the British—probably because its rock-climbing potential, compared to that of Mont Blanc or the Bregaglia, is poor. It is not an ideal area for the tyro however, for even the easier routes can be serious and access is often long and over complex glacier terrain. But, for the alpinist with a modicum of experience, it can be a most rewarding range.

The massif of Mont Blanc seen from the slopes of Mont Gelé above Verbier

On the far left is the Grandes Jorasses and right beneath the westering sun is the great dome of Mont Blanc some 26 miles (42km) distant. To the right are the clustered peaks of the Tour Noir, Les Courtes and Les Droites and the very distinctive isolated wedge of the Aiguille du Chardonnet, and, finally, the Aiguille du Tour just 14 miles (22km) away. A sea of cloud fills the Val d' Entremont below.

We were shooting a ski movie in Verbier, a pleasant purpose-built ski-resort perched on a ledge above Martigny at the far north-western corner of the Pennine Alps. For filming it was ideal—quiet enough for us to get on with the job yet with superb skiing and a really useful series of interconnecting lifts. But for me, however, as one who is more interested in skis as a means of moving among the mountains rather than as a means of returning as swiftly as possible to their base, the location proved frustrating. The slopes above Verbier provide magnificent views not only across the Rhône Valley to the western end of the Bernese Alps, but also to the Himalayan-looking Grand Combin walling the head of the Val de Bagnes and to Mont Blanc with its attendant ranks of shapely summits rising over the deep Val d' Entremont (up which runs the St Bernard highway). Excellent winter conditions prevailed among the high peaks and I was itching to complete the assignment and get among them.

Late one afternoon as we were swooping homewards towards the cloud-filled valley, I stopped to take this picture. At least I could photograph the Mont Blanc peaks even if I couldn't climb them! A party stopped ahead of me, adjusted their bindings and left the piste to move off southward across the hillside, their long shadows gliding effortlessly beside them. Carrying ropes, axes and rucksacks, they were aiming no doubt for an ascent of Mont Fort or the Rosablanche on the morrow. I watched enviously until their trail, the only mark in the textured snow, disappeared over a distant crest in the direction of the Mont Fort hut before setting off into the gathering dusk. In winter the High Alps are a new world again and every journey, even among the most familiar mountains, is a fresh voyage of exploration.

Overleaf: **The 'Argentière Wall', seen from the summit of the Aiguille du Chardonnet**

Left to right are the northern faces of the Aiguille de Triolet, at the head of the Argentière Glacier, the Col des Cristaux, Les Courtes with the North Face of the Grandes Jorasses looming behind the little Tour des Courtes, the great mass of Les Droites and, finally, the Aiguille Verte. Some of the finest ice and mixed routes in the Alps surmount this wall.

The Chardonnet itself is a fine peak and a good viewpoint and its traverse, via the Forbes Arête, is a popular and easy classic. Those aspiring to the big walls across the glacier, however, should reach the top by the excellent little North Face, a mixed climb whose final ice-wall leads spectacularly right to the summit. It is sobering to then discover that the Chardonnet's North Face has actually been descended on skis—albeit by a rather different line!

The Bernese Oberland—the north wall of the Bernese Alps

The Wetterhorn—with the meadowy pass of Grosse Scheidegg lying between it
and the dark Schwarzhorn (9,606ft/2,928m)—is seen over the Grindelwald Valley
from Kleine Scheidegg. The Eigerwand is out of the picture to the right. Usually in
the Alps the visiting mountaineer is a bird of passage: rarely does he stay long in one
place and then only when the weather clamps right down. He is usually too busy
trying to climb as many mountains as possible in his all-too-short holiday. It was
interesting, for a change, to spend six weeks in one place—the famous hotel perched
on the grassy saddle at Kleine Scheidegg—while we filmed *The Eiger Sanction.*
This picture is the view from my bedroom window. I photographed it many times,
at dawn, at dusk, in sun and in snow and it was different every time. It was a novel
and fascinating experience for an old alpine hand!

On the North Face of the Doldenhorn in the Bernese Oberland

The Doldenhorn (11,952ft/3,643m) is the final peak of the Blümlisalp chain above
Kandersteg and its 2,300ft (701m) North Face gives a fairly straightforward ice-
climb graded 'TD inf' – not that gradings of ice-climbs mean much! One
season Bill O'Connor and I chose the face as our first climb and, eschewing the
expensive and claustrophobic comforts of the Fründenhütte nearby, we bivouacked
at its foot and bombed up the ice in double-quick time. But a 100ft (30m) rock-band
guards the summit—it is limestone, steep and loose and damp, and the way through
it starts with a strenuous little overhang! Bill removed his crampons to lead, leaving
them with me to send up on the rope. Eventually the steep rock blended into steep
ice and, poised in a precarious position, he called down for his crampons. When
they were almost within his grasp, something slipped. The crampons went flying
outward and downward. They went singing down the ice and disappeared far
below. No doubt it was my fault, somehow, and the extremely awkward change of
lead in our fearsome situation that resulted provided an entertaining ending to an
otherwise uneventful climb. There is a moral somewhere here I think?

In the picture the left skyline is the North East Ridge, the 'Galletgrat'. It is the
classic ice-*arête* so well illustrated in that beautiful and well known photograph by
the doyen of aerial photographers, Bradford Washburn.

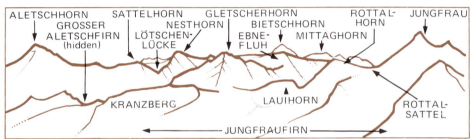

ALETSCHHORN   SATTELHORN   GLETSCHERHORN   ROTTAL-   JUNGFRAU
GROSSER   NESTHORN   BIETSCHHORN   HORN
ALETSCHFIRN   LÖTSCHEN-   EBNE-   MITTAGHORN
(hidden)   LÜCKE   FLUH
KRANZBERG   LAUIHORN   ROTTAL-
SATTEL
JUNGFRAUFIRN

Looking south west from the summit of the Mönch

The North Face of the savage Gspaltenhorn is over 5,000ft (1,524m) high. To the right of the summit can be seen the snowy tops of the beautiful Blümlisalp above Kandersteg

Situation: Switzerland—Cantons Berne and Valais, with a small part in Canton Vaud

Most Important Peaks

1 Finsteraarhorn (14,022/4,274) 1829: F. J. Hugi and party
2 Aletschhorn (13,763/4,195) 1862: E. Ruppen, M. Jossen, A. Eggel
3 Jungfrau (13,642/4,158) 1813: Meyey brothers and party
4 Mönch (13,448/4,099)1857: S. Porges with Christian Almer and party
5 Schreckhorn (13,379/4,078) 1861: Sir Leslie Stephen and party
10 Eiger (13,025/3,970) 1858: C. Barrington with Christian Almer, etc
14 Bietschhorn (12,907/3,934) 1859: Sir Leslie Stephen and party
Lauterbrunnen Breithorn (12,408/3,782) 1865: E. von Fellenberg and party
Wetterhorn (12,142/3,700) 1844: M. Bannholzer and J. Jaun
Blumlisalphorn (12,021/3,664) 1860: Sir Leslie Stephen and party—a member of which, J. K. Stone, was American and this was therefore the earliest first ascent in the Alps by an American!

Major Passes

Grimsel Pass (7,136/2,175) the eastern boundary of the range and a major north-south road link
Gemmi Pass (7,618/2,322) north-south—taken as the western boundary of the major eastern area, an easy and much frequented mule-trail dating to before AD1252
Lotschen Pass (8,825/2,690) north-south—an ancient and easy mule-trail but crossing a straight-forward glacier: the oldest glacier-pass in the Alps?
Lotschelücke (10,427/3,178) an easy east-west glacier-pass

Tschingel Pass (9,209/2,807) an easy east-west glacier-pass said to have been crossed on horseback in 1742!
Strahlegg Pass (10,960/3,340) classic and useful east-west glacier-pass
Wetterlücke (10,427/3,178) important north-south glacier-pass
Grunhornlücke (10,781/3,286) popular and easy east-west glacier-pass
Oberaarjoch (10,600/3,230) easy north-south glacier-pass
Beich Pass (10,259/3,127) easy and much frequented east-west glacier-pass
Jungfraujoch (11,401/3,475) classic and difficult north-south glacier-pass of historic importance, but now abandoned because of the railway

Major Glaciers

Grosser Aletsch system—15½ miles (25km)—the longest glacier in the Alps
Fiescher—9¼ miles (15km)

Major Centres

Kandersteg—pleasant and unpretentious resort
Lauterbrunnen—rambling village with good facilities, with two major ski resorts, Murren, the cradle of British skiing, and Wengen, close above
Grindelwald—large and fairly glossy resort and ski centre
Brig—rather sleepy small town gives good access to southern side of range

Huts

More than thirty-one huts, most owned by the Swiss Alpine Club

Access

By air
To international airports at Zurich or Geneva. Helicopter and light aircraft may be chartered from Interlaken or Sion

By rail
From Geneva or Lausanne the main line up the Rhône Valley to Brig gives access to the south side of the range.

From Geneva via Bern and Thur to Kandersteg from where the train continues to Brig via the Lötschenberg Tunnel or to Interlaken where the local train connects to Grindelwald or Lauterbrunen

By road
Easy access to all three centres on north side and connections to south side (Brig) by Grimsel Pass (east) or Col du Pillon (west) or car-ferry train through the Lötschenberg Tunnel. Brig is otherwise on the main road from Lake Geneva up the Rhône Valley

Maps

The excellent Swiss National *Landeskarte* are readily available in 1:100,000, 1:50,000 and 1:25,000 scale

Guide-books

The Swiss Alpine Club publish a set of five German-language guide-books to the Bernese Alps of which vol I covers the area west of Gemmi Pass. A sixth volume, *Alpes Vaudoises*, covers the far western end of the chain in French.

In English *Selected Climbs in the Bernese Alps* is published by the Alpine Club (London) and *Bernese Alps West*, by Westcol (UK)

Central Alps

Beyond the Grimsel and Furka Passes the south-east quarter of Switzerland is entirely mountainous and its major feature is the head waters of the mighty Rhine. Round its valley and its spreading upper tributaries the mountains sweep in a great arc, occasionally continuous, but usually in separate groups. To the alpinist from beyond the Swiss frontier few of these mountains hold much of interest—with some notable exceptions—and the area is left largely to the Swiss themselves for whom access from the populated lowlands and the cities of Zurich, Luzern and St Gallen, is easy.

The main Alpine watershed, here between the Rhône and the Po, follows much of the crest of the arc in its western half before passing to the crest of another mountain chain outside it to the south east. The Swiss/Italian frontier extends as much as 50 miles (80km) southwards of the watershed to encompass that peculiar Italianesque salient of Switzerland that borders Lakes Maggiore and Lugano—Canton Ticino. Not surprisingly the language of Ticino is Italian, while there are several enclaves in this basically German-speaking region, notably the Val Tavetsch east of the Oberalp Pass, where Romansch is spoken.

This is an area where the British have figured but little in the exploration. Mountaineering has a long history here, however, in which perhaps the outstanding figure was the Disentis monk, Father Placidus à Spesecha, who made a remarkable series of ascents in the late eighteenth and early nineteenth centuries. As an old man on Tödi (King of the Little Mountains) in 1824, he was unable to continue but had the satisfaction of watching members of his party reach the summit for the first time. Today the north-east and north-west faces of this inelegant mountain give notable and difficult climbs.

The most interesting mountains in the area are those in the north west, clustered round the little Göschen Tal. The Rhône rises on the west flank of the Dammastock, an impressive rock-and-ice-peak which dominates the area and boasts a savage east face notorious for its huge cornices. Close by is the fine and isolated Galenstock which gives a good selection of climbs on rock, snow and ice. Titlis, just across the Susten Pass to the north, rising almost from Lake Lucerne, is famed for its ski-mountaineering, but the pride of the region is really the excellent granite of its smaller peripheral peaks. Popular among Swiss rock-specialists are the towers of the Gelmerhörner above the Grimsel Pass, the sawblade ridge of the Büelenhörner

above the Furka Pass, and the Bergseeschijen (9,237ft/2,815m) and Feldschijen (10,502ft/3,200m) pinnacles to the north and south of the Göschen Tal lake.

Pride of place, however, must go to the superb Salbitschijen above the entrance to the Göschen Tal. Its long, pinnacled South Ridge, pioneered in 1935 by Alfred and Otto Amstad with Guido Masetto, is one of the classic rock-climbs of the Alps and as such is internationally famous. The same team pioneered many other good routes in the area, but the exceptionally long and fierce West Ridge, with its five huge towers, was not traversed until 1948. There are many modern top-class rock-climbs in the vicinity, many of them discovered by local experts, Max Niedermann, Kurt Gruter or Moses Gamma—the latter a member of the family that runs the Salbit Hut and has been guiding in the region for ninety years.

Southward the mountains are of little interest to the serious climber, the rock is often poor and shales and slates abound. But there are a host of smallish peaks which hold several considerable glaciers—which seem to be among the few in the Alps currently advancing—and which give easy ascents and often some excellent spring ski-touring and ski-mountaineering. Prominent among these ski-peaks are Monte Leone in the Lepontines and the Rheinwaldhorn in the Adula group. Perhaps the most popular summit in the Lepontines is the Ofenhorn which boasts a near-classic North Ridge pioneered in 1891 by the ubiquitous Coolidge and Christian Almer. Twelve miles north east the Witenwasserenstock (10,112ft/3,082m) is a source of three rivers—the Rhône, the Rhine and the Ticino (a tributary of the Po)—which flow, respectively, into the Mediterranean, the North Sea and the Adriatic.

Elsewhere there is good climbing but often on limestone, the North Face of the Windgälle above Altdorf, for instance, or on the brittle Dolomite-like Spannort chain. North of the Wallensee, the seven fantastic miniature mountains of the Churfirsten chain offer some superb modern climbs on their vertical and overhanging southern faces, climbs up to 1,600ft (487m) in length. To the far south, in Ticino, weird limestone pinnacles rise from broadleafed woods. Typical are the Dentes della Vecchi (the Widow's Teeth), not even 5,000ft (1,525m) above the sea but a stamping ground of the great Comici. A far cry from the High Alps!

The Salbitschijen from the east. The classic and many-spired South Ridge is the left-hand skyline, while the easy way up this fine rock peak is via the glacier col just visible on the far right

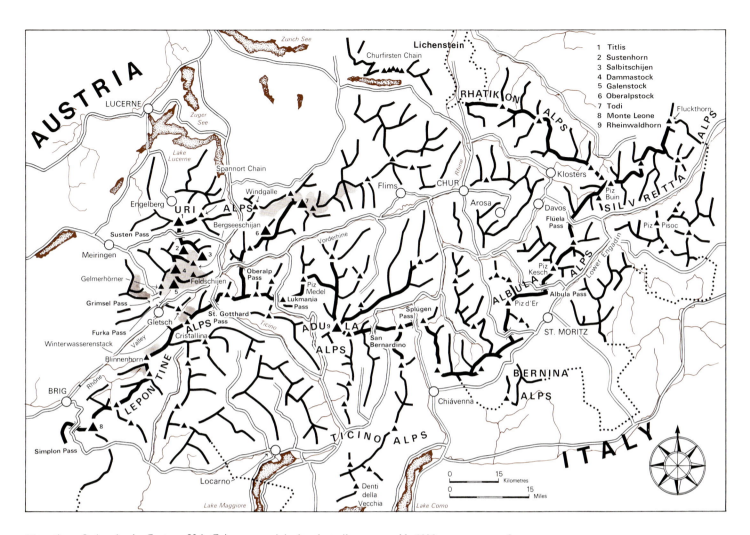

Situation: Switzerland—Cantons Uri, Grisons, Ticino and small parts of others

Most Important Peaks

Dammastock (11,906/3,628) 1864: A. Hoffmann-Burckhardt with A. von Weissenfluh and J. Fischer

Tödi (11,877/3,620) 1824: Placidus Curschella and August Bisquolm, members of Father Placidus à Spesecha's party

Galenstock (11,755/3,582) 1845: E. Desou, D. Dollfuss-Ausset and D. Dollfuss with Hans Wähun, etc

Monte Leone (11,658/3,553) 1859: J. J. Weilenmann, solo

Sustenhorn (11,496/3,503) 1841: Gottlieb Studer with J. & H. von Weissenfluh

Rheinwaldhorn (11,162/3,400) 1789: Father Placidus à Spesecha

Oberalpstock (10,915/3,326) 1799: Father Placidus à Spesecha

Titlis (10,627/3,240) 1744: Fathers Hess, Waser and two other monks from Engelberg

Salbitschijen (9,780/2,980) 1889: Probably E. Huber and Jos. Gamma

Major Passes

Grimsel (7,100/2,164) important transalpine road-pass, north–south

Furka (7,969/2,428) major transalpine road-pass, east–west, also with railway

Oberalp (6,709/2,044)

St Gotthard (6,919/2,108) major transalpine road-pass, north–south, tunnelled by major rail link, and perhaps the busiest road-pass in the Alps: the

original mule-trail was opened in 1293

Lukmania (6,286/1,915) minor road-pass, north–south

Susten (7,411/2,258) important road-pass, east–west

San Bernardino (6,759/2,060) transalpine road-pass, north–south

Splugen (6,939/2,115) minor transalpine road-pass, north–south

Julien (7,169/2,185) important transalpine road-pass, north–south

Albula (7,589/2,313) minor road-pass, north–south, tunnelled by railway

Flüela (7,877/2,400) minor road-pass, north–south

Major Glacier

The Rhône Glacier—4½ miles (7km) in length

Convenient Centres

Andermatt—also a ski resort
Engelberg
Davos—primarily a ski resort
Airolo—small but busy town

Huts and Bivouacs

Sixty plus, belonging largely to the Swiss Alpine Club

Access

By air

There is an international airport at Zurich, small airports at Samedan, near St Moritz, and Locarno and several small airstrips elsewhere. Light planes and helicopters may be chartered from Samedan

By rail

Andermatt can be reached on the St Gotthard express line from Zurich to Lugano

Chur is easily reached from Zurich, whence small mountain lines run to St Moritz, Davos and Thusis. The so-called 'Glacier Express', another small mountain line, connects Chur to Andermatt, Gletsch and Brig via the Operalp and Furka Passes—a distance of some 90 miles (145km). Linthal is served by rail from Zurich as are Engelberg and Meiringen via Luzern

By road

The region is well served by roads from all directions

Maps

The excellent Swiss National *Landeskarte* are available in Switzerland and in specialist stores abroad. Available in 1:100,000, 1:50,000 and 1:25,000 scale

Guide-books

Climbing is well documented in the German language in the series published by the Swiss Alpine Club. Westcol (UK) publish in English—*Central Switzerland* (Dammastock region), *Mittel Switzerland* (Lepontine, Ticino and Adula Alps) and *Engelhörner and Salbitschen* (the former group is part of the Oberland)

33

The Bregaglia

West of the Muretto Pass the peaks rise again, sharper and more rocky, as the Bregaglia or Bergell. The Swiss–Italian border follows much of its crest-line and the water from both flanks drains into Lake Como and so southward to the Po. The lusher vegetation and generally better weather than the Western Alps suggest a 'southern alpine' climate and the Badile in particular seems prone to violent thunderstorms which sweep up from the hot Lombardy plains.

To the south the mountains rise from the deep trench of the Valtellina only 1,000ft (305m) above the sea, but the main peaks lie well to the north and thrust down two major ridges which flank long and narrow glens subsidiary to that valley. The Swiss side is generally steeper and bold glacier-filled *cirques* seem actually to hang high above the forested walls of the Val Bregaglia below, which, at Bondo, is only 2,600ft (792m) above sea level. This valley, which at its head climbs, almost as a cliff, a thousand feet to the Maloja Pass, continues the line of the Engadine to the Italian frontier and beyond.

The Val Bregaglia, where Italian itself is spoken, is one of the most beautiful valleys in the Alps, despite the major international road which traverses it. Tiny cobbled villages, some on the valley floor, some perched high on the sunny northern side, cluster round their tall-towered churches. Fountains play and flowers bloom in village squares and the tall faces of the houses are often decorated with religious murals or coats-of-arms. While there is some tourist traffic, the region is largely agricultural apart from some extensive quarrys in Italy with their associated industry such as cement works, and the long-completed hydro-electric reservoir in the Albigna *cirque*.

While the relatively small Piz Badile is internationally famous, the highest mountain of the group is relatively unknown: Monte Dizgrazia, isolated on a branch ridge southward, entirely in Italy, is quite out of character with the rest of the Bregaglia. It is an elegant snow-peak, aloof and grand, with a splendid northern wall of hanging ice on which the first rather indirect line, the Spigolo Inglese, was made by the Scots,

Raeburn and Ling, in 1910. The latest 'super direct' was added by Diemberger in 1958. The arcing north-north-east ice-arête, the Corda Molla, is a beautiful climb—a classic of the area.

Elsewhere rock predominates, although there are several excellent ice-climbs worthy of the connoisseur, such as the shapely North Face of the Cima di Rosso, the easier North Face of the Cima

di Cantun and Klucker's fierce North Couloir of the Colle del Badile. The name of Christian Klucker, in fact, dominates the early history of the Bregaglia even more so than does that of Count Aldo Bonacossa a generation later.

The *cirques* on the Italian side of the crest, above the Val Masino, are a rock-climber's paradise. Many of the great Italian climbers of the 1920s and 1930s were active here, Bonacossa, of course, and men such as Bramani, Gevasutti and Molteni, and there are many superb rock-routes of all standards, particularly in the Allievi *cirque*. On the northern side there are two impressive routes, one pure rock, one mixed, on the twin Pillars of Ferro in the Albigna *cirque*, but the best climbing is clustered around the

Sciora *cirque* from which it is divided by the four improbable-looking towers of the Sciora chain, the Fuori, the Pioda, the Ago and the Dentro which give excellent climbs of up to 1,800ft (549m). The classic slabs of the Bugelisen or 'Flat Iron', are part of the 2,700ft (823m) long north-north-west ridge of the Piz Gemelli but the *cirque* is dominated by the huge bulk of Piz Cengalo: its north face is a full 3,800ft (1,158m) high and gives an awkward rock-route, spiced with ice, much more in the style of the Western Alps than the Bregaglia! Its smooth north-west Pillar is a magnificent and difficult pure rock-climb of nearly 3,000ft (914m) and one of two choice climbs of Bregaglia. The other is Cassin's Route on the north-east face of

The Sciora Cirque seen from Soglio to the N.W. across the deep Val Bregaglia. Left to right: the Sciora Peaks, the Bondasca Glacier, the Piz Gemelli, the Piz Cengalo—its magnificent N.W. Pillar clearly visible—and the famous Piz Badile. The classic N. Ridge divides the dark shadow of the N.E. Face from the sunny N.W. Face on the right

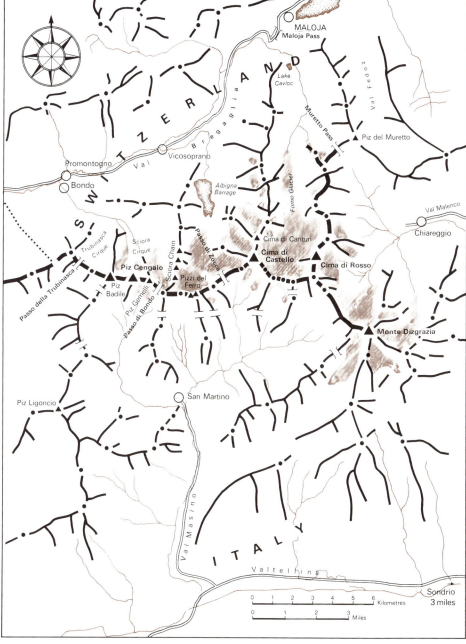

The Bregaglia

the Piz Badile alongside—a huge 3,000ft (914m) sweep of steep slabs which give a delectable and sustained climb of a fairly hard grade. The epic story of its first ascent in 1937 is well known. It is one of the 'six classic north faces' of the Alps and such is its reputation that in good summer weather there may be several parties on the climb together: it has been soloed in extremely short times by several Continental and British climbers. Of increasing reputation is Bonatti's fine route on the same face which has had far fewer ascents.

There are other superb but far less popular climbs in outlying areas of Bregaglia such as the Trubinasca *cirque* with its great grey buttresses and its peculiar lush vegetation, or on the long ridge of the Badile that extends over 7 miles southwards to the Valtelline. Near its end, Piz Ligoncio holds a little known north-west face which gives a climb of similar style and length to the Cassin Route on the Badile. This area is little frequented by other than Italian climbers and there are plenty of surprises for those who look for them!

In short the Bregaglia holds something for everyone, the superb rough grey granite favours novice and expert alike and it is no wonder that it is a popular area, particularly among the British who seem to cherish it second only to Chamonix, and who have made several important new routes in recent years. But it is not difficult to escape from other climbers, for there is little of the Chamonix-style rat-race, and for those prepared to explore there is still ample scope for new rock-climbs of high standard.

Situation: Switzerland—Canton Ticino; Italy—Bergamo Province of Lombardy Region

Most Important Peaks
1 Monte Dizgrazia (12,067/3,678) 1862: Leslie Stephen, E. S. Kennedy with Melchior Anderegg and Thomas Cox
3 Cima di Castello (11,129/3,392) 1866: Douglas Freshfield, C. C. Tucker with F. Devouassoud and A. Fluri
4 Piz Cengalo (11,056/3,370) 1866: Douglas Freshfield, C. C. Tucker; with F. Devouassoud
5 Cima di Rosso (11,043/3,366) 1867: W. Coolidge with F. and H. Devouassoud
6 Piz Badile (3,000/914) 1867: W. A. B. Coolidge with F. and H. Devouassoud

Major Passes
Muretto Pass (8,406/2,562) divides the Bernina and Bergell groups, an old and easy transalpine pass with a good trail. Dates to fourteenth century
Maloja Pass (5,935/1,809) a major transalpine road-pass
Passo di Zocca (9,019/2,749) an old and easy smugglers' pass across the main Bergell crest
Passo di Bondo (10,397/3,169) an important high glacier-pass across the main Bergell crest, but difficult to find
Passo della Trubinasca (8,868/2,703) an important link between the Swiss and Italian sides of the range, easy but steep and rocky. Normally used in conjunction with Passo Porcellizzo (9,390/2,862) which gives east–west access on the Italian side

Major Glacier
Forno Glacier—3½ miles (5½km). One of the few advancing alpine glaciers

Monte Dizgrazia, Bregaglia's highest peak, rises isolated on the Italian flanks of the Range. In this view, photographed from the Cima di Rosso, the classic Corda Molla arête falls to the left of the summit. Between it and the conspicuous Spigolo Inglese lies the steep ice of the North Face. The *voie normale* reaches the N.W. ridge from the (unseen) southern side at the saddle between the summit and Monte Pioda, the subsidiary summit to the right

Convenient Centres
Maloja—convenient for both Bernina and
Bregaglia
Vicosoprano—delightful small village
Promontogno—another pleasant small village
San Martino—Italian valley-head village
Chiareggio—the village centre for Monte
Dizgrazia

Huts and Bivouacs
Twenty-three, many of them bivouacs belonging
to the Italian Alpine Club

Access
By air
To Zurich international airport and thence by
charter to Samedan (St Moritz). Light aircraft and
helicopters may be chartered from here and it is a
popular gliding centre

By rail
Major line from Zurich to Chur and then on to
Samedan and St Moritz. In Italy a line up Lake
Como links Bergamo with the Valtellina towns of
Sondrio and Tirano with a branch to Chiavenna. A
mountain line links Samedan to Tirano via the
Bernina Pass

By road
The Bernina and Bregaglia are encircled by good
roads from which, on the Swiss side, there is
virtually no vehicular access southwards. On the
Italian side public roads run to the heads of each
valley. Excellent bus services run from St Moritz
via Maloja and the Val Bregaglia to the Italian
border from whence a good Italian service continues to Chiavenna. There are bus services up the
Italian valleys from the relevant Valtellina railway
stations

Maps
The excellent Swiss National *Landeskarte* are
easily available in Switzerland at 1:100,000,
1:50,000 and 1:25,000 scale. They cover enough of
the Italian side of the area to fill most requirements.
A British climbers' map—scale 1:35,000, covering
the Bergell on one sheet—is published by Westcol
(UK)

Guide-books
The Swiss Alpine Club publish one volume in
German; the Italian Alpine Club publish one in
Italian; Rudolf Rother, Munich, publish *Selected
Climbs*, 1 volume, in German (1968).

In the English language Westcol (UK) publish 2
volumes, *Bregaglia East* (1971) and *Bregaglia West*
(1974)

Bernina Alps

Tucked away on the Italian frontier in the far south-eastern corner of Switzerland, and outside the arc of the Central Alps, lie two small yet superb mountain groups, the Bernina Alps and the Bregaglia. The former, high, compact and almost entirely ice-draped, contrasts strongly with the bold rock scenery and serrated ridges of its neighbour. But beautiful valleys, impressive peaks and great climbs have ensured both groups of a place in any list of the very finest mountains of the Alps.

The border runs along the crest of both massifs but the main alpine watershed, now between the Danube and Po, follows only the Bernina. The Inn rises in the twin lakes of Silser and Silvaplana amid the green meadows of the Maloja Pass and its valley, the Engadine, which the Bernina peaks flank to the south, runs north east towards the Austrian frontier, falling at first only imperceptibly. From the high peaks the northward-running valleys cradle easy-angled and sometimes long glaciers, while on the Italian side wider, stubby glaciers and more complex terrain hang over the double-headed Val Malenco and the Swiss salient of Val Poschiavo south of the Bernina Pass. Both valleys are tributaries of the long and deep Valtellina.

Although German is usually understood, the Engadine is the heart of Romansch-speaking Switzerland: the tongue is an ancient one akin to the Latin of Ancient Rome and is one of the four official languages of Switzerland.

The region is largely given over to the tourist trade. Its major centre, St Moritz, is perhaps the plushiest and most wealthy resort in Switzerland and its facilities, not only hotels and shops, but those for winter sporting, are superb. The skiing is among the best in the Alps, there are horse races on frozen lakes and here is the home of the famous Cresta Run. Pontresina is smaller, rather more casual and much more mountain-orientated.

The monarch of the area is Piz Bernina itself, the highest peak—indeed the only four thousand metre peak—in the Alps west of the Lauteraarhorn in the Bernese Oberland. Its first ascent, in 1850, via the Labyrinth ice-fall and East Ridge was ostensibly for survey purposes. Its most famous climb, however, an alpine classic, is the North Ridge, the beautiful Biancograt, a long arcing snow-arête, presenting no serious difficulty, first climbed in 1876 and actually ascended and descended solo in six hours from the Tschierva Hut, for a wager, by Herman Buhl.

Two and a half miles to the east, Piz Palu is by any standards a distinctive mountain—and a popular one too. Its summit ridge holds three tops from each of which, to the north, a bold pillar of rock and ice falls some 2,400ft (731m) to the Pers Glacier below. Each gives a superb mixed climb, the most interesting being the Centre Pillar or Bumiller-grat, and the hardest the Western Pillar which, surprisingly, seems to have had no British ascent between the first in

1899 and the next in 1970. The steep hanging glacier between the East and Central Peaks provides an interesting, but very serious, ice-climb.

To the west Piz Scersen is a difficult peak by its easiest line but is famous for its long North-West Spur—the Eisnase, a magnificent medium-grade ice-climb of 1887 vintage. Its neighbour, Piz Roseg, boasts a north-eastern ice-face of 2,300ft (700m) and of international repute, first ascended in 1890 by Norman-Neruda and Christian Klucker; this was not repeated for thirty-four years. Today this broad and beautiful face is crisscrossed with lines, some of the modern ones very difficult. The traverse of the frontier ridge, 1½ miles (2½km) from Roseg, over Scersen to Piz Bernina, ranks as one of the finest expeditions of its kind in the Alps. Serious and strenuous climbing over mixed ground, it was first completed in 1932.

The Bernina is another group where the British were prominent among the pioneers, but most notable of all was the Engadine's greatest son—the renowned guide, Christian Klucker. Among other famous mountaineers who figure in Bernina's history were Norman-Neruda, Paul Gussfeldt, Professor Graham Brown, Alfred Zurcher, Walter

Seen from Diavolezza to the north east, the three North-Face Pillars of Piz Palu rise from the Pers Glacier. In the centre of the picture are the summits of Bellavista and the distant fang of Crast Agüzza. On the far right is Piz Bernina with the classic Biancograt as its right skyline

Anstutz and, more recently, Kurt Diemberger.

While there are good rock-routes in the Bernina, usually on the Italian flanks, it is for snow and ice that the group is renowned and its main appeal is to the middle-grade **alpinist**. The competitive spirit that pervades the Mont Blanc area is here absent, there are no obvious 'last great problems' but many of the harder climbs see little traffic. There is good winter climbing and some fine ski-mountaineering.

The Unter or Lower Engadine is not without interest. On its south-eastern side, adjoining the Bernina Alps, are a group of beautiful small peaks of Dolomite limestone culminating in Piz Pisoc (10,427ft/3,178m). There is good ridge-climbing but the whole area is a National Park containing large herds of steinbock among other animals, and also of great geological importance. There is more to do than just climb! The Albula Alps, rising to Piz Kesch (11,211ft; 3,417m), and the Silvretta Alps on the Austrian border reaching just over 11,000ft (3,353m) at the Flucht Horn and containing the well known Piz Buin (10,866ft/3,312m), line the north-western side of the Upper and Lower Engadine respectively. Both are famous for their ski-touring.

Situation: Switzerland—Canton Ticino
Italy—Bergamo Province of Lombardy region

Most Important Peaks
1 Piz Bernina (13,284/4,049) 1850: Johann Coaz with J. and L. Ragut Tschamer
2 Piz Zupo (13,109/3,995) 1863: L. Enderlin and party
3 Piz Scersen (13,028/3,971) 1877: Paul Gussfeldt and party
5 Piz Roseg (12,917/3,937) 1865: A. W. Moore, H. Walker with Jacob Anderegg
7 Piz Palu (12,812/3,905) 1866: K. E. Digby and party or A. W. Moore, H. Walker with J. Anderegg

Major Passes
Bernina Pass (7,621/2,323) transalpine pass crossed by road and railway and marking the eastern extremity of the Bernina Alps
Fuorcla Crast Aguzza (11,814/3,601) the most important glacier-pass across the crest of the major Bernina peaks
Sella Pass (10,725/3,269) an important link across the range but necessitates crossing badly crevassed glacier
Muretto Pass (8,406/2,562) divides the Bernina and Bergell groups, an old and easy transalpine pass with a good trail. Dates to fourteenth century
Maloja Pass (5,935/1,809) a major transalpine road-pass

Major Glacier
Morteratsch Glacier—5 miles (8km)

Convenient Centres
St Moritz—also a fashionable ski resort
Pontiesina
Franscia—small village at Italian valley head
Maloja—convenient for both Bernina and Bregaglia

Huts and Bivouacs
Eight—four Swiss; four Italian

Access
By air
To Zurich international airport and thence by charter to Samedan (St Moritz). Light aircraft and helicopters may be chartered from here and it is a popular gliding centre

By rail
Major line from Zurich to Chur and then on to Samedan and St Moritz. In Italy a line up Lake Como links Bergamo with the Valtellina towns of Sondrio and Tirano with a branch to Chiavenna. A mountain line links Samedan to Tirano via the Bernina Pass

By road
The Bernina and Bregaglia are encircled by good roads from which, on the Swiss side, there is virtually no vehicular access southwards. On the Italian side public roads run to the heads of each valley. Excellent bus services run from St Moritz via Maloja and the Val Bregaglia to the Italian border from whence a good Italian service continues to Chiavenna. There are bus services up the Italian valleys from the relevant Valtellina railway stations

Maps
The excellent Swiss National *Landeskarte* are available everywhere in Switzerland at 1:100,000, 1:50,000 and 1:25,000 scale. They cover enough of the Italian side of the area to fill most requirements

Guide-books
The Swiss Alpine Club publish one volume in the German language and the Italian Alpine Club one volume in Italian.
In the English language Westcol (UK) publish *Bernina Alps* (1 vol)

Eastern Alps

Filling most of Austria and much of north east Italy with mountains, the Eastern alps stretch some 250 miles (402km) from the Swiss frontier to the hills outside Vienna and, through this sea of peaks, three main and roughly parallel mountain chains, each of very different character, can be distinguished. The central chain is the major one and it continues the line of the Bernina and Engadine mountains into Austria with the Ötztal, Stubai, Zillertal, and Hohe and Niedere Tauern groups. It continues too the important watershed between the Danube and the Adriatic. Although draining entirely southward, the compact Ortler massif is geographically an offshoot of the Engadine and—together with the isolated granitic Adamello-Presanella massif further south still—can be considered, certainly in character, as part of this central chain. Built predominantly of crystalline rocks, gneiss, schists, shales and some limestones, the mountains hold snow, ice and some sizable glaciers and include all the higher summits of the Eastern Alps.

To the north, and separated by the east–west valleys of the Inn, the Salzach and the Enns, lies the chain of the northern limestone ranges—the Kalkalpen. Relatively small rock peaks, they stretch in narrow ridges like a series of sawblades along, or close to, the Bavarian frontier.

The southern chain, once again limestone rock peaks, is not so orderly. The tangled spires of the Dolomite complex rise above the deep valley of the Adige and then run north east until they fade into the east–west line of the Carnic Alps. On the Yugoslav frontier the mountains form a final knot as the Julians. Here the Alps end but the high ground tumbles south into the Balkans.

Except for the Hohe Tauern, the central chain lies in the Austrian Tirol and the Italian frontier follows its crest—although it has not always done so. Until the First World War the Alto Adige, including most of the Dolomites and much of the Ortler and Adamello massifs, and indeed the cities of Bolzano and Trento, was Austrian territory—the South Tirol. During the war bitter fighting took place throughout the area and many of the scars, from rock-hewn fortifications to rusted barbed wire and old boots, are still visible among the mountains. Today much of the population is still German-speaking and the South Tirol is a source of friction between the two nations.

Historically the Tirol, north and south, was a smiling corner of the Habsburg realm well patronized by a succession of emperors and empresses and Innsbruck—and Bolzano to a lesser extent—echo this past glory. It seems a pastoral land of orchards, hayfields and wild flowers, the mountains not so dominating as among the Swiss valleys. Certainly the weather is better than it is in the Western Alps.

The wealth of climbing is, of course, incredible. Most famous to foreigners are the Dolomites. The topography of these dramatic limestone peaks seems confusing. Fairytale spires and impossible walls of yellow, grey and brown soar above flower-covered meadows and glaring white scree-fields apparently

The Zillertal Alps: a winter view looking south west up the deep Tuxer Tal towards the peak of the Tuxer Hauptkamm, dominated by the pyramid of the Olperer. The small resort of Hintertux, noted for its summer skiing on the Gefrorne Wand Glacier – just catching the sun below the Olperer – lies at the head of the valley

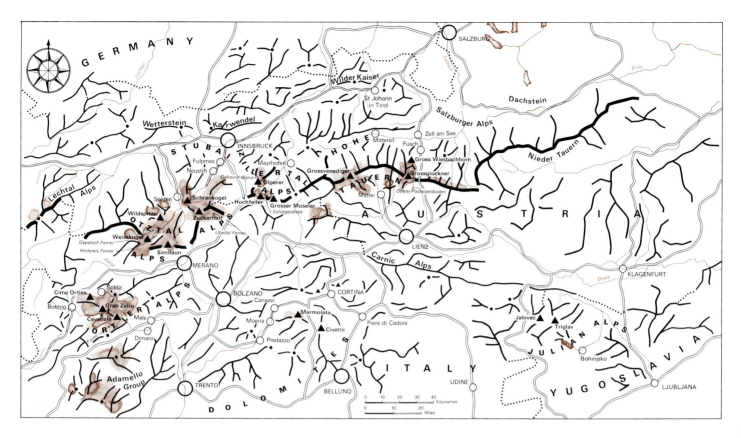

without rhyme or reason. In winter the skiing is excellent, both on piste, at centres like Cortina, and touring amid splendid scenery: in summer the only snow worth mentioning is the small glacier on the north flank of the Marmolata.

Dolomite climbing has had much influence on the development of rock-climbing, and indeed mountaineering, elsewhere. Mind-boggling steepness, extreme exposure, great length and often friable rock are characteristic. Pitons and bolts are common on many climbs and no regard is paid to the ethical differences between 'free' and 'aid' climbing—most of the harder climbs require 'aid' of some sort at some stage. The most famous face in the 'Dollies' is the 1,600ft (487m) North Face of the Cima Grande of which the first 720ft (219m) are continuously overhanging. The first—and easiest—line on the face, Comici's 1933 route, is the classic and one of the 'great six' Alpine north faces. Other major, but far larger, faces are the South Face of the Marmolata and the battlemented 3-mile (5km) long North–West Face of the Civetta.

In Yugoslavia the limestone peaks of the Julian Alps, imposing but less surprising than the 'Dollies', also give excellent and long rock-climbs. The region is wild and extremely beautiful. But it is the northern Kalkalpen that can be considered the crucible of modern alpine

rock-climbing and they attract thousands of climbers every year as they have for over half a century.

Many of the techniques and gadgets familiar to us today were invented and developed here by Bavarian and Austrian climbers, men like Dülfer and the tigers of the 'Munich School', before and after the Great War, paving the way for the great advance in technical standards in the Western Alps during the thirties. Notable are the 6,000ft (1,829m) East Face of the Watzmann—the highest rock-face in the Eastern Alps—and the mile long, 2,500ft (762m) high, Laliodererspitze in the Karwendel.

Despite much first-class rock-climbing and fine ridge traverses amid, for instance, the spiky fangs of the Zillertal Alps (peaks such as the Zsigmondyspitze—10,128ft/3,087m) it is for snow-, ice- and mixed-climbing that the mountains of the long central chain are best known. The imposing snowy peaks of the Ortler hold many excellent routes, the classic being perhaps the steep and difficult 2,000ft (609m) ice-rib on the North Face of the Gran Zebu (or Königsspitze). The summit is guarded by the famous 'whipped cream roll' cornice which has been climbed direct by Kurt Diemberger. Among the best ice-walls elsewhere are those of the Wildspitze, the Hochfeiler, and the Grossvenediger. On the impressive

North-West Face of the Grosses Wiesbachhorn, Willo Welzenbach made a classic ice-climb in 1924 when ice-pegs were used for the first time. Today extremely popular, it has even been descended on skis! Pride of place must go, however, to the magnificent Grossglockner whose exquisite icy cone is Austria's highest summit. One of the most elegant peaks in the Alps, its easier routes are now immensely popular tourist climbs, but its northern face holds major and serious lines. The Pallavicini-Rinne—Austria's classic ice-climb—is a 2,000ft (609m) couloir and was a remarkable ascent for 1876. It was unrepeated for forty-five years! Close by, Welzenbach's North Face route is a formidable climb on mixed ground. The Hohe Tauern contain some fifty summits above 10,000ft (3,048m) and offers a great range of easy and difficult climbs. But the immediate Glockner region itself is owned by the Austrian Alpine Club as a nature reserve and the Grossglockner 'high alpine toll road' guarantees that accessible areas are crowded throughout the tourist season. In winter, however, the central chain becomes a paradise for ski-touring and winter-climbing second to none, and the mountains regain the peace they lost fifty years ago.

41

Eastern Alps

The Italian Dolomites. The North Faces of the famous Tre Cime di Lavaredo. On the left the Cima Piccolissima, Punta di Frida and Cima Piccolo clump together, while at the centre stands the massive Cima Grande, and on the right the Cima Ovest. There are many spectacular climbs on these great overhanging walls

Most Important Mountain Groups

Ortler Alps

Situation: Italy—Alto Adige Region
1 Cima Ortles (12,792/3,900) 1804: Joseph Pichler and party—by command of Archduke John of Austria
2 Gran Zebu (Grosse Königsspitze) (12,661/3,859) 1854: S. Steinbeger and party
3 Monte Cevedale (12,395/3,778) 1865: J. Payer and J. Pinggera

Major Glacier
Forno system—3 × 3 miles (5 × 5km)

Huts and Bivouacs
Some thirty-three, mostly owned by CAI

Convenient Centre
Solda—a small village

Guide-book
Ortler Alps, West Col (UK)

Ötztal Alps

Situation: Austria—Tirol Province; Italy—Alto Adige Region
1 Wildspitze—Nordgipfel (12,375/3,772) 1861: L. Klotz (South Peak—1848: L. Klotz)
2 Weisskugel (12,267/3,739) 1850: J. Specht with L. Klotz and J. Raffeiner
3 Similaun (11,831/3,606) 1834: T. Kaserer with J. Raffeiner

Major Glaciers
Gepatsch Ferner—5½ miles (8¼km)
Hintereis Ferner—5½ miles (8¼km)

Huts and Bivouacs
Some forty-three, belonging to OAV, CAI, etc

Convenient Centre
Solden—large resort village

Guide-book
Ötztal Alps, West Col (UK)

Stubai Alps

Situation: Austria—Tirol Province; Italy—Alto Adige Region
1 Zuckerhutl (11,499/3,505) 1862: A. Specht with A. Tanzer
2 Schrankogel (11,470/3,496) 1824: J. Harpasser

Major Glacier
Ubeltal Ferner—2.5 × 2.5 miles (4 × 4km)

Huts and Bivouacs
Some fifty, belonging to OAV, CAI, etc

Convenient Centre
Neustift—large village, Fulpmes

Guide-book
Stubai Alps, West Col (UK)

Zillertal Alps

Situation: Austria—Tirol Province; Italy—Alto Adige Region
1 Hochfeiler (11,516/3,510) 1865: Paul Grohmann with P. Fuchs and H. Joseler
2 Grosser Moseler (11,411/3,478) 1865: Tuckett, Freshfield and party with F. Devouassoud
3 Olperer (11,404/3,476) 1867: Paul Grohmann with Georg Samer

Major Glaciers
Schlegeiskees—2.5 miles (4km) wide
Gefrorne Wand—1.8 × 1.4 miles (3 × 2km)

Huts and Bivouacs
More than 40 huts, both Austrian and Italian, are owned by OAV, CAI, etc

Convenient Centre
Mayrhofen—important large resort village

Guide Book
Zillertal Alps, West Col (UK) in preparation

Hohe Tauern

Situation: Austria—Salzburg, Ost Tirol and Kärnten (Carinthia) Provinces
1 Grossglockner (12,461/3,798) 1800: Count von Salm, Prince Bishop of Gurk and his party of sixty
Grossvenediger (12,054/3,674) 1841: Forester Rohregger and party
Grosses Wiesbachhorn (11,713/3,570) 1798(?): Zanker and Zorner

Major Glacier
Oberer Pasterzenboden system—5.6 miles (9km)—the longest in the Eastern Alps

Huts and Bivouacs
More than 47 throughout the region

Convenient Centres
Zell am See—important resort, Mittersill

Guide-book
Glockner Region, West Col (UK)

Dolomites

Situation: Italy—Alto Adige Region and Belluno Province
1 Marmolata (10,965/3,342) 1863: P. Grohmann with Dimai bros
  di Rocca 1860: J. Ball and Birkbeck with V. Tairraz
Civetta (10,558/3,218)
Cima Grande di Lavaredo (9,839/2,999) 1869: P. Grohmann with F. Innerkofler and P. Salcher

Huts and Bivouacs
A large number throughout the region mostly owned by the CAI

Convenient Centre
Cortina d'Ampezzo—major international resort

Guide-book
Dolomites, 2 vols, Alpine Club (London)

Julian Alps

Situation: Yugoslavia—Slovenia; Italy—Venezia
1 Triglar (9,393/2,863) 1778: Lorenz Willnotzer Jalovec (8,671/2,643) 1875: C. Wormb and party

Huts and Bivouacs
Over 40 huts are owned by Jugoslav and Italian Alpine Clubs

Convenient Centre
Bohinjska Lake resorts, or Bled

Guide Book
Julian Alps, West Col (UK)

Northern Limestone Ranges
(Kalkalpen)

Situation: Austria—mostly Tirol and Salzburg Province; Germany—Bavaria
Lechtal Alps: Parseierspitze (9,961/3,036)
Wetterstein: Zugspitze (9,718/2,962)—highest mountain in Germany
Karwendel: Birkkarspitze (9,019/2,749); Lalidererspitze (8,474/2,583)
Wilder Kaiser: Ellmauer Halt (7,690/2,344); Fleischbank (7,175/2,187)
Salzburger Alps: Hochkönig (9,649/2,941); Watzmann (8,901/2,713)
Dachstein and Torstein: Hohe Dachstein (9,826/2,995)

Guide books
At present 2 volumes, *Karwendel* and *Kaisergebirge* are published by West Col (UK).

Eastern Alps
Apart from the English volumes above, Rudolf Rother (Munich) publish guides to all areas in German and CAI/TCI publish guides to the Ortler, Dolomites and Julians in Italian

Maps
Most of the Eastern Alps areas are available from the following publishers: 1:2,5000 scale—AV (Austria); 1:50,000 scale—*Kompass* (Austria) and Freytag-Berndt (Austria) or Rudolf Rother (Munich) and some areas from TCI (Italy)

English Lake District: Ian Howell on 'Eliminate A' on Dow Crag

Dow Crag is in the Coniston Fells and looks out eastwards over the little tarn of Goats Water to Coniston Old Man (2,635ft/803m). Although it is a mountain crag, the walk up to it is not a long one; the rock is sound and compact—although very greasy when wet—and it holds a good variety of long (350ft/107m) climbs, and is therefore understandably popular. The first climb here was made by Haskett-Smith in 1886.

'Eliminate A' takes a direct line up the most southerly of the four massive main buttresses and is about 380ft (116m) long. One of the best climbs on Dow Crag, it was completed as early as 1923 by George Basterfield and H. S. Gross and still retains a good VS grading. Ian Howell is seen on the sixth pitch—an exposed and rather delicate traverse which I found very precarious with a camera slung round my chest. With a large paunch too I would certainly have been off!

Overleaf: **Scotland: the Cuillin of Skye**

This is a variation of that classic view of the Black Cuillin from Elgol – the roadhead and crofting hamlet at the tip of the Strathaird Peninsula in southern Skye. It is dusk in early June and the sun has dropped behind the mountains, but at this time of year it will remain twilight until dawn. The serrated 7-mile (11km) ridge of the Cuillin runs from Garsbheinn (2,935ft/895m)—the large pyramid to the left—to Sgurr nan Gillean (3,167ft/965m)—the peak second from the right with a pinnacled right-hand ridge. Sgurr na Stri (1,632ft/497m)—the peak on the far right—is an outlier rising sheer from the sea.

From this angle, 5 miles (8km) to the south east across the great inlet of Loch Scavaig, one sees right into the heart of the Cuillin. Here, ringed by 3,000ft (914m) rock walls, lies Loch Coruisk, a freshwater loch linked to Scavaig by a short and tumultuous river. The wild grandeur of the naked ice-smoothed rock contrasting with the clear green skerry-studded sea, the silver strand and the unexpected wild flowers make this sanctuary perhaps the most beautiful place in Britain. With luck it will remain unspoilt, for, apart from boat trips run by an enterprising Elgol fisherman, it is only accessible to climbers and hardy mountain walkers.

Skye is known as 'The Island of Mists' and it is notorious, unfairly perhaps, for its poor weather. Certainly my first five visits to the Cuillin were extremely wet and for the first two, over a period of no less than four weeks, we never saw the mountains, although we climbed on them every day! But all these visits were in August which is not a good month for Scottish weather in any case, and more recently I have spent some time on the island in May and June and not seen a cloud! Those who know Skye and the other Hebridean islands find little difficulty in echoing the sentiments of Sir Walter Scott:

'. . .mountains divide us, and the waste of the seas . . .
. . .and we in dreams behold the Hebrides.'

Snowdonia: Tryfan seen from the Glyders to the south east

Friendly, compact and, for me at any rate, very much the mountains of home
(Tryfan was my first summit as a small boy). This picture was taken on a raw winter
day when I had the mountains to myself; unusual in this area. The three large
buttresses of Tryfan's East Face are seen from the frosted saddle near the tiny Llyn
Caseg-fraith, while on the left Bristly Ridge rises to Glyder Fach (3,262ft/994m). In
the Carneddau, across the Ogwen valley to the right, Cwm Lloer nestles between
the shoulders of Pen-yr-oleu-wen (3,211ft/979m) and Carnedd Dafydd.

   Tryfan (3,010ft/917m) is the only top in Wales that cannot be reached without the
use of hands, although with some cunning route-finding someone could prove me
wrong! Two enormous blocks—Adam and Eve—crown its summit, the central one
of the three peaks, and it is traditional to leap from one to the other: a slip would
lead 600ft (183m) down the East Face! The first recorded ascent of the mountain
was in the 1790s by a Mr Bingley, but no doubt local shepherds had been there
years before. By the 1850s it was well known that the traverse of Tryfan's North and
South Ridges—the right and left skylines in the picture—followed by the ascent of
Bristly Ridge, made one of the finest 'expeditions' in Wales and even today, under
hard winter conditions, it can provide good fun. Among the earliest rock-climbs in
the area were the South and North Gullys, those either side of the summit, and by
1914 the great classic lines on the three buttresses had been made. These are routes
that I hold in high affection for it was on them that I learnt to climb, in sun and in
snow, and they hold memories galore.

Ben Nevis from the Great Glen

Once again this is a classic view taken from the heights above the Caledonian
Canal on the west side of the Great Glen, a couple of miles up from Banavie. We are
looking into the great north-eastern corrie of the Ben—the valley of the Allt
a'Mhuilinn. Walling it is the greatest crag in Britain, some 2 miles (3km) long and
up to 2,000ft (610m) high. The North-East Buttress forms the skyline and the
summit of the mountain lies close to its top: high up on its face the still snow-filled
upper sections of Zero and Point Five Gullys may be discerned. The line of famous
Tower Ridge parallels the Buttress in the sun, while Carn Dearg Buttress and
Castle Ridge loom in the shadow.

   The picture was taken in mid June and good snow conditions are often found well
into May: snow lingers throughout the summer in most years, especially in the deep
recess between North East Buttress and Tower Ridge. Some years ago we were
actually forced to retreat from a climb in early September by powder avalanches of
new snow.

   A tiny climbing hut, owned by the Scottish Mountaineering Club, lies near the
base of Tower Ridge: provisioned in the past by pack-horses and tracked vehicles,
it is now serviced by helicopter. While climbing from the hut one December, Tony
Smythe and I were unable to relocate it in a white-out after completing our climb
and were forced to descend to spend the night in Fort William, only to discover,
when we returned in calm weather the next day, that our footprints passed inches
from the snow-drifted door! Ben Nevis (4,406ft/1,343m) is a very serious mountain
and proposals to build another larger hut are, I feel, a step in the wrong direction.
No hut is strictly necessary; major routes can be completed safely from the valley,
and those unprepared to face the long pre-dawn walk are surely unfitted to attempt
the Ben's demanding climbs.

Europe

Coire an t'Sneachda, the Snowy Corrie, one of the two great corries of Cairn Gorm. Ringed by dark cliffs, it cradles two small lochans amongst its boulders

Caucasus

The southern bastion of Europe, the Caucasus stretch for 550 miles (168km) from the Black Sea to the Caspian. No great continental divide this, however, and today not even a political one, for the range merely separates the plains of Russia from the highlands of Asia Minor and the rivers born among the mountains are neither long nor important.

Although in extent and character comparable to the European Alps, the range is narrower and less complex besides being 5 degrees (250 miles/402km) further south and generally nearly 3,000ft (914m) higher. The snow-line is higher too and, although the loftier regions are heavily and extensively glaciated, the glaciers are if anything rather smaller than comparable alpine ones. In its great length the narrow crest is crossed only by four major passes and the long lateral ridges which rise from it often tend to bend sharply parallel to their parent effectively making two or even three lines of mountains.

With natural divisions at the important Klukhor and Krestovy Passes the Caucasus breaks easily into three sections. The western is alpine in height and rises gradually from the Black Sea which controls its warm and humid climate: it is consequently heavily forested. The eastern section is a little higher and rather arid, particularly at its far extremity where it fades into semi-desert on the Caspian shore. Most important is the 160 miles (257km) of the central section where all the higher peaks lie and where the weather is notoriously unsettled and the scenery alpine, with high meadows and valley pine woods. Characteristic are the great glacier basins, in the style of those of the Mont Blanc Massif, but walled, with great peaks standing proud more in the manner of the Pennine Alps: the Bezingi, Maragom, Dykh-su and Tsanner basins are typical. The peaks themselves are mostly formidable with wide, well buttressed rock- and ice-faces and long, high and serrated linking arêtes. Of the major tops of the central chain, only Elbrus and Kazbek at its two limits give easy access, via straightforward snow-slopes, to their summits—both are extinct volcanic cones.

Blocking the corridor from Asia to Europe, the Caucasus have suffered repeated incursions over the centuries: Romans, Persians, Arabs and Turks from the south, Huns, Tartars, Imperial Russians, Soviets and—most recently—Nazis, from the north. Not surprisingly the people are traditionally fierce, war-like and stubbornly independent and—paradoxically—those on the Asian flank, once the Kingdom of Georgia, are Christian, while those on the northern or European flank, Muslims.

The first climbers were British, for the close of the so-called 'Golden Age' in the Alps coincided with the arrival of settled times in the Caucasus in the wake of Imperial Russian conquest. Freshfield's powerful 1868 party made a reconnaissance in force of the whole range and some easy ascents. Members of the Alpine Club—with their alpine guides—were extremely active in the decade from 1886, with 1888 as the vintage year—as the list below shows. It was marred by tragedy however: Donkin and Fox, two well known climbers, vanished with their two guides during an attempt on Koshtan-Tau. Rumours spread of foul play and kidnapping by bandits and an 'international incident' almost occurred. But a search party the following year, led by Freshfield, discovered their last camp high on the peak and it was obvious that they had died in a climbing accident. Some of the search party continued to the summit. Hungarian alpinist de Déchy and the great mountain photographer, Vittorio Sella, also made climbs and, by 1896, most of the great peaks had been ascended. German and Austrian climbers made many good climbs before the Great War and during the thirties, but the Russians themselves date the start of their own Caucasian mountaineering to a mass ascent, by eighteen people, of Kazbek in 1923.

The areas of most interest to climbers lie near the heads of the Baksan and Bezingi Valleys. Above the former rises the twin-headed fang of Ushba—the 'Matterhorn of the Caucasus'. Its traverse in 1903 by Hans Pfann's party—a six-bivouac tour-de-force—paved the way to what has since become a Caucasian speciality, a big traverse linking several peaks. Ushba's easiest route is quite hard and its north–west face contains a 6,600ft (2,012m) aided climb! Shkhelda is a saw-blade of rock and ice rising above the Ushba glacier, and the famous traverse over its five summits and countless gendarmes is set a 'control time' of twelve days by the Russians! Hamish MacInnes, who made the first foreign traverse in 1961, described it as a cross between the Himalaya and the Dolomites.

The Bezingi Basin contains no fewer than eleven of the fourteen '5,000m' (16,400ft) peaks in the range. Famous climbs here include the 'mixed' twin south buttresses of Dykh-Tau whose South Face is similar in appearance to

The saw-tooth ridge of Shkhelda, seen from the Baksan Valley. The 'control time' for a traverse of this ridge is in the region of twelve days

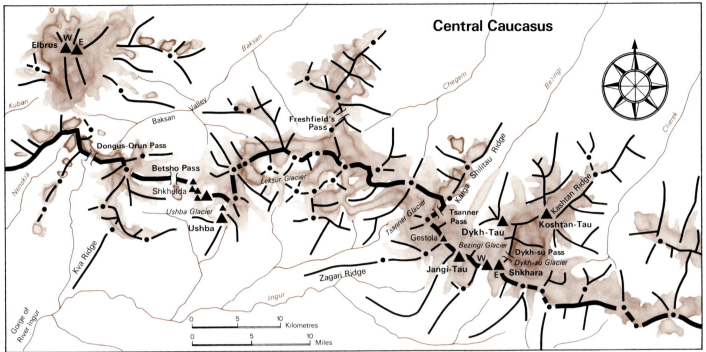

Central Caucasus

the North of the Grandes Jorasses: the right-hand buttress was a British first ascent of 1958 (M. Harris, G. Band) and the left a Polish route of 1959. It is interesting to note that Mummery's first ascent of the mountain finished via the upper section of the Polish route. Longstaff compared the South Face of Shkhara to the Macugnaga Face of Monte Rosa. It is a mile-long ridge with a major summit at each end and its Tomaschek Buttress (1930), finding its way through the tangle of *séracs* and ice-gullies of its 6,500ft (1,981m) North Face is classic. Jangi-tau too has a famous route on its huge northern face—the Schwarzgruber Rib (1935). Both these great climbs were first made by Austrian parties and have been repeated by foreign teams, including British and French, in recent years. With its huge walls the basin gives fantastic traverse possibilities: the traverse over Dykh-Tau and Koshtan-Tau is nearly 7 miles (11km) and fairly popular, but the formidable 'Bezingi Wall' gives over 10 miles (16km) of sustained climbing from the Dykh-su Pass to the Tsanner Pass and is technically hard and continuously high. First completed in six days by an Austrian team in 1931, and not often repeated, it is considered the greatest expedition in the range.

Modern Russian climbers are extremely good and have achieved great things in their mountains and obviously the potential for difficult climbing, both new and repeat ascents, is still tremendous in so large a range. In terms of seriousness and commitment, climbing on the higher peaks must be considered

as lying between the Alps and the Himalaya: poor weather and high altitude are major factors. The Russians make visiting Western mountaineers very welcome, but the bureaucratic difficulties and the expense of visiting the Caucasus, coupled to the Russian style of organized and closely controlled climbing, very foreign to the anarchistic freedom Western climbers enjoy, ensures that few ever reach the Caucasus, which is a pity because it does offer some of the finest mountaineering in the world.

Situation: USSR—Georgia and Azerbaijan SSR's to the south and various small Soviet republics to the north

Most Important Peaks
1 Elbrus W (18,481/5,633) 1874: Moore, Gardiner, Grove and Walker—the highest summit in Europe
Elbrus E (18,442/5,621) 1868: Freshfield, Moore, Tucker
2 Dykh-Tau (17,074/5,204) 1888: A. F. Mummery with H. Zurfluh
3 Shkhara E (17,064/5,201) 1888: J. G. Cockin with Ulrich Almer
Shkhara W (16,529/5,038) 1903: Tom Longstaff and L. W. Rolleston
4 Koshtan-Tau (16,877/5,144) 1889: H. Wooley and party
5 Jangi-Tau (16,571/5,050) 1888: J. G. Cockin with Ulrich Almer
6 Kazbek (16,558/5,047) 1868: Freshfield, Moore, Tucker
Ushba South (15,453/4,710) 1903: Schulze and von Ficker
Ushba North (15,400/4,694) 1888: J. G. Cockin with Ulrich Almer
Shkhelda (14,173/4,320)

Western Caucasus
1 Dombai-Ulgen (13,255/4,040) 1914: Schuster and Fischer

Eastern Caucasus
1 Tebulos-Inta (14,744/4,494) P. Merzbacher

Major Glaciers
Bezingi system—9½ miles (15km)

Major Passes
Marukh Pass (9,085/2,769)
Klukhor Pass (9,140/2,786)—road-pass, west boundary of Central Caucasus
Dongus-Orun—road-pass
Mamison Pass (9,281/2,829)—road-pass
Krestovy Pass (7,835/2,388)—Georgian military road and eastern boundary of Central Caucasus

Huts and Bivouacs
The Russian system does not use huts and climbers are expected to establish their own high camps and bivouacs.

Convenient Centres
Climbers operate from permanent 'mountaineering camps' established at suitable locations. Some of these are: Elbruz area in the Aksant and Amanauz Valleys—headwaters of the Kuban river; Ushba area in the Adyr Su and Adyl Su Valleys—headwaters of the Baksan river and in the Bezingi valley

Access
(a) By official invitation to a country's senior club from the Mountaineering Federation of the USSR
(b) By personal invitation from a Trade Union mountaineering Club to stay at one of their mountain centres
(c) As tourists through Intourist, the official Russian travel agency
After this initial approach all access problems are taken care of

Guide-books
The Exploration of the Caucasus, Douglas Freshfield (Edward Arnold, London, 1896)

Good guides are published in East Germany particularly to the Elbrus region. The Austrian Alpine Club provides two *Kammkarte* maps covering Central Caucasus.

Tatra

The Carpathians curve for nearly 900 miles (1,448km) along the borders of Czechoslovakia, Poland and the Ukraine before curling into the heart of Romania. Cradled within this horseshoe lie the lush plains of Hungary where the mighty Danube meanders on its long journey from the Black Forest to the Black Sea. A major continental divide, two great rivers rise from its northern slopes, the Vistula flowing north to the Baltic, while the Dniester flows south east to the Black Sea. Only in two places do these forested highlands rise high: Negoi reaches 8,360ft (2,548m) above the craggy Fagarasulin plateau of the wild Transylvanian Alps where gothic legend locates the home of Dracula and Frankenstein—a mere 70 miles (113km) north west of Bucharest. In the north, however, the Tatra or Tatry, a small rugged massif astride the Czechoslovak–Polish frontier, rises to 8,373ft (2,552m)—the highest point between the Alps and the Caucasus—and, although occupying an area only some 37×12 miles (59×19km), the Tatra holds a position in the world's mountain hierarchy out of all proportion to its size.

Once the border between the ancient kingdoms of Poland and Hungary, the mountain fastness of the Tatra was the reputed lair of brigands and outlaws until well into the nineteenth century. Exploration was slow, although several travellers, notably British, did penetrate the region early on. Today the Gurals—the local mountain peasants—are shepherds and farmers who still cling to their traditional costume and dances, for progress has less affected them than it has their alpine counterparts. Now the range is enclosed within National Parks—two-thirds of the Tatra are Slovak territory—and both Polish and Slovak Park Authorities work closely together. Chamois and deer abound and, in the several areas set aside as strict game sanctuaries, wild boar, European lynx and bears still flourish.

The range forms three mountain groups of very different character: the East or Belanske Tatra, the High or Wysokie Tatra and—to the west—the Zachodnie Tatra. The Belanske group is a relatively small area of Dolomitic and sedimentary rocks but the Zachodnie Tatra occupies nearly half the range. Predominantly limestone, it is gentler country than the High Tatra. Fine little peaks and steep walls of white rock rise above broad green uplands and dark pines: this is fine country for hiking and ski-touring and the climbing—neglected

until recently in favour of the High Tatra—is excellent with plenty of scope for new lines. Typical perhaps is the mile-long limestone wall that culminates in Mnich Raptawicki (*c*6,000ft/1,829m), virgin until an Anglo-Polish party made a 500ft (152m) route on it, using aid, in 1972. This is also cave country and the Sniezna ('Snow') system is one of the deepest yet discovered, over 2,000ft (609m) deep and 4 miles (6km) long.

By contrast the Wysokie Tatra are rugged mountains of naked granite. Ten summits top 8,500ft (2,591m) and form a dramatic and jagged skyline from which crags often fall over 2,000ft (609m) into deep gouged corries floored with scree and bejewelled with the beautiful tarns for which these mountains are famous. The High Tatra have been compared to a scaled-up Cuillin (Skye), but here snow lies throughout the summer in the gullies and hollows among the peaks and winter brings heavy falls and plenty of ice: winter climbing in fact, as in Scotland, is a speciality of the Tatra. Below the corries there are alpine meadows, and forests of beech, rowan, birch and

spruce rise up to meet them around the 4,000ft (1,219m) level.

Much of the best climbing is concentrated in the three large corries on the Polish side—the greatest concentration of long and hard routes being clustered around the *cirque* of Morskie Oko—the 'Eye of the Sea' tarn. Notable is the great peak of Mieguszowiecki with its several summits, a grade IV traverse in summer. The classic route of its North Face is the North–East Spur, grade V and giving nearly 3,000ft (914m) of climbing—in 1955 its first winter ascent took four days. Other climbs on the face range from Orfowski's Route, 1,260ft (380m) of grade IV, to Alligator's Route, the same length, but grade VI. Rising from the face of one of the Mieguszowiecki summits is Kazalnica (the Pulpit), a pinnacle on whose blank 1,500ft (457m)

Gerlach: the picture is taken from Rysy, Poland's highest summit. The sharp ridges and rocky summits of these fine little mountains are clearly visible

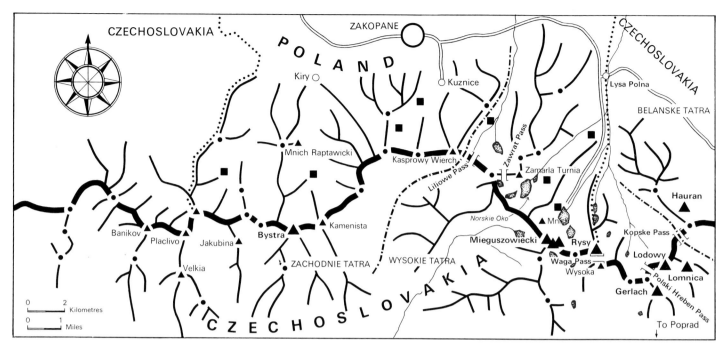

North Face expansion bolts were first used in the Tatra—it is probably the range's most difficult wall. Mnich (the Monk) is a small spiky peak on a short ridge jutting into the corrie with a classic line, only grade IV, on its North–West Face but with other climbs some free, some which require aid, but all hard which force a line of roofs on its East Face. Across the corrie the fine slabs of the South Face of Zamarla Turnia are popular and the first grade V climb in the Tatra was put up here in 1910. In the Hala Gasienicowa corrie to the west there are many easier and shorter climbs.

The Slovak flank is more complex and Czechoslovak territory extends to both sides of the crest. Gerlach has a fine and straightforward climb up its North-West Ridge and Lomnica, its summit, unfortunately marred by a *téléphérique* station, has a superb West Face. The famous Hokeyka Route on it crosses the great slab shaped like a hockey stick which is its main feature. Many of the hard routes put up in the 1930s are classic nowadays and one such is Stanislawski's Chimney on the North Face of magnificent Maly Kiezmarski (8,281ft/2,524m). He was one of the great climbers of the period and the 2,800ft (853m) route is still graded VI. The Freundschaft Weg, not very hard, on the 1,500ft (458m) North-East Face of Gerlachousy Stit (8,711ft/2,655m) was made in 1969 by Ian Clough, climbing with a Czechoslovak-Norwegian party.

Nowadays most summer routes in the Tatra are repeated in winter and the winter traverse of the entire range is, of course, the finest expedition. It had been completed only five times to 1975 which is not surprising as it involves some 30 miles (48km) of sustained climbing, some of it very hard indeed, and thirteen bivouacs! Really a very major undertaking. It is climbs of this sort which train Polish mountaineers to be among the world's best, despite Poland's lack of high mountains.

Unfortunately the Tatra weather leaves much to be desired in summer: the granite, usually of excellent quality, is notoriously slippery when damp. But the heavy snows of winter provide—besides superlative winter climbing—excellent skiing both on and off pistes. A Polish cable car runs to the summit of Kasprowy Wierch (6,500ft/1,981m) but, despite World Ski Championships twice held in Zakopane, other uphill facilities are considered locally to be inadequate.

Pressure on the Tatra is great: the National Park authorities must cope with over 4 million visitors a year within this very limited area. Strict rules are enforced which govern all activities and good facilities are provided—in the form of excellent hostels, well maintained signposted paths, a professional guide service and excellent mountain rescue facilities. Fixed ropes and iron handrails decorate difficult sections of the more popular easy peaks. Tourists are forbidden to leave the marked trails and only bone fide climbers—'Taterniks'—may stray off them. To Western mountaineers these may seem iron-handed tactics, but at least they preserve these wonderful little mountains for those best able to appreciate their delights.

Situation: Poland and Czechoslovakia

Most Important Peaks
High Tatra—Tatry Wysokie
1 Gerlach (8,737/2,663) c1855: Z. Bosniachi and W. Grzegorzek (entirely in Czechoslovakia)
2 Lomnica (8,642/2,634) 1793: Robert Townshend
3 Lodowy (8,622/2,628) 1843: John Ball
Rysy (8,205/2,501) c1840: E. Blasy (highest peak in Poland)
Mieguszowiecki (7,999/2,438)
Bystra (7,382/2,250) highest in Zachodnie Tatra
Hauran (7,067/2,154) highest in Belanske Tatra

Major Passes
Although there are many fine passes over its main divide the mountain frontier is closed and only properly designated border posts may be used with all formalities—e.g. visas, etc.

Huts and Bivouacs
In Poland there are eight 'mountain house' hostels belonging to the National Park Authority in High and West Tatra. In Czechoslovakia there are huts in every major valley

Convenient Centres
North (Poland): Zakopane—bustling resort town
South (Czechoslovakia): Tatransca Lomnica

Access
By air to Warsaw International Airport or to Cracow airport thence by road or rail to Zakopane via Cracow or to Prague International Airport or Kosice airport and thence by road or rail to Poprad, which is linked to Zakopane by road via Lysa Polna

Maps
The Polish Map Institute (PPWK) publishes 1:30,000 and 1:75,000 maps of the Northern (Polish) flank.
The official Czechoslovak maps (USGK) are to 1:50,000 and 1:500,000 scale. There are also ST 1:50,000 sheets of High Tatra

Guide-books
An English guide-book to selected climbing is published by Fregata Travel, the official Polish travel agency in London. The Polish climbing guide-book lists some 3,000 routes in no less than 17 volumes for High Tatra alone, but there is also 1 volume of selected climbs in 'topo' format.

Pyrenees

Effectively cutting off the Iberian Peninsula from the body of western Europe, both physically, politically, ethnically and culturally, the long and narrow chain of the Pyrenees stretches for some 270 miles (434km) from the Mediterranean to the Bay of Biscay. While lower and less extensive than the Alps it is the second of Europe's great ranges west of the Caucasus. Only three main peaks top 11,000ft (3,353m) but more than fifty rise above 10,000ft (3,048m). In summer the snow cover is relatively small but the several little glaciers that cling to the northern flanks of the mountains have now stabilised.

The mountain crest, except for one notable instance, forms the watershed between the Garonne and the Adour to the north and the Ebro to the south and is usually followed by the political frontier. The crest rises steeply from France, presenting almost a mountain wall to the north but from the south it is masked by ranges of foothills falling gradually away to the plains of Aragon. The Garonne itself rises in Spain and cuts back deeply into the crest near its centre where the eastern section of the chain actually overlaps the western. Otherwise the crest is continuously high over its central 180 miles (290km) where it is breached only by four other road-passes—indeed for the 70 miles (193km) immediately west of the Garonne by no such pass at all! The Aneto Glacier on the southern side of the watershed is actually one of the sources of the Garonne but its out-flow disappears underground into the Trou de Toro pothole to reappear several miles later on the northern side of the watershed! The exploration of this cave system and others in this most important cave region is well described in Norbert Casteret's book *Ten Years under the Earth*. For practical purposes the pass situation has been eased by the construction of two road-tunnels.

Scenically the Pyrenees are extremely beautiful and some 75 miles (121km) of the northern flanks of the chain lie within the French Parc National des Pyrenees with a Centre in the Val d'Azun. Smaller areas, notably the Encantados and Ordesa Canyon are included in Spanish National Parks. The geology is complex, but most of the peaks are built either of granite or limestone or both and it is the scenery of the latter that perhaps most characterizes the range forming the great cliff—encircled amphitheatres—such as the Cirque de Gavarnie—which often head the dead-end lateral valleys. Tremendous waterfalls are another fea-

Pic du Midi d'Ossau is seen here over the little Lac d'Ayous

ture. On the Spanish flank the Ordesa Canyon with its huge walls of many-hued limestone beneath snow-covered summits is considered the most beautiful valley of the range. Interesting animal species include the isard—a Pyrenean chamois—wild boar and brown bear, while ibex, vultures and lammergeior may occasionally be seen. The climate, tending to oceanic in the west and Mediterranean in the east, favours a wide ranging and often rare flora, while the weather in summer is generally fairly settled and, certainly on the Spanish side, hot.

At its western end, on both sides of the frontier, the range is the home of the ancient Basque people, and their unique language, together with Bearnais and

This view of the North Face of the Vignemale shows the great gash of the Couloir de Gaube. The Refuge des Ouletes lies hidden in the cwm in the foreground

Bigourdan patois, is still spoken in some areas. Similarly Aragonese patois is spoken in some Spanish valleys. Roman, Vandal and Islamic invasion has swirled round the mountains and romantic legends associate (incorrectly) the Brèche de Roland above the Cirque de Gavarnie with the epic of Charlemagne's retreat: in more recent times the high frontier has been traversed by smugglers and refugees in both directions.

Many of the most interesting peaks actually lie south of the frontier. The Encantados is a complex granite group isolated in Catalonia with many good rock-climbs on small peaks rising from an attractive area of pine woods and rocky lakes. Best known are the two formidable looking needles of Els Encantats (9,102ft/2,774m), the lower of which, while probably the most difficult major Pyrenean summit, presents little problem to the experienced rock-climber.

Nearby the difficult Agulles (Aiguilles) d'Amitges also give good routes. Nearly 20 miles (32km) west, and again entirely in Spain, Pico Aneto rises from the granite Maladeta massif. As the highest Pyrenean summit it is a popular and easy ascent and the sweeping rock-ridges that surround it give pleasant scrambling above four small glaciers. The unfrequented Pico de Posets and Monte Perdido are both limestone peaks standing on short subsidiary ridges south of the main crest. Both are easy walks but the latter holds a classic ice-climb on its northern hanging glacier from which the ice has retreated since its first ascent in 1880, making the route harder. Close by is the famous Cirque de Gavarnie topped by an arc of limestone peaks, the highest of which is Marbore (10,656ft/3,248m). The walls of the *cirque* are over 5,000ft (1,524m) high, but broken into tiers by two large horizontal

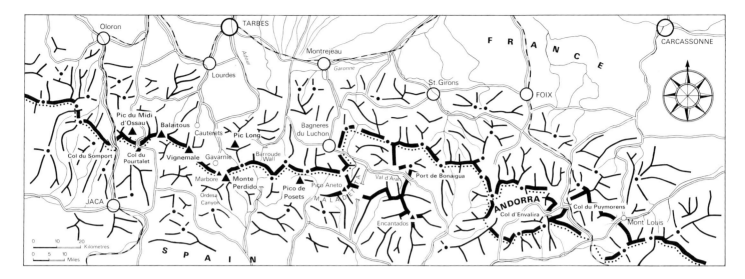

terraces, and they hold a host of popular modern rock-climbs up to the highest grades.

North of the main crest in the remote Neouvielle area, Pic Long is the highest Pyrenean summit entirely in France. Its fine granite North Face on which ice-fields separate rock-bands, rises above little Lac Tourrat and was opened up in 1933 by Ollivier and Mailly: there are several newer lines. Further west on the main chain is the massive rusty granite cone of Balaitous. It has a fine West Face but is especially noted for the excellent traverses afforded by its long pinnacled ridges which give some of the best climbs in the range.

Certainly the most interesting peaks are the Vignemale and the Pic du Midi d'Ossau. The former is the highest frontier summit, a huge plateau of schistose limestone surrounded by steep walls. Its North Face in fact is the highest un-broken Pyrenean wall and a full 2,500ft (762m): it is climbed by several modern routes of medium to highest grade and is split by the deep gash of the Couloir de Gaube, a difficult ice-climb rather Scottish in style first climbed in 1889 and not repeated in its entirety until 1946! The Voie Normal however is easy. Vignemale is famous for its association with the eccentric Count Henry Russell, the famous Pyrenean pioneer who made some thirty-three ascents and in the 1880s spent much time living—indeed even receiving dinner guests in evening dress—in grottoes blasted from the rock below the tongue of the Glacier d'Ossoue.

The Pic du Midi d'Ossau stands alone above the pastures, a fine double-headed pyramid of purple-brown granite, and not unlike Mount Kenya. It gives magnificent climbing: the *Voie Normale* is easy but there are many classic rock-routes of all grades to the hardest, the first of which were pioneered by Ollivier and Mailly in the 1930s—they were the first to use aid techniques in the Pyrenees. A recent 2,000ft (609m) winter ascent on the Pic took three days and much is still being achieved on the mountain. Elsewhere there is notable rock-climbing in the Ordesa Canyon, on the limestone Barroude Wall in the Cirque de Troumouse and on several of the granite peaks on or close to the frontier south of Bagneres de Luchon.

To sum up then: because of good walking and easy access from hut or camp, straightforward routes to virtually all summits and reasonable altitude coupled to relatively settled weather, the Pyrenees are ideal country for less experienced mountaineers or backpackers. There is fine rock-climbing and a little ice of sorts and much of the range is still wild and remote country, while *nordic* ski touring can be really excellent.

Opposite above: **The northern flanks of Balaitous: the pinnacled West Ridge and the long East Ridge are clearly visible**

Right: **Les Encantats seen over the Lac de San Mauricio: these fine** *aiguilles* **are probably the best known of the Encantados peaks**

Situation: France, Spain and Republic of Andorra

Some important Peaks

1 Pico de Aneto (11,168/3,404) 1842: Albert de Franqueville and Platon Chihacher and party. Entirely in Spain

2 Pico de Posets (11,073/3,375) 1856: M. Halkett

3 Monte Perdido (11,007/3,355) 1802: Laurens and Rondou of L-F Ramond's party

Vignemale (10,820/3,298) 1837: H. Cazeaux and B. Guillembet—the highest entirely French peak

Pic Long (10,472/3,192) 1846: Duc de Nemours, son of King Louis Philippe, and the guide Marc Sesquet

Balaitous (10,322/3,146) 1825: Lts Peytier, Hossard and their party

Pic du Midi d'Ossau (9,465/2,885) *c*1787: unknown but in 1797 Guillaume Delfau with Mathieu

Major Road Passes

Col du Puymorens (6,281/1,914)

Col d'Envalira (7,897/2,407) from France to Andorra

Port de Bonaigua (6,797/2,072) across the watershed at the head of the Garonne but both sides are in Spain

Col du Pourtalet (5,768/1,758)

Col du Somport (5,354/1,632)

Col du Tourmalet (6,936/2,114) between the Gave de Pau and Adour valleys

All these passes carry important roads linking France to Spain

Largest Glacier

Ossoue Glacier (below Vignemale)—1 mile (1.6km)

Huts and Bivouacs

Some sixty and more huts and refuges are owned by the CAF, the French Pyrenees National Park authority, the Catalan Alpine Club and others

Convenient Centres

There are villages near the heads of most valleys on both French and Spanish sides of the frontier—Gavarnie, Cauterets and Bagneres du Luchon are among the more important on the north side. There are several ski resorts notably those in Andorra, Formigal and Candanchu on the south side of the central chain, and La Mongie, Gourette and St Lary, all in France.

Access

Southern Spanish side—nearest airport is Zaragoza; northern, French side—nearest airport is Tarbes-Lourdes

By rail: (France) via Montrejeau Junction to Bagneres du Luchon or (Spain) via the Pau to Jaca line

Bus services link villages in many valleys but public transport is not very comprehensive and east-west communications, especially on the south side of the frontier, are poor

Maps

French IGN maps in 1:50,000, 1:25,000 and 1:20,000 scales; Spanish IGC maps in 1:50,000 scale give comprehensive coverage; Spanish 'Editorial Alpina' maps at 1:25,000 not always accurate but easier to obtain

Guide-books

In English: *Pyrenees East and West* (2 vols) published by Gastons—West Col (UK)

The excellent and comprehensive French 'Ollivier'/FEM series covers the area in 6 volumes and an equally good Spanish series is published by the Catalan Alpine Club in Barcelona

Scandinavia

Mountains cover over 70 per cent of Norway and those that do not rise from the sea never lie far from it. None are high by world standards, but the height above their base of many summits compares favourably with important alpine peaks. A length of over 1,000 miles (1,609km) makes these mountains the longest chain in Europe: on the west they rise steeply from an incredibly indented coastline, while to the east they fall away gradually across Sweden to the Baltic some 150 miles (241km) from the crest. The topography is complex; the whole country was under a huge ice-sheet only 10–12,000 years ago, and the frontier between the two countries bears only a vague relationship to the watershed between Atlantic and Baltic. In several places vestigial ice-caps remain and there are numerous glaciers but the warm Gulf Stream ensures that the climate is not as extreme as it might be at such latitudes—one-third of the mountains lie north of the Arctic Circle—and, despite unsettled oceanic weather with heavy precipitation, the glaciers continue to retreat.

The Norwegians are an 'outdoor' people but there are only 4 million of them scattered over a huge area, 25 per cent of which is forest and less than 3 per cent cultivable. The mountains are empty compared to other European ranges. Naturally, early development, which started with the climbs of Cecil Slingsby ('father of Norwegian mountaineering') and his Alpine Club colleagues and the Danish climber, Carl Hall, concentrated on 'peak bagging', and it was not until

fairly recently that rock-climbing developed as a specialist sport. Climbers have tended to concentrate on several particular areas, but there is an incredible amount of steep rock and there is scope for climbing virtually everywhere, if no longer of virgin summits then on virgin faces and crags.

The most southerly important group is the Jotunheimen, the 'Home of the Giants'. Here are the highest peaks, some 250 rising above 6,000ft (1,829m), and more than sixty glaciers. Galdhøppigen—Norway's highest—is an easy ascent, as is the shapely Glittertind standing across the Visdalen valley, but more interesting is the Hurrungane area some 20 miles (32km) to the south west. Here is the formidable tower of Store Skagastolstind, climbed at Slingsby's third attempt after his companions were unable to continue. The *Voie Normale* is still a serious climb (grade III) and there are other excellent but harder climbs of around 2,000ft (609m) on the peak, including two made in 1935 by that great pioneer, Arne Naess, the 'elder statesman' of Norwegian mountaineering. The rock here is gabbro and there is fine climbing on some twenty surrounding summits.

Westward lies the huge Jostadals Breen Ice-Cap—the largest glacier in continental Europe—with several long valley-glaciers glowing off it. Its highest point is the Ladalskapa (6,834ft/2,083m)—a protruding nunatak—and there is good scrambling on other similar features as well as a variety of interesting ski-traverses.

A rock-climbing area of worldwide fame is Romsdal where, fanning out behind the small town of Andalsnes at the head of the Romsdalsfjord, are the rock-walled valleys of Isterdal, Romsdal, Vengedal and Grovdal. These cliffs

are gneiss and they vary from small roadside crags to the Troll Wall itself, plumb vertical for over 4,000ft (1,219m), the highest such wall in Europe. Rock-climbing here was developed by the famous guide, Arne Randers Heen, and others in the 1920s and '30s, after Slingsby and Hall had 'bagged' the summits two generations before. Heen teamed up with young Ralph Hoibakk, today probably Norway's most prolific climber, to make the first grade VI route in Romsdal, the 4,600ft (1,402m) East Pillar of Trollryggen, in 1958. The Troll Wall—the north face of Trollryggen—succumbed to a British team, Amatt, Howard, and Tweedale, in 1965: five bivouacs were made on the 5,000ft (1,524m) climb, most of it sustained free climbing but with several major aid pitches. It has since become a classic. A French 'direct' route made two years later used siege tactics over twenty-one days, and many other 'big wall' climbs were made on this and other huge faces in the area. But Romsdal is not just big walls: new and long climbs of more traditional character were being made by other British and Norwegian teams, among them Joe Brown and Tom Patey.

The most beautiful mountain in Romsdal is Vengetind, an attractive pointed summit with several pleasant routes on it rising above Vengedal, while nearby Kvandalstind, the summit of a spiky ridge, gives a traverse of medium difficulty. The Romsdalshorn itself, an impressive rock-tower with superb views across deep Romsdal to the Trolltind peaks, gives several good climbs.

South and north of Romsdal are the areas of Sunnmore and Nordmore, respectively. In Sunnmore, isolated gabbro peaks of over 5,000ft (1,524m) rise between a series of long fjords and give excellent scrambling, while, in the latter area, very popular with local climbers, is the immense wall of Harstadnebba, no longer virgin, and the imposing fang-like peak of Dalatarnet (4,573ft/1,394m).

North of the Arctic Circle the country becomes more remote, access is more difficult and mountaineering takes on a more expeditionary character. There are fine peaks in the Svartisen Ice-Cap area and round the Sjunkfjord just north of Bodø, while, rising sheer from the waters of the Tysfjord, just south of Narvik, is the improbable chisel-shaped obelisk of Stetind—considered by Slingsby, most uncharitably, to be 'the ugliest mountain in the world'. In 1935 Arne Naess climbed the 1,600ft (488m) South Pillar (grade V +) a superb route of excellent

The view into the Jotunheimen from near the summit of Memurutind, looking west south west over the Heillstugguhöe and Tverrbottinden Peaks to the Hurrungane (left skyline, with Skagastolstind)

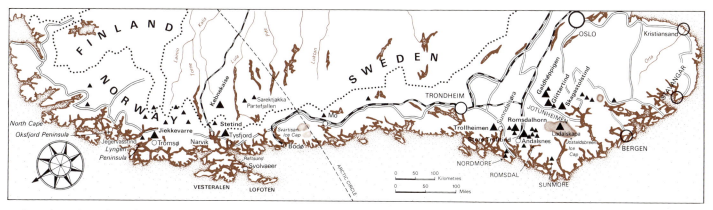

rock and, no less than thirty-seven years later, forced the formidable North Face. Other mountains here are not so high but there are still virgin 2,000ft (609m) rock-faces close above the Arctic Highway.

Across the Swedish frontier, in landscape rather more Arctic, rises Kebnekaise, a mountain holding a small ice-cap and famous for its ice-caves. Some winter climbing has been done in the area and in the Sareks National Park 40 miles (64km) southward.

Off the coast lie the eighty islands of the Lofoten and Vesterlen archipelago where a myriad gabbro peaks rise, often to 4,000ft (1,219m), straight from the sea. The passage of the narrow Raftsund, between the two major island groups, must be one of the most impressive short voyages in the world. Among the first climbs on the islands was Slingsby's ascent of Goat Pinnacle—crowned with two horns—1,000ft (305m) sheer, above the village cemetary of Svolvaeer, a feat for which he was awarded the freedom of this little fishing port. More recently Geoff Cram's party ascended the highest face, the 3,000ft (914m) East Face of

Breiflogtind, in 1968. The islands are quite frequently visited.

In the far north the Lyngen Peninsula has attracted many expeditions over the years. Here is the highest peak in Arctic Norway, Jiekkevarre—Slingsby's 'Mont Blanc of the north'—crowned with its ice-cap, hung with glaciers and with an imposing East Face that has recently been climbed. Nearer the peninsula's tip the Jegervasstind group gives good alpine-style climbing on shapely gabbro peaks. Towards North Cape there are some interesting coastal peaks, notably on the Oksfjord Peninsula with its three small ice-caps, first visited by Hastings in 1898.

So much is still untouched and opinion among Norwegian mountaineers is that regions so far 'undeveloped' should remain so and that climbers visiting these areas should be able to enjoy exploratory mountaineering for its own sake, without the rash of guide-books and commercialism that has followed 'development' elsewhere in Europe.

Situation: kingdoms of Norway and Sweden

Jotunheimen
1 Galdhøppigen (8,098/2,468) 1850: L. Arnesen, S. Flotten, S. Sulheim
2 Glittertind (8,045/2,452)
3 Skagastolstind (7,888/2,404) 1876: W. C. Slingsby, alone

Huts and Bivouacs
There is a good system throughout the area belonging to the DNT, the Norwegian Mountain Touring Association

Convenient Centres
Small summer hamlets with guest houses and stores are scattered throughout the area but Spiterstulen in Visdalen Valley is central for Galdhøppigen and Glittertind while Turtegro is the centre for the Hurrungane

Sunnmore
Kviteggja (5,548/1,691)

Convenient Centres
Orsta and Oye—small fjord-side villages

Romsdal
Store Vengetind (6,045/1,842) 1881: W. C. Slingsby and J. Vigdal
Store Trolltind (5,888/1,795) 1882: Carl Hall, M.

Soggemoen, J. Venge
Kvandalstind (5,822/1,774) 1885: W. C. Slingsby, C. Hopkinson, I. Jensen
Romsdalshorn (5,102/1,555) 1827: Christen Hoel and Hans Bjermeland

Convenient Centre
Andalsnes—small town with excellent facilities

Nordmore and Trollheimen
Trollheimen (5,469/1,667)
Dalatarnet (4,573/1,394)

Convenient Centre
Sunndalsora—small town
Mountain lodge at Innerdal

Tysfjord
Stetind (4,530/1,381) 1910: A. B. Bryn, C. W. Rubenson, F. Schjelderup

Convenient Centres
Tysfjord village, or Narvik—an important town and port

Lofoten and Vesteralen Islands
Moysale (4,154/1,266) c1910: J. Norman Collie
Higrafstind (3,809/1,161)
Trolltindan (3,428/1,045)
Hermannsdaltind (3,392/1,034)

Convenient Centres
Fishing ports on each island

Lyngen
Jiekkevarre (6,053/1,845) 1897: G. Hastings and H. Wooley
Store Jegervasstind (5,545/1,690) 1951: Tom Weir, Adam Watson, Douglas Scott

Convenient Centres
Crofting settlement of Lyngseidet or Tromsø—important port and town

Sweden
1 Kebnekaise (6,965/2,123)

Major Glaciers
1 Jostadals Breen ice-cap system: 340 square miles (547 sq km)
2 Svartisen ice-cap system: 100 + square miles (161 + sq km)

Guide-books
Walks and Climbs in Romsdal Cicerone Press (UK)
Mountain Holidays in Norway (Per Praag) Norway Travel Association, Oslo
Mountain Touring Holidays in Norway (Erling Welle-Strand) Norwegian Mountain Touring Association
Norway—the Northern Playground W. C. Slingsby (1904)

There are several paperback guides provided by the Norsk Tindeklub (Norwegian Alpine Club)

Access
There are rail links from Oslo to Andalsnes, Trondheim, Bodø and to Narvik from Boden (Sweden). The Arctic Highway links Trondheim to North Cape

Rulten, one of the finest peaks in the Lofoten Islands, first climbed in 1903 by J. N. Collie and party

British Isles: Lake District/Wales

In terms of size alone the mountains of Britain are insignificant. In terms of world mountaineering, however, their influence has been tremendous and although they offer superlative rock-climbing and fine—if small-scale—mountaineering in their own right, it is as a crucible of men and ideas, of techniques and equipment, that the British mountains are remarkable. Notwithstanding, in an island whose geography and geology—and hence scenery—is so rich and varied, the mountains are of exceptional beauty and can be considered great ranges in microcosm. The three major mountain areas, while having much in common, are sufficiently different to demand separate treatment.

South of the Scottish border, the high country lies west and north of a line linking the Exe to the Humber and reaches an apex at two points—knots of ancient igneous and volcanic rock—the mountains of Snowdonia and the Lake District. Both groups are the product of glacier ice which sculpted the once rounded or whale-backed hills with deep-cut cwms, walled with crag and scree and often floored with small tarns. Between the cwms rise ridges, sometimes broad and grassy, occasionally narrow and rocky, leading to the mountain tops. In England and Wales only one real summit cannot be reached hands-in-pockets and yet, within a few feet, cliffs may fall away sheer for 500ft or so. The main valleys between the mountains often hold moraine-dammed lakes.

The Lake District

Cumbria—or 'the Lakes'—contains only four summits above 3,000ft (914m) but they are the highest in England and there are 108 other separate summits topping 2,000ft (610m) in the range. Generally speaking the Lakeland 'fells' (as the mountains are known) are more gentle and the crags smaller and less obvious than those of Snowdonia. The main valleys radiate from the central hub of the Scafell massif and tend to be pastoral, chequered with small stone-walled fields, dotted with sheep and cattle and with white-walled farmhouses surrounded by tall sycamore and ash trees. These valleys hold the tranquil lakes for which the region is famous. It is a smiling landscape much extolled by the Romantic poets—the native Wordsworth, Ruskin, Shelley, Tennyson and others.

It has been claimed, with some justification, that the 'sport' of rock-climbing was invented in the Lakes. The alpine

pioneers of the 'Golden' and 'Silver' ages who visited the British hills in winter, alpenstocks in hand, ascended snow-gullies and steep snow-slopes as 'training' for sterner stuff abroad. But, in 1882, Walter Haskett Smith, not yet an alpinist, began a systematic series of rock-climbs around Wasdale, above Langdale and on Pillar Rock, for their own sake—climbing just for the fun of it rather than for the utilitarian purpose of reaching a summit. The idea caught on and, by the time of his famous ascent of Napes Needle on Great Gable in 1886, the new sport was 'off the ground'. He produced the first rock-climbing guidebook in 1894. Other early Lakeland rock-climbers, men who were to influence world mountaineering in one way or another, were Norman Collie, Cecil Slingsby, Geoffrey Hastings, the Hopkinsons, the Pilkingtons and Herman Wooley, not forgetting the redoubtable local Abrahams brothers—the greatest 'action' mountain photographers of early years.

Today there are over 1,500 rock-climbs listed in the Lakeland guidebooks on some forty important, and many more less important, crags and only singularly talented and imaginative

leaders can hope to make new routes. The finest crag is the great North-West Face of Scafell—England's second highest peak—and its classic route—indeed the classic of the Lake District—is Central Buttress. First climbed by Herford in 1914, it features a strenuous and gymnastic lead up a huge overhanging flake and is still considered hard (VI). Other popular crags include the Napes Ridges (above the Needle) on Great Gable, Gimmer Crag above Langdale, Pillar Rock above Ennerdale, Dow Crag above Coniston, and various low-level crags in Borrowdale. Probably today's hardest route is Livesey's 'Footloose Crow' on Goat Crag in Borrowdale: its crux is a fingery 190ft (53m) diagonal traverse, virtually unprotected—an exceptionally bold lead few climbers can emulate. With such a climb the sport has returned to its beginnings and the early edict that a leader must not fall!

Fell-walking—which is a Lake District speciality—is extremely popular and the traverse of Helvellyn by the narrow and scrambly Striding Edge is a notable outing. Fell-running, a comparatively new and nationwide mountain sport—a cross between true orienteering and basic mountaineering—was born in the Lakes

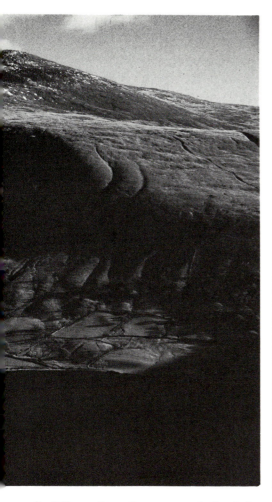

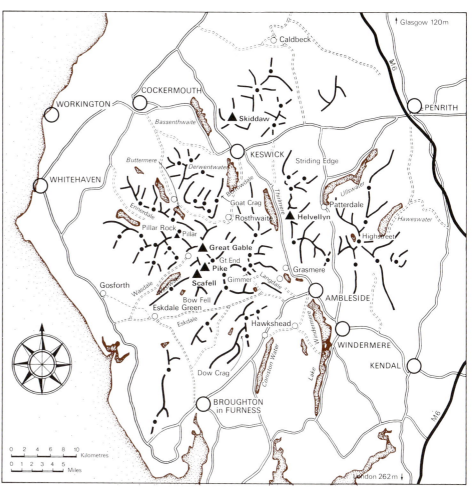

Scafell, seen from the west over the head of Wast Water; in the centre is Scafell Pike and on the left Lingmell. The cliffs of Scafell Crag are seen dropping into the cwm of Hollow Stones. Late Autumn

out of the shepherds' fell races held on village sports days and is also a popular if especially gruelling pastime! Its most famous manifestation is the '24-hour record' the aim of which is the ascent of the greatest number of 2,000ft (610m) tops returning to the starting point within twenty-four hours. First run in the last century, the current record of seventy-two tops was set by shepherd Joss Naylor in 1975. In winter the Lakeland fells seem to hold more snow than Snowdonia and, besides a few good ice-gullies, on Great End (2,984ft/910m) in particular, it is usually possible to make ski ascents of the higher tops on several days each year.

During the season the Lake District is packed with tourists, especially the central region within easy road access of the M6 motorway. Luckily environmental protection is not neglected in this very delightful and so English area and a crucial 866 square miles lie within an efficiently run and fairly unintrusive National Park.

Snowdonia

Virtually the whole of Wales is hill country—168 tops rise over 2,000ft (610m)—and, although there are several groups of attractive small mountains (containing little serious climbing) in the south, it is with the culminating mountain fastness of the north—Eryri or Snowdonia—that we are concerned. Here lie the highest mountains south of the Scottish Highlands, and no less than fourteen summits top 3,000ft (914m). These mountains are more rugged and more shapely than those of the Lakes and the scenery wilder and more dramatic, despite the fact that deep valleys containing major roads separate the area into small massifs. Rocky hillsides above bare valleys of moorland or rough pasture lead upwards to narrow ridges and sharp summits. Naked rock is much in evidence. While there are pockets of pastoral tranquility, some ancient woods of ash and oak and several attractive valley lakes, the overall atmosphere is mysterious and secretive which history, the rich store of local legends, and the now ubiquitous Welsh tongue of the local people do nothing to dispel.

In the early days the alpinists visited Snowdonia even more frequently than the Lakes and even formed a 'Society of Welsh Rabbits' in 1870—based on the hostelry of Pen-y-Gwryd—to foster the winter exploration of the district. One of their number, T. W. Wall—with A. H. Stocker—made the first ascent of the North Face of Lliwedd (2,947ft/898m) an 800ft crag of quite formidable appearance—the highest in Wales—in 1883. Roderick Williams climbed both South and North Gullys on Tryfan in 1887 and 1888. But it was not until the early 1890s that rock-climbing in Wales really got under way, becoming crystallized by the formation of the Climbers Club—the first domestic club devoted to rock-climbing—in 1898. The presiding genius of these years, until his death in 1912, was J. M. Archer Thomson. It was he who produced the first CC guidebook in the now standard 'pocket format'—*Lliwedd* in 1909. Influential, also, were members of the Christmas and Easter parties organized at Pen-y-Pass, the other famous climbing hostelry, by Geoffrey Winthrop Young—the greatest alpinist of the period—which included great names like Mallory and Eckenstein.

The finest crag in Snowdonia is Clogwyn Du'r Arddu, a dark and daunting

600ft (180m) precipice on the north flank of Snowdon. Virtually inviolate until 1927, when Fred Pigott's team forced a line up its vertical East Buttress, and 1928 when Jack Longland's party (which included Pigott and Frank Smythe) succeeded on the overlapping slabs of the West Buttress, it is the most important single crag in Britain today. Crisscrossed with well over eighty major routes, none of them easy, it reflects all the great exponents and technical advances of British rock-climbing since 1927.

Dominating the Llanberis Pass, flanked as it is by a line of small and steep crags with a concentration of fine technical routes, is the huge blank dièdre of Cenotaph Corner—splitting the small but impressive crag of Dinas Cromlech. First climbed in 1952 by Joe Brown, it is perhaps the 'status symbol' of Welsh rock-climbing—a popular test piece (VI). Brown and his sometime companion, Don Whillans, dominated British rock-climbing for well over a decade

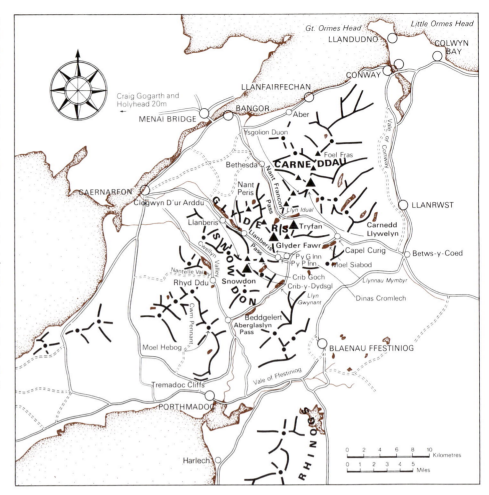

The peaks of the 'Snowdon Horseshoe' seen from the north east over the choppy waters of Llynnau Mymbyr. On the left is Lliwedd; centre Y Wyddfa (Snowdon summit); to the right Crib Goch and Crib-y-ddysgl above the cleft of Pen-y-Pass

from 1951—both are great alpinists who have made their mark on mountains all over the world. A major concentration of climbs, generally easier, lies around or above the Ogwen Valley, particularly on the 600ft (180m) East Face of Tryfan—a splendid little rock peak whose easiest ascent does just require the use of hands—and on the 450ft (140m) slabs of Cwm Idwal. The long line of crags at Tremadoc, almost at sea level and usually climbable whatever the mountain weather, are important today and there are hundreds of interesting climbs on over fifty other crags scattered throughout Snowdonia as well as on the outlying Arans and beautiful Cader Idris to the south.

Despite the fact that it is a sea-cliff and nearly 30 miles from the nearest mountain, recently discovered Craig Gogarth demands mention. Over half a mile of extremely intimidating rock, always vertical, often overhanging and up to 400ft (120m) high, Gogarth has been the scene of big developments in the late 1960s and 70s. There are no easy routes but the cliff is in condition year-round and its resultant popularity has advanced Welsh rock-climbing standards in a most significant way.

Hill-walking in Snowdonia tends to be rather more serious than in the Lake District. The classic is the 'Snowdon Horseshoe', along the rocky ridges of Lliwedd, Y Wyddfa—Snowdon summit which suffers the indignity of a cafe and railway station—and on over Crib-y-ddysgl (3,496ft/1,066m) and Crib Goch (3,026ft/922m). The traverse of the last two peaks involves rock-scrambling and is actually knife-edged over a short section. Under winter conditions this is a superb expedition, as are many of the other Snowdonia 'scrambles'. At irregular intervals there is quite good winter climbing in the area, Lliwedd, Cwm Idwal and Ysgolion Duon (the Black Ladders) being notable locations.

A popular long-distance walk is the traverse of the fourteen Welsh 3,000ft tops, starting from the summit of Snowdon and ending on Foel Fras (3,092ft/942m). First completed in 1919 with a time of 20 hours, the current record for this gruelling 22-mile endurance piece is 4 hours 46 minutes, set in 1973 by Joss Naylor.

Although the roads and Snowdon itself are thronged with tourists at holiday times it is possible still to find peace and solitude in these popular mountains. Most of the region lies within the Snowdonia National Park.

England

Most important mountains
1 Scafell Pike (3,210/978)
2 Scafell (3,162/964)
3 Helvellyn (3,116/949)
4 Skiddaw (3,054/931)
7 Great Gable (2,949/899)

Huts
Some twenty-five belong to a variety of clubs

Convenient centres
For rock-climbing, Wasdale Head and Langdale, but for general fell-walking and for climbs outside this central area Ambleside, Keswick and Coniston as well as numerous small villages and farms are convenient

Guide-books
Rock-climbing Guide to the English Lake District—9 vols—is the very comprehensive master guide published by the Fell and Rock Climbing Club (FRCC)
Rock Climbing in the Lake District is a useful volume of selected climbs published by Constable (London)
Wainwright's Pictorial Guide to Lakeland Fells —in 7 vols—is an extremely comprehensive guide from a fell-walking standpoint—it is published by Westmorland Gazette
So-called 'pirate' rock-climbing guides are published by various people from time to time and new developments are written up in the bi-annual journal of the FRCC and in various magazines, notably *Crags*

Maps
The Ordnance Survey publish usually excellent 1:25,000, 1:50,000 and 1:250,000 maps. Currently (1978) some are still suffering from the effects of metrication. Westcol publish a special climbers *kammkarte* map, at 1:25,000, to the central area

Access
Nearest airports are Tyne-Tees and Manchester, the latter probably more convenient for connecting travel by road or rail. Main railway stations at Kendal, Penrith and Carlisle, link to London and Manchester direct and branch lines run round the west coast (to Whitehaven etc) and to Windermere. A 'Mountain Goat' shuttlebus service operates in season in the more popular areas and there are some seasonal road restrictions for private vehicles. An otherwise fair road network with many narrow lanes tends to be peripheral owing to the nature of the topography. Windermere is easily reached by an excellent link road from the M6 motorway. Further information of a general nature can be obtained from the Lake District National Park

Wales

Most important mountains
1 Snowdon—Y Wyddfa (3,560/1,085)
3 Carnedd Llywelyn (3,485/1,062)
4 Glyder Fawr (3,279/999)
14 Tryfan (3,010/917)
17 Cader Idris (2,927/892)

Huts
Some thirty-three belonging to a variety of clubs

Convenient centres
The most important Snowdonia villages are: Capel Curig, Bethesda and Llanberis—all with good facilities. Nant Peris, Beddgelert and Rhyd Ddu are smaller. Less important for rock-climbers are Betws-y-Coed, Porthmadoc and Dolgellau

Guide-books
Climbers Club Guide to Wales, in 11 volumes, is published for the club (the CC) by Cordee (Leicester). Several volumes covering supplementary areas are published by Cicerone Press (Manchester), Westcol (Reading) and others. *Rock-climbing in Wales*, published by Constable (London), is a useful volume of selected climbs. Westcol also publish a series of 'district guides' giving hill-walking and general mountain information, 3 vols cover Snowdonia. New developments are recorded in the annual Climbers Club *Journal* and in various magazines, notably *Crags*

Maps
The official Ordnance Survey 1:50,000 series are generally excellent despite still suffering from recent metrication.
Other good coverage is the OS 1:25,000 and 1:250,000.
Westcol publish a special climbers map in *kammkarte* format at 1:25,000 scale. Two sheets cover Snowdonia

Access
North Wales is served by good roads but, in some parts of central Wales, main roads are few and far between. For the main mountainous area of Snowdonia, the nearest airport is Manchester and there are direct rail links from that city, and from London, to Colwyn Bay and Bangor. A branch line continues to Betws-y-Coed and Festiniog. Bus services link most villages to the towns of Bangor and Caernarfon. Further information of a general nature can be obtained from the Snowdonia National Park

Great Britain: Scotland

The Scottish Highlands, Western Europe's greatest wilderness, cover no less than one-fifth of the land area of the United Kingdom. From the granite ridges of the Isle of Arran the mountains stretch some 215 miles (346km) to the quartzite walls of Foinaven, and nearly 140 miles (225km) from Mount Keen's cone of scree and heather to the naked gabbro fangs of the Skye Cuillin. Carved largely from ancient Pre-Cambrian rocks these mountains owe their rich diversity of form to the erosion, by both ice-sheet and local valley glacier, of a rolling plateau—itself the roots of a great primeval mountain range. Text-book examples of post-glacial scenery, corrie and crag, moraine and erratic, fjord and tarn, occur almost everywhere. Snow lies on the mountains for several months each winter and, in one or two places, usually persists throughout the summer: recent research has indicated that the last vestigial glacier finally disappeared from the Cairngorms less than three centuries ago. Although the peaks are not high, their latitude is that of the Alaska Panhandle and their climate has been described as 'arctic-alpine', and yet, because of the benign Gulf Stream, the coastal and valley climate of the west is rarely extreme. The best weather seems to be in spring, early summer and the early autumn.

The fault line of the Great Glen divides the Highlands in two. To the north and west the mountains, while generally of lower altitude, tend to be upstanding and of more spectacular form than those to the east and south, especially near the deeply indented west coast where they often rise steeply from the sea. Off-shore the archipelagos of the Inner and Outer Hebrides also contain shapely peaks. Many of the glens cradle fine lochs. The north west is a land of haunting beauty.

While the coastal scenery continues south of the Great Glen, the inland mountains—the Grampians—usually form large massifs, high plateaux cut with deep corries, having a desolate charm all their own. Here are concentrated all seven separate 4,000ft (1,220m) summits in Britain: the Highlands contain 276 summits (known as 'Munros') and no less than 543 tops above 3,000ft (914m).

Climbing traditions in Scotland have always been more those of 'mountaineering' than of 'technical rock gymnastics' although there are many superb rock-climbs to all standards. 'Munro-bagging'—the ascent of all 276 summits—although technically straightforward, is no mean feat. The many fine ridges and arêtes which provide rocky scrambles in summer can become difficult alpine climbs in winter when arctic conditions of snow and ice, wind and whiteout, avalanche and short daylight hours demand proper mountaineering expertise. Major winter routes can be long and extremely serious undertakings with technical ice-climbing as difficult as that found anywhere in the world.

The great cliffs of Creag Meaghaidh line the head of Coire Ardair. April

Ben Nevis, merely a huge whale-back when seen from the south, boasts—as its North-East Face—the greatest cliff in Britain, some 2 miles long and 2,000ft (600m) high. Some of the climbs on this complex of ridges, buttresses, walls and gullys are very long and, although the summer rock-climbing—on porphyry—is excellent, 'the Ben' is especially notable for its winter climbing. As in summer there are routes of all standards, classics being the 2,000ft (609m), alpine-style Tower Ridge and the more modern Zero and Point Five Gullys, each 1,000ft of difficult and very serious steep ice.

Glencoe has the largest concentration of rock-climbs, many of them on the firm rhyolite of the Buachaille Etive Mor, the great rock pyramid guarding the head of the glen. There are more than 150 routes of up to 1,000ft (305m), old classics like Crowberry Ridge Direct (Abraham brothers, 1900) and hard new ones like Shibboleth (Robin Smith, 1958). The winter climbing on the Buachaille, and elsewhere in Glencoe, is good, easily accessible and very popular.

Offering virtually no summer climbing, the remote mica-schist crags of Creag Meaghaidh (3,700ft/1,128m) are notable in winter, especially for Tom Patey's incredible 1½-mile girdle traverse—the Crab Crawl—one of the best winter expeditions in Britain.

Eastward is a great expanse of high granite plateau—the Cairngorms—an area of outstanding ecological interest. There are many climbs in the easily accessible northern corries, particularly good in winter, but the central area of the massif is extremely remote and winter conditions are the most serious in Britain. The imposing 800ft (244m) tower of Shelter Stone Crag, above Loch Avon, provides some of the best climbs, both in summer and winter. Another good winter crag is Lochnagar, a Cairngorm outlier above the Royal residence of Balmoral Castle, while nearby Creag an Dubh-loch is a hugh and intimidating wall with a collection of long and hard rock-climbs. Other developed areas south of the Great Glen are the Cobbler (2,891ft/881m) at Arrochar—close to Glasgow—and the Isle of Arran in the Firth of Clyde.

The north-west Highlands are almost secret country: some areas are developed and there are some guide-books, but many climbers do not publicize their activities up here and there is still great scope for exploration. Perhaps it should remain thus. Well documented areas in-

clude the impressive Torridonian sandstone cliffs of Applecross, the remarkable Triple Buttress of Coire Mhic Fhearchair high on Beinne Eighe (3,309ft/1,009m) where white quartzite tops the red sandstone, and the fine cliffs amid most spectacular scenery near remote Carnmore at the head of Fionn Loch. Much has been done recently on the steep quartzite of Foinaven in the far north.

Skye, however, is unique. The wild gabbro peaks of the Cuillin form a high horseshoe ridge, gashed, gendarmed and, in places, knife-edged. Its traverse is a superb expedition over 7 miles (11km) long, taking in thirty-one summits, and more than 10,000ft (3,048m) of ascent from sea level. Real—but never very difficult—rock-climbing is involved. A party led by Patey and MacInnes completed the traverse in winter, with one bivouac, in 1965—but good winter conditions are rare. Some of the Cuillin's best rock-climbs, and over 300 have been recorded, are the long classic routes, many over 1,000ft (305m), of no great difficulty, yet pioneered before 1914. Other, but shorter and less demanding, ridge traverses on the mainland are those of An Teallach and Liathach, beautiful sandstone peaks.

Of the other islands, Harris and Rhum have especially fine mountains and the climbing on the former is noteworthy. Huge sea-cliffs ringing remote St Kilda and several of the Orkney and Shetland Islands await serious exploration, although the difficult ascent of The Old Man of Hoy stack (450ft), off Orkney, is now classic.

Scottish skiing can be surprisingly good, often lasting into May in the Cairngorms. There are lift facilities at Glencoe and Glenshee while the well developed resort of Aviemore backs the complex of facilities on the northern flanks of popular Cairn Gorm. Ski-mountaineering, the preserve of a few enthusiasts, can be very rewarding particularly among the high Grampian massifs.

It was the discovery of the Cuillin by the Alpine Club in the 1870s, when there were still virgin peaks to climb, that really started mountaineering in Scotland. Although the Scottish Mountaineering Club was founded in 1889, the birth of 'climbing' *per se* is usually dated to the 1894 climbs of Norman Collie's party, Tower Ridge on Ben Nevis and the first routes in Glencoe. Scottish climbing went from strength to strength and its tough schooling has produced some of the finest all-round mountaineers of recent times.

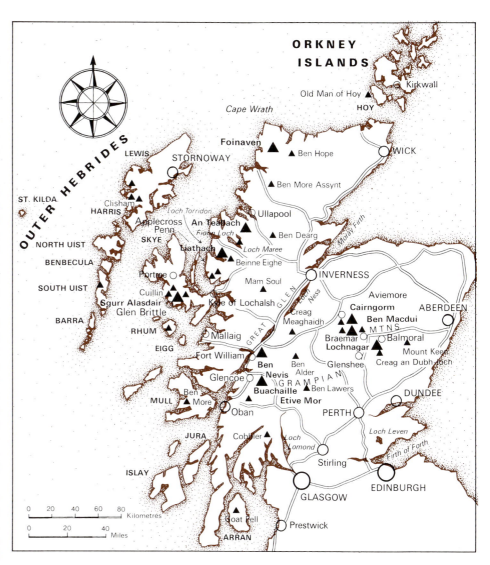

Scotland

Some Important Mountains

1 Ben Nevis (4,406/1,343)
2 Ben Macdui (4,296/1,309)
5 Cairn Gorm (4,084/1,245)
20 Lochnagar (3,786/1,154)
69 An Teallach (3,483/1,062)
71 Liathach (3,456/1,053)
106 Buachaille Etive Mor (3,345/1,020)
117 Sgurr Alasdair (3,309/1,009)
Foinaven (2,980/908)

Huts and Bivouacs

The SMC, JMCS and BMC own some seven huts and several clubs own private cottages, while there are some convenient youth hostels. In many areas it is traditional to climb from 'bothies' or 'howffs'

Convenient Centres

Fort William and Aviemore are bustling small towns with all facilities for climbers. Glencoe has basic facilities and Glen Brittle, on Skye, minimum facilities. Elsewhere there are villages, inns and guest houses within reasonable motoring distance of most mountains

Guide-books

The Scottish Mountaineering Trust publish some 14 volumes of guides covering both summer and winter climbs, as well as a series of nine 'District Guides' giving more general mountain information.

Cicerone Press publish 2 volumes of selected winter climbs and Westcol a guide to ski-mountaineering. Constable publish 2 useful volumes of selected climbs covering the whole of Scotland in summer and winter. New climbs and developments are noted in the excellent annual journal of the SMC

Maps

The official Ordnance Survey 1:50,000 series still suffer from recent metrication. Also OS 1:25,000 and 1:250,000.

Special maps of the Skye Cuillin at 1:15,000 and approximately 1:21,000 and Ben Nevis at approximately 1:16,000 are distributed by Westcol

Access

This is often difficult. Glasgow and Prestwick are international airports and there are regular services to Edinburgh, Aberdeen, Inverness, Wick and the Northern and Western Isles. Rail links from the south, via Edinburgh and Glasgow lead to Inverness, from whence branch lines lead to Wick and to Kyle of Lochalsh, to Fort William, with a branch on to Mallaig, and to Oban. Roads are often few and far between and sometimes necessitate ferry crossings. Local bus services are poor. Good ferries link all the important islands to the mainland

Africa

Many of the high points in Africa's Great Rift Valley are active volcanoes. This one is O1 Doinyo Lengai (9,443ft/2,878m) which stands guard over the southern end of Lake Natron in Tanzania. The last eruption was in 1966. On the right is seen the steep western escarpment of the Rift

Atlas

The most northerly of Africa's mountains, the Atlas forms a broken chain of high ground behind the Mediterranean and Atlantic coasts of Tunisia, Algeria and Morocco, stretching 1,300 miles from Cape Bon to Ifni. Much of the eastern half of the chain is high plateau, the Atlas Saharien rarely rising above 5,000ft (1,500m), although there are some small groups of pleasant mountains along the coast, such as the Djurdjura, close to Algiers, the Medjerda near Bone and, south of Constantine, the Aures which reach 7,631ft. The most important mountains, however, lie in Morocco in the western half of the chain, and here three major sub-ranges, running parallel, can be distinguished. The Middle Atlas is a high region of plateaux, gorges and cedar forests south of Fès, the wild and barren Anti Atlas run inland from the Atlantic coast south of Agadir, while between the two lies the High Atlas—most important of them all.

A complex of jagged ridges and deep narrow valleys running 250 miles (400km) almost across the country, the High Atlas contain the highest peaks in North Africa—a dozen of them over 13,000ft (3,900m). The range is a frontier between the semi-arid Mediterranean littoral and the huge expanse of real desert wilderness, the Sahara, that stretches south for over a thousand miles. Northward the mountain torrents fall to the sea, southward they disappear, swallowed by the scorching sand.

Subject to great seasonal variations of temperature, in summer harsh and waterless beneath a hot sun, but in winter crisp and white and icy with heavy snow cover, these mountains now hold no glaciers. From the ancient walled city of Marrakech 50 miles (80km) to the north, the long line of the glittering winter snows, framed by palm trees, presents a justly famed prospect.

Unlike the Arabs of the plains the inhabitants of the High Atlas are Hamitic Berbers, a Muslim people, aloof and independent, who wrest a hard living from a rigorous, if enchanting, environment. Basically pastoral, they tend sheep and goats, grow maize and fruit and their flat-roofed houses cluster in villages where the mountain valleys widen and soil becomes plentiful. Here in spring the surrounding orchards are bright with blossom and trout streams flow through green terraces and groves of poplar and walnut. Although the local tongues are Berber and Arabic, French is still the language of commerce and culture.

Roads are few and far between and there are only three road-passes across the entire length of the mountains. Europeans did not penetrate the High Atlas until well into the nineteenth century and the highest summit was not located until 1922. Even today most of the range is comparatively little known to mountaineers, the exception being the Massif du Toubkal, lying due south of Marrakech between the two principle trans-Atlas passes and where all the higher mountains, barring only Ighil M'Goum, 100 miles (160km) to the east, are concentrated.

Here the peaks are massive rather than elegant, often displaying high and steep rocky faces and many of the summits are points, either on a high ridge crest or on wide plateaux. There is only one lake, the attractive little Lac d'Ifni. The rock of the Toubkal Massif is volcanic of various kinds and, while often excellent, is sometimes poor, particularly on southern faces. Much development took place in the twenties and thirties, a local CAF section was formed in 1922, several huts were built and skiing was started. Naturally the French were the chief pioneers, particularly Louis Gentil and

Jebel Toubkal the highest summit in North Africa—seen here from the west. A popular massif with both climbers and skiers, it is served by a system of mountain huts

the Marquis de Segonzac, and later the de Lépiney brothers, L. Neltner and A. Stofer, although several climbers from other countries were also active, notably Bentley Beetham, Rand Herron, Anderl Heckmair and a strong Polish team. Political upheavals followed the Second World War and, despite the widespread explorations of Roger Mailly and a productive visit by the guides Charlet and Contamine in 1956 which publicized the excellence of the rock-climbing, it has not been until recent years that mountaineers have again been active, among them some notable British parties led by Hamish Brown, a Scot particularly interested in the good winter mountaineering. Ski-touring in the massif is becoming popular and Oukaïmeden, now linked to Marrakech by a spectacular new road, has become established as Morocco's downhill ski resort with quite respectable facilities.

There are two good climbing seasons, the winter–spring period, from February to May, when snow cloaks the large expanses of boulder and scree round the valley heads and skis can be useful, even for hut approaches, and the early autumn when the weather is cool again before the winter storms—which can be ferocious—set in.

Virtually all the major summits can be reached easily and Toubkal itself, the highest peak, is a popular ascent from the

Neltner Hut at the head of the Mizane Valley, also offering a fine ski-traverse. Its *arêtes* are famous climbs, the classic being the 'OSO' (West South West) above the Tizi Ouanoums (tizi means pass or col) with rock at about grade IV. In fact the traverse of the long ridge crests of many of the peaks, with their towers and pinnacles and usually excellent rock, gives superb sport. The traverse of Anrhemer is an example which involves two miles of climbing, all above 12,000ft (3,650m) and has been likened to the Cuillin Ridge of Skye. The long Crête de l'Ouanoukrim with its many summits and Clochetons Pinnacles is another fine expedition and Wilfred Noyce continued it for some 6 miles over the peaks to the north before descending from Tasserhimout to Imlil. Multi-day traverses of the remoter ridges offer unusual enjoyment, notable being that from Iferouane to Taska-n-Zat, a distance of over 15 miles (24km).

Many of the best rock-climbs to have been done so far are close above the little Lépiney Hut at the gorge-like head of the Azzaden Valley. The massive faces of the Tazarhart 'plateau-mountain' tower 2,000ft (600m) over the hut and give good routes, some by Charlet and Contamine, while the opposite wall of Ouanoukrim has some major climbs besides easy ways to the crest. The hut at Tachddirt, one of the very highest Atlas villages, is also a good climbing centre for routes on Angour—another plateau-mountain—which has a fine West Ridge bounding the long South Face where several climbs have been made of up to 3,500ft (1,000m). Across the valley Aksoual boasts a classic winter climb up its North Ridge whose snowy 5,000ft (1,524m) flanks offer great winter-climbing potential.

Elsewhere there is much to climb, but the remoter mountains and cliffs necessitate long approaches linking valleys via, perhaps, several tizis and maybe several bivouacs. This style of travel in fact lends itself to excellent 'trekking' and ski-touring and several marvellous circuits can be made: that from Imlil via Tachddirt to Timichi, continuing up the Ourika Valley, through the narrow Kissaria Gorge and over to Lac d'Ifni, returning to the Mizane Valley over the Tizi Ouanoums is a fine expedition and well known. Meanwhile other areas of the High Atlas beckon and it is worth noting that superb climbs have been made on the great limestone wall of Aouii, on Jebel Azourki, 120 miles (190km) east of Toubkal.

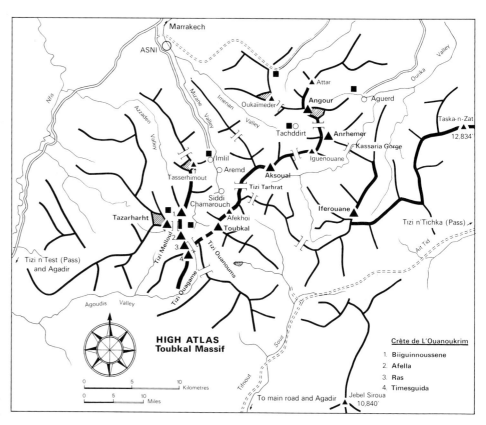

HIGH ATLAS
Toubkal Massif

Crête de L'Ouanoukrim
1. Biiguinnoussene
2. Afella
3. Ras
4. Timesguida

Situation: Kingdom of Morocco; Republics of Algeria and Tunisia

High Atlas
1 Toubkal (13,665/4,165) 1923: V. Berger, M. Dolbeau, Marquis de Segonzac, first European ascent
2 Crête de l'Ouanoukrim
Timesguida (13,415/4,089)
Ras (13,396/4,083)
Afella (13,264/4,043)
Biiguinnoussene (13,130/4,002)
3 Jebel Ighil M'Goum (13,356/4,071)—only 4,000-metre peak outside Toubkal Massif
5 Tazarharht (13,058/3,980)
7 Aksoual (12,828/3,910)
8 Anrhemer (12,773/3,893)
9 Jebel Ayachi (12,260/3,737)—most easterly major summit of High Atlas
10 Jebel Azourki (12,106/3,690)
11 Jebel Igdet (11,873/3,619)—20 miles (32km) west of Toubkal Massif

Major Passes
By road
Tizi n'Test (6,890/2,100) links Marrakech to Agadir through the High Atlas, forming western limit of Toubkal Massif
Tizi n'Tichka (7,448/2,270) links Marrakech to Ouarzazate and southern desert through the High Atlas and forms eastern limit of Toubkal Massif
Tizi n'Talrhemt at far eastern end of High Atlas

On foot
Tizi Ouanoums (11,910/3,630) crosses main crest of Toubkal Massif linking Mizane and Sous Valleys
Tizi Ouagane (12,187/3,715) links Mizane and Agoudis Valleys
Tizi Tarhrat (11,220/3,420) links Mizane and upper Ourika Valleys

Tizi Tachddirt (10,407/3,172) links Tachddirt to Ourika Valley
Tizi nou Addi (9,606/2,928) links Tachddirt to Oukaïmeden

Huts and Bivouacs
At least six huts belong to the CAF and several shelters are owned by the Marrakech Syndicate d'Initiative

Guide-books
Le Massif du Toubkal (1938), published by the Office Cherifien de Tourisme, Rabat, and *Villes et Montagnes Maroccaines*, published by La Porte, Rabat (1965)—both out of print.

Also articles in *Alpine Journal, Climber and Rambler* magazine, the CAF journal *La Montagne,* and *Appalacia*

Maps
Official IGN sheet of 1:100,000 scale covers the Toubkal area, but maps covering areas outside this are hard to come by. Carte Michelin sheet 169 is useful

Convenient Centres
Marrakech is a busy city with all facilities including public baths, post offices and car rental. Imlil, at the head of the paved road, has a CAF hut, and mules and porters may be hired here and local food purchased

Access
There is an international airport at Casablanca and airports at Marrakech and Agadir. Excellent and inexpensive train and bus services connect Tangier, Rabat and Casablanca to Marrakech, while a local bus service runs from Marrakech to Asni with a connection to Imlil. There are also bus services over the Tizi n'Test to Taroudannt and over the n'Tichka to Ourzazate. There are several alternative car-ferry services to Morocco both across the Straits of Gibraltar and the Mediterranean, and personal motor transport can be useful in the Atlas

Mount Kenya

Only 10 miles south of the Equator, Mount Kenya rises in regal isolation some 12,000ft (3,658m) above the surrounding plateau country. The glint of its ice-hung fang above the horizon, visible sometimes from as far off as 100 miles, is an astonishing sight above the hot savannah of East Africa. Mount Kenya must be one of the world's most distinctive mountains.

The peak itself is the eroded plug of a huge and ancient volcano, estimated to have topped 23,000ft (7,010m) and since cut back by a million years of largely glacial erosion. Batian and Nelion, the twin summits separated by the icy gash of the Gate of the Mists, are surrounded by a cluster of satellite aiguilles and cradle no fewer than fifteen glaciers, mostly tiny and all shrinking fast. The summits rise, some 2,000ft (609m) of steep rock, from the apex of a huge dome some 60 miles (96km) across, deeply runnelled by the radiating valleys of mountain torrents and clothed with a rich diversity of vegetation. The tussocky moorland above about 11,500ft (3,505m) is dotted with weird plants. Humble groundsel grows to 20ft trees, while silky lobelia reach 5ft, and there are colourful clumps of everlasting Helichrysum: a zone of giant heather, 20–30ft high, separates this moorland from the tall, thick mountain forest with its bamboo thickets which covers the lower slopes up to some 10,000ft. Elephant, rhino, buffalo and leopard are among the rich fauna of the forest and they occasionally penetrate to the moorland where the characteristic inhabitant is the little rock hyrax, resembling the alpine marmot. Strung like a necklace around the base of the peaks are a series of beautiful tarns, another characteristic of the mountain.

Because of its equatorial position, the climate of the mountain is peculiar: the southern flank experiences summer conditions throughout the whole of Kenya's January–February 'dry season', while in August–September the northern side is 'in condition'. Meanwhile the opposite flank is plastered in snow and ice. Early on it was realized that the rock-climbing was superb. The syenite which forms the precipitous inner peaks is coarse and granite-like and loose rock becomes rare as the angle steepens. The mountaineering afforded by this combination of rock, snow and ice compares very favourably with that provided by the Chamonix Aiguilles, but it is only since the late sixties that the potentials of the winter flank of the mountain have been realized.

Perhaps the first white man to see Mount Kenya's distant snows was the missionary Dr Krapf in 1849, but he was not believed until thirty years later when various explorers managed to reach the mountain and to penetrate, in one case, actually to glacier level. In 1899 a large expedition, led by Sir Halford Mackinder, the geographer, reached the mountain after a difficult march from the railhead camp at Nairobi, during which two of his native porters were killed by hostile tribesmen. After several unsuccessful attempts, MacKinder and his two Courmayeur guides finally reached the summit of Batian via a complex and awkward route, crossing the South-East and South Faces of Nelion before cutting up the steep and exposed Diamond Glacier. There were no further successful ascents for thirty years until the first ascent of Nelion was made, *en route* to Batian, by what is now the 'standard route'—the South-East Face—still a serious enough climb, often verglassed and demanding proper rock-climbing skills (grade III). A few routes were added during the ensuing two decades, notably by Arthur Firmin, a local climber who dominated East African mountaineering throughout the 1940s and early '50s. A famous attempt was made by escaped Italian POW's in 1943, who managed to ascend Point Lenana, now considered an easy 'snow plod' and a popular goal for tourists doing the East African safari circuit.

Of the early routes classic today, the long North-West Ridge of Batian, pioneered by Shipton and Tilman in 1930, is perhaps the greatest. It starts at the Firmin Col to give over 2,000ft (609m) of fine climbing, up to grade V, over several gendarmes and notches to the summit. In 1964, Rusty Baillie and Tom Phillips approached the Col via the South Ridge of Point Pigott and continued over Batian to Nelion and down its long South-East Ridge to Point John: this 'Grand Traverse' is the finest expedition on the mountain, two bivouacs are usual and it is rarely completed.

Two relatively straightforward climbs (grade IV), each 'in condition' at different seasons, are the Firmin-Hicks Route (1944) on the north side of Batian, which follows the North-East Rib to Firmin's Tower and the final section of the North-West Ridge and is often used in descent, and Firmin's South Face route (1950) which reaches as far as MacKinder's Diamond Glacier traverse by a direct line on Nelion's South Face.

The steepest rock on the mountain is the impressive eastern face of Nelion above the Krapf Glacier. Two hard and now classic routes were made here by local climber, Barry Cliff, and visiting Austrians in 1963: the East Face is a very direct line of 1,200ft (366m) (VI; A3) while the North-East Pillar is rather longer but a little easier. Less serious and shorter climbs are offered by the smaller peaks, John, Peter and Midget in particular, and the former boasts two notable aid-routes, both requiring two bivouacs, on its blank and overhanging 1,200ft North and West Faces.

Due largely to a small nucleus of powerful expatriate climbers in the MCK, knowing the mountain well and sufficiently acclimatized to snatch first ascents in long weekends from Nairobi, the 1970s have seen a great spate of new activity on Mount Kenya. Among the best of such recent climbs have been Northern Slabs (V; A1), forced up the great amphitheatre below the northern side of the Gate of the Mists by Ian Howell and John Temple in 1972, and the same team's Diamond Buttress (1976) a very sustained and hard line alongside the South-West Ridge and said to provide the finest rock-climbing on the mountain. It is rare for visiting climbers to be in a position to accomplish new routes today, but recent exceptions are Doug Scott and Tut Braithwaite's North-East Face Direct on Nelion in 1977, and Bob Barton and Dave Morris's new ice route on the West Face made in 1978.

The most spectacular of the new modern routes, however, have been on ice. Among them the Diamond Couloir and the Ice Window are classic climbs of world standing. Small and steep, the Diamond Glacier hangs from the southern side of the Gate of the Mists: below its overhanging snout a 1,200ft (366m) ice-channel drops in a sequence of almost vertical steps to the Darwin Glacier below. This is the Diamond Couloir. Long considered suicidal because of objective dangers, its pitches change season by season. Ian Howell and Phil Snyder first cracked all its major problems in safety during the 'southern winter season' of 1971. But darkness forced a retreat and, after several further attempts by strong parties, Snyder finally reached the Gate in 1973 with Ranger

The South-West Face of Mount Kenya seen from near Mackinder's Camp in the Teleki Valley. The twin summits are Batian (left), and Nelion (right), on either side of the Diamond Glacier and Couloir. On the right is Point John

Mount Kenya

Thumbe. Yvon Chouinard added a direct finish up the vertical ice of the headwall in 1975. Aesthetic beauty and simplicity of line make the Couloir the most obvious ice-climb in Africa and certainly one of the greatest. Running up a series of ice-gullies on the southern flank of Nelion, parallel to the Couloir, the Ice Window route finds its way on to the jutting upper lip of the Diamond Glacier through an ice-cave with a peculiar exposed exit 'window'. This surprising expedition gives 1,500ft (500m) of climbing, is rather easier than the Couloir and more often in condition.

Mountaineers unfamiliar with Mount Kenya are often troubled by altitude sickness, and several tourists every season have to be brought down by the skilled African rangers of the National Park Rescue Team. The weather is usually milder than the altitude would suggest and standard conditions are clear mornings and misty, often snowy, afternoons; forced bivouacs are not too serious but darkness, here on the Equator, lasts a full twelve hours.

Mount Kenya rises isolated and impressive above the high moorlands. In this view, taken from Naro Moru River Lodge, some 20 miles (32km) due west, the Forel Glacier is seen immediately below the summit of Batian. On the left sunlight strikes the Josef Glacier below Point Dutton, with Point Peter seen as a sharp peaklet to its left. On the right there is a glimpse of the Darwin Glacier and beyond is the sharp aiguille of Point John

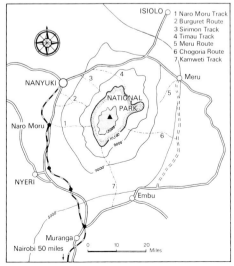

ISIOLO
1 Naro Moru Track
2 Burguret Route
3 Sirimon Track
4 Timau Track
5 Meru Route
6 Chogoria Route
7 Kamweti Track

NANYUKI
Meru
NATIONAL PARK
Naro Moru
NYERI
Embu
Muranga
Nairobi 50 miles

0   10   20
Miles

Situation: Republic of Kenya—Central and Eastern Districts.

Most Important Summits
1 Batian (17,085/5,199) 1899: Halford MacKinder with C. Ollier and J. Brocherel
2 Nelion (17,022/5,188) 1929: Eric Shipton and Percy Wyn Harris
3 Point Lenana (16,355/4,985) 1899: C. B. Hausburg with C. Ollier and J. Brocherel
4 Point Pigott (16,265/4,957) 1930: Eric Shipton and H. W. Tilman
5 Point Dutton (16,025/4,885)
6 Point John (16,020/4,883) 1929: Eric Shipton and R. E. Russell
8 Point Peter (15,605/4,757) 1930: Eric Shipton and H. W. Tilman

Largest Glacier
Lewis–Gregory system 0.8 mile in length

Huts and Bivouacs
Nine huts belonging to the Mountain Club of Kenya are situated strategically round the peak or among the surrounding moorland hills. Two emergency bivouacs are sited on Nelion, one on the summit and one on the *voie normal*. Shipton's Cave is a useful 'howff', and there are other caves elsewhere

Guide-books
The climbing guide is *Mount Kenya and Kilimanjaro*, while *Mountains of Kenya* is a general hill-walking guide to the whole country. Both are published by the MCK (Nairobi). Details of new climbs are published in the Annual Bulletin of the MCK and sometimes in authoritative international magazines such as *Mountain*

Maps
The official Survey of Kenya publish 1:250,000, 1:125,000 maps of the whole area and a special 1:25,000 sheet of Mount Kenya itself. While adequate for the moorland approaches, this is of no use for climbing. A 1:10,000 special map of the central peaks was once published by Schriebl and Schneider (Vienna)

Convenient Centres
The small township of Nanyuki is convenient for northern and western approaches and there are hotels at Meru, Embu and Nyeri, all on the encircling road at a distance 30 miles (48km) from the mountain. Naro Moru River Lodge, where climbers are understood and welcomed, is extremely convenient and offers good facilities

Access
Nairobi has an international airport and air charter facilities are available from Wilson Airport in the city. There are airstrips at Naro Moru and Nanyuki. These townships can also be reached by rail, bus or chartered taxi from Nairobi. There are seven main approach trails from the encircling main road and it is possible to drive some way up each. The Naro Moru and Sirimon tracks are the most important and in good conditions, it is possible to drive above 10,000ft (3,048m) on both. Four-wheel drive taxis may be hired from Naro Moru and Nanyuki for these approaches. On other routes mules have been used and pony trekking is popular on the northern moorland

All ground above 10,500ft (3,200m) lies within the Mount Kenya National Park for which entrance fees must be paid, and, in season, firebond permits issued, at the Naro Moru, Sirimon or Timau entry gates

Kilimanjaro

The highest mountain in the great African continent is a dormant volcano, one of the largest in the world. Its immense truncated cone, aloof and ice-covered, is famous in story and familiar as the back drop to countless films and pictures of African wildlife. From the arid steppes of the Masai country just 200 miles South of the Equator, it rises more than 15,000ft (4,500m) to an astonishing 2½ square miles at 18,500ft (5,600m): a huge area of high ground. Few mountains in the world are so high and yet so isolated.

There have been three important centres of volcanic activity of Kilimanjaro. Kibo, the major peak, is an old crater, 1½ miles (2.5km) in diameter, in the centre of which a small inner crater, complete with 400ft (122m) deep ash pit, still emits sulphurous fumes. In places the rim of the main crater has gone, notably at several 'notches' on the east side and at the wide Western Breach. One ice-field crowns the northern rim while another hangs from the high ridge of the south rim, the highest point of which—an eminence of brown angular scree falling as steep cliffs into the crater—is Uhuru Peak, the summit of Kilimanjaro.

The Western Breach, floored with steep scree and small glaciers, and girded with considerable cliffs is a most imposing *cirque*. On its southern side the Breach Wall rises over 4,000ft (1,200m) and is nearly 1½ miles long—a face of vertical rock and steep ice worthy of Africa's highest peak. Beside it the three tortured tongues of the southern ice-field pour precipitously through a line of crags in a series of impressive ice-falls.

Eastward of Kibo, across the flat desert of the Saddle, rears the striking pinnacled rock crest of Mawenzi—the remnants of volcanism older than Kibo. While its West Face is impressive, its East Face is stupendous, falling steeply into the moorland as a 4,000ft (1,200m) complex of tangled gullys, ribs and towers cleft by two great gorges, the Greater and Little Barrancos.

To the west of Kibo lies Shira, the collapsed remains of an ancient caldera now forming a beautiful moorland plateau at between 11 and 12,000ft (3,350–3,650m). A forestry track climbing up to it is passable to 4-wheel drive vehicles.

A thick belt of tall montane forest encircles Kilimanjaro below 10,000ft (3,000m), but on the southern and eastern flanks coffee and banana shambas often penetrate as high as 6,000ft (1,800m). Elephant, buffalo and rhino live in the forest. Above the trees a wide zone of heather forest, taller and denser than that of Mount Kenya, fades into 'alpine desert' at around 13,000ft (4,000m): here among the dry lava screes there is little vegetation save only moss, Helichrysum and the occasional giant groundsel.

The first ascent of Kaiser Wilhelm Spitze—now Uhuru Peak—by the Leipzig geographer Hans Meyer and his Austrian guide Ludwig Purtscheller via the Saddle and the southern rim, came forty-one years after the missionary John Rebmann first claimed to have seen the snows of Kilimanjaro in 1848. By 1914 there had been several ascents, the Marangu Route had been established and the first huts had been built. Today the ascent is very popular and large numbers of tourists reach the Saddle and Kibo Hut by the Marangu Route, many continuing to Gillmans Point on the crater rim. However, altitude sickness takes a heavy toll and few press on the further mile and 700ft (213m) to Uhuru. While the Marangu Route is straightforward, it is a long and tiring slog and the crater is usually not reached until the fourth day. Park fees and huts are expensive so too is the hire of guides and porters. Unfortunately, at the time of writing, the shorter and more interesting Loitokitok Route, from the Kenyan Outward Bound School, has been officially closed for some years.

Of the several straightforward routes up Kibo, the finest—through the Western Breach—involves interesting rock-scrambling amid awe-inspiring scenery and an approach via the spectacular Umbwe Route. Opened in 1963 and not often used, this remote trail follows a narrow forest ridge between deep gorges and utilizes a succession of caves for bivouacing. Water is scarce and route-finding difficult, but it is a superb wilderness expedition for experienced mountaineers and a really fit party can make the ascent of some 8,000ft (2,400m) from roadhead to No 2 cave in twelve hours. The same party would probably require two further bivouacs to reach Uhuru and return to the roadhead. Another fine expedition is the circumnavigation of Kibo via the Saddle at around the 14,000ft (4,300m) level: this should take about four days of hard, rough walking from the Shira Plateau roadhead.

There are excellent routes of around 4,000ft (1,200m) on Kibo's southern glaciers, and the classic is perhaps the Heim: a fairly straightforward ice-climb in a fantastic situation alongside the Breach Wall, it can be completed by a swift party in one day. Next to it the steep, broken and wide Kersten Glacier holds several lines: the west edge, by Welsch and Herncarek in 1962 (grade V) took three days, the Direct—straight up the centre—by Howell, O'Connor and Cleare in 1975 involved spectacular aid-climbing on a hanging icicle (grade VI; A1), while in 1976 Allan and Savage discovered an attractive line towards the eastern side. The latter two climbs both required one bivouac on the ice. Less difficult climbs have been made on the Decken and Penck Glaciers.

The massive South-West Face of Kibo towers over the Barranco Bivouac high on the Umbwe Route. In the centre is the Breach Wall; on the left the *cirque* of the Western Breach, and on the right the Heim and Kersten Glaciers

One of Africa's major mountaineering problems is presented by the great Breach Wall. Its innermost facet, a high featureless crag, was climbed in 1971 by Fritz Lortscher, but the main Wall has defeated several very powerful parties. The high-angle Balletto Ice-field separates a lower tier of steep mixed ground from a vertical upper tier down which huge icicles hang from the Diamond Glacier above, one actually linking with the Balletto. John Temple, climbing with Tony Charlton in 1975 and Dave Cheesemond in 1976, forced two very difficult lines up the Wall—the latter after four days' climbing—which if linked would make a fairly direct route, but it was not until 1978 that Reinhold Messner managed to surmount the challenging icicle.

Across the Saddle there is no easy way to Mawenzi's summit, although the climb is not difficult and there are over a dozen interesting rock routes on the ridges and buttresses of the west and north flanks, mostly of medium difficulty. Unfortunately the rock, largely volcanic tuff and breccia, is not good, and ideal conditions require a sprinkling of snow and ice. A traverse over all eleven tops of the summit ridge is a worthwhile and fairly difficult three-day climb. Even reaching the base of Mawenzi's stupendous East Face is a major expedition and there have been only a handful of ascents. Edwards and Thomson threaded the first line up this complex mountainside in 1964, emerging in an ice-gully above the Lesser Barranco; in 1968 Howell and Higgins forced a more elegant route, with three bivouacs, via the Downie Ridge which divides the two Barrancos, and in 1970 Lortscher made a rambling progress across the upper face.

One of the most interesting expeditions yet made on Kilimanjaro was the complete traverse of Kibo and Mawenzi made in eight days in 1971 by Howell and Snyder. They ascended the Western Breach via the Umbwe Route, traversed Kibo and the Saddle and climbed Mawenzi to descend the downie ridge and the Lesser Barranco—much of it by rapelle—to end up eventually at Loitokitok.

High and alone above Africa, Kilimanjaro is a unique mountain. Its scale is Himalayan and altitude, bitterly cold twelve-hour bivouacs, remoteness and long approaches with the paucity of rescue facilities render technical climbing a very serious and, indeed, almost expeditionary undertaking. But the scope for rewarding and difficult mountaineering is tremendous.

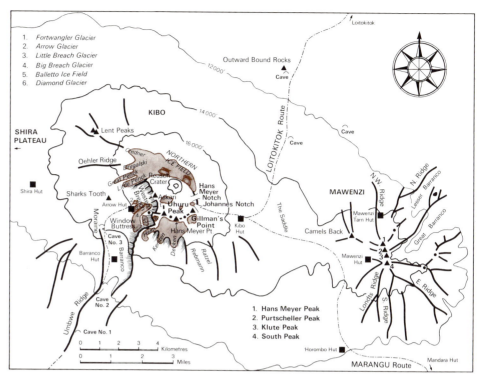

1. Fortwangler Glacier
2. Arrow Glacier
3. Little Breach Glacier
4. Big Breach Glacier
5. Balletto Ice Field
6. Diamond Glacier

1. Hans Meyer Peak
2. Purtscheller Peak
3. Klute Peak
4. South Peak

Situation: Kilimanjaro Region, Republic of Tanzania

Most Important Summits
1 Kibo—Uhuru Peak (19,340/5,895) 1889: Prof Hans Meyer with L. Purtscheller
Gillman's Point (18,640/5,685)
2 Mawenzi Hans Meyer Peak (16,890/5,148) 1912: E. Oehler and F. Klute
Purtscheller Peak (16,800/5,121) 1938: E. Eisenmann and R. Hildebrand
Klute Peak (16,710/5,095) 1889: H. Meyer and L. Purtscheller
South Peak (16,350/4,983) 1924: G. Londt with African guide, Oforo
3 Shira Plateau (13,140/4,005)

Largest Glaciers
Northern ice-field system—$3\frac{1}{4}$ miles (5km) in length

Huts and Bivouacs
There are nine huts or bivouacs on the mountain, some belonging to the Kilimanjaro Mountain Club and some to the National Park authority who are building more. There are many caves strategically situated which are useful

Guide-books
Guide-book to Mount Kenya and Kilimanjaro published by Mountain Club of Kenya (Nairobi)—also new developments are noted in the *Bulletin* of MCK and authoritative international publications such as *Mountain Magazine*

Maps
The Government of Tanzania 1:100,000 Kilimanjaro special sheet (by DOS) gives a good idea of the approaches but is little real use above about 14,000ft (4,267m). A 1:50,000 map has also been published by the same source but is no longer available

Convenient Centres
The town of Moshi has some basic facilities and there are two hotels at Marangu which specialize in catering for would-be ascensionists of that route

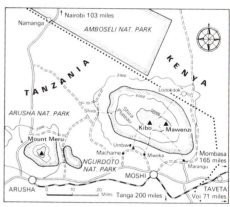

Access
There are international airports at Dar es Salaam, near Arusha (Kilimanjaro International Airport), as well as smaller airports at Moshi and Tanga. A daily train service links Tanga and Dar es Salaam to Moshi and Arusha. Local bus services do exist between Moshi and some of the townships on the southern flanks of Kilimanjaro near the roadheads. Cars can be hired in Moshi. At the time of writing the Tanzanian Government has closed its border crossings with Kenya at Namanga, Taveta and elsewhere.

Kilimanjaro now lies within a National Park and permits are required to climb the mountain. Routes other than the Marangu Route are frowned on and the northern Loitokitok Route from Kenya has been closed for some years

Ruwenzori

In 500 BC Aeschylus wrote of '. . . Egypt nurtured by the snow.'. A first reference perhaps to the mysterious Ruwenzori? More than 600 years later Ptolemy, the great geographer, suggested on his map that the Nile was born from a snow-fed lake cradled among high mountains deep in Central Africa: he labelled them the 'Mountains of the Moon'. Although the Nile has many sources, the Ruwenzori, where there are several such lakes, are by far the highest mountains to feed that mighty river.

The Ruwenzori is a 'block mountain' of ancient Pre-Cambrian rock that rose out of the Western Rift Valley some 5 million years ago and has since been eroded to the form we know today: a series of large massifs each crowned with several summits and rising steeply around 3,000ft (900m) above deep and narrow valleys, and surrounded by a wide belt of tangled foothills extending 70 miles (112km) north to south and half that distance east to west. Apparently 15,000 years ago the glaciers poured down below 7,000ft (2,000m) but the glacial retreat of recent years seems now to have halted—today the lower glacier snouts nudge the 14,250ft (4,343m) contour. No less than ten peaks top 16,000ft (4,800m) and the six higher massifs hold permanent ice.

The moody charm of the Ruwenzori, the ice, the vegetation, the bog, indeed the very atmosphere, is due to the weather. Although there are two concentrated rainy seasons—from March to May and September to December—a typical dry season day might start clear and frosty, but by midday the mountains might be in cloud with snow falling throughout the afternoon and the sky clearing again at dusk. Sometimes the weather can be superb, though it is rarely settled.

A characteristic of the higher peaks is the spectacular encrustations of ice-rime that build up on the rocks and ridges, forming weird mushrooms and huge cornices. The tall cliffs and slabs which

Among the South Stanley peaks: Philip (16,140ft/4,919m) rises above the little hanging Coronation Glacier. On the left is Nyabubuya and on the right Kitasamba (both c15,950ft/4,860m), while on the far right, across the East Gully first climbed by Firmin and Busk in 1953, lies the wall of Savoia (16,330ft/4,977m). The East Gully of Nyabubuya has also been climbed, but in summer conditions. The picture was taken from the east, across the lower Elena Glacier in winter conditions – late December

wall the valleys below the ice are usually lichen-covered high up and draped with moss at lower levels. Dark and placid tarns mirror the surrounding stands of monster tree groundsel and giant silvery lobelia, and the hillsides are cloaked with often impenetrable thickets of woody Helichrysum—5ft high and covered with white 'everlasting' flowers—and groundsel jungle. Dense groves of giant heather, hung with luxuriant moss and ferns extend above 12,000ft (3,600m), while the foothills descend into tangled bamboo and, ultimately, to high montane forest.

Characteristic, too, is Ruwenzori bog. It is ubiquitous, deep and slimy—mud to the knees and wet feet are a fact of life. Elephants, ants, giant hogs and monkeys live in the forest, besides peculiar giant earthworms some 2ft long. The plentiful hyrax are hunted by both leopard and the local Bakonjo tribesmen—who also provide the porters without whom Ruwenzori expeditions could not operate.

Although Stanley, in 1876, was the first recorded European to catch a distant sight of the eternal snows, it was not until the turn of the century that European explorers first probed to the snowline, among them Freshfield and Mumm of the Alpine Club. It was not long before the first full-scale expedition was led into the Ruwenzori by the Duke of the Abruzzi; his strong party included four Courmayeur guides, Vittorio Sella—already a renowned mountain photographer—and some 150 porters, and they climbed nearly all the major summits and made the first map. Since then there have been regular visitors but numbers have, understandably, never been large. Much exploration was done in the 1920s and '30s by local expatriates, notably G. N. Humphreys, and since the war by the once active Mountain Club of Uganda who built seven huts at convenient locations. But the current state of development is much as was that of the Pennine Alps in 1890. All the summits and major ridges have been climbed, but little else.

While the approaches to the heart of the Ruwenzori are long and arduous, the chain of huts and rock-shelters makes the usual Bujuku Valley Route—boggy but nowhere steep—a relatively pleasant three-day march to the strategic Bujuku Huts.

Much of the best climbing is on Mount Stanley which consists of two groups of peaks at either end of the Stanley Ice Plateau. From the Plateau the ascents of Alexandra and Margherita and the onward traverse to Albert are straightforward snow-climbs with spectacular scenery, but there are more difficult and far longer mixed routes on either flank. Two of the very best climbs in the range are the beautiful North-West Ridge of Albert, a mainly rock route that compares favourably with any classic Zermatt ridge, and the difficult 2,000ft (600m) ice-gully that runs directly up its fine North Face. As elsewhere in the range, the metamorphic rock is typically excellent. An easy classic on ice is Alexandra's West Face glacier. These climbs are actually in Zaire, as are other good ones on the western flanks of these peaks: the frontier is hypothetical and does not follow the summit crest of Stanley and, unfortunately, the Zairean Park authorities seem to disapprove of climbing.

On the Stanley Plateau, Moebius is a mere pimple, but its steep western glacier is the Ruwenzori's longest and makes an interesting straightforward ice-climb. The Plateau is easily reached from the tiny Elena bivi huts, an excellent base for the South Stanley peaks. Here the little Coronation Glacier, discovered by Firmin and Busk in 1953, is a jewel cradled by Savoia, Elizabeth and Philip and the rock and ice architecture is among the best in the range—there are some good modern rock and mixed climbs too, both easy and hard, and a fine difficult traverse linking all the South Stanley peaks.

So far no difficult climbs have been made on Mount Speke, but the South-West Ridge of Johnston is an interesting climb, mainly on rock, and the traverse onwards to Vittorio Emanuele, after locating the awkward rapelle from the summit, makes a worthwhile outing.

Mount Baker boasts the most impressive walls in the range: the extremely steep and blank West Face of Semper, just south of the Scott Elliot Pass, is over 2,000ft (600m) high and has yet to be climbed—part of it is overhung by the Y Glacier. Overlooking Lake Bujuku, the great North Face is a mile-wide mountainside seamed with gullys and buttresses and it has given several serious mixed climbs, the first by Shipton and Tilman in 1932. Baker's Classic, however, is the complete traverse of its crest via the South Ridge of Edward: the ridge continuing over Semper and the Monks Head is very narrow in places with several steep steps and gives fine mixed climbing reminiscent of the best alpine ridges. Descent is from Moore or Wollaston via the awkward Moore Glacier. The whole expedition, from Kitandara to the Bujongolo cave is over 9 miles (14km).

Mounts Emin and Gessi are rarely visited and, while their scenery is less impressive than that of the higher massifs, their rock-ridges are jagged and narrow and provide exhilarating scrambles.

Mount Stanley: looking north across the Stanley Plateau towards Alexandra (left) and Margherita (right). The standard route on both peaks lies up the right-hand, or eastern, ridges

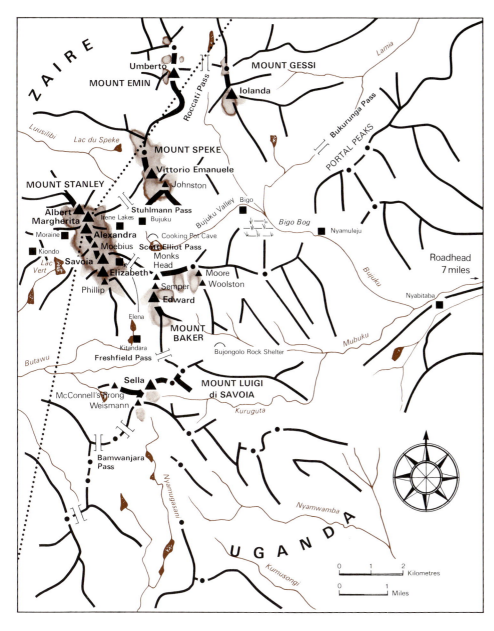

Little has been climbed on Mount Luigi di Savoia except the easiest ways to the summits, a notable exception being the short but difficult ascent—using aid—of McConnell's Prong in 1971, but the glacial *cirque* heading the Kuruguta Valley, below the East Face of Weismann, is the most impressive in the range.

Five further groups of peaks, all with summits over 14,000ft (4,200m), and some with no recorded ascents, outlie the central massifs, while there are other lesser groups virtually unexplored. Potential for new routes, both easy and difficult, among the larger peaks is still great but conditions could render hard multi-day ascents very uncomfortable. A Uganda Ski Club exists—eligible only to those few who have skied on the Stanley Plateau—but it is currently inactive, and potential for other ski ascents is nil.

Situation: Republics of Uganda and Zaire

Mount Stanley
1 Margherita (16,763/5,109) 1906: Duke of the Abruzzi with J. Petigax, C. Ollier and J. Brocherel
2 Alexandra (16,703/5,091) 1906: as above
3 Albert (16,690/5,087) 1932: X. de Grunne, J. de la Vallee-Poussin, W. Ganshof with J. Georges
4 Savoia (16,330/4,977) 1906: Duke of the Abruzzi with J. Petigax, C. Ollier and J. Brocherel
Elizabeth (16,170/4,929) 1953: Arthur Firmin and Douglas Busk

Mount Speke
10 Vittorio Emanuele (16,042/4,890) 1906: Duke of the Abruzzi with J. Petigax and C. Ollier

Mount Baker
13 Edward (15,889/4,843) 1906: Duke of the Abruzzi with J. Petigax, C. Olier and J. Brocherel

Mount Emin
14 Umberto (15,740/4,798) 1906: Duke of the Abruzzi with J. and L. Petigax

Mount Gessi
17 Iolanda (15,470/4,715) 1906: Duke of the Abruzzi with C. Ollier and J. Petigax

Mount Luigi di Savoia
20 Sella (15,178/4,626) 1906: Vittorio Sella, with J. Brocherel and E. Botta

Major Passes—all are stiff walking
Stuhlmann Pass (13,650/4,161) links Bujuku Valley to Luusilubi Valley (Zaire)
Scott Elliot Pass (14,350/4,374) links Bujuku Valley to Kitandara
Freshfield Pass (14,050/4,282) links Mubuku Valley to Kitandara
Bamwanjara Pass (14,050/4,282) links Mubuku Valley to Kitandara
Bamwanjara Pass (14,650/4,465) links Kitandara to Nyamugasani Valley and Chapmans roadhead
Roccati Pass (13,500/4,115) links Bigo area to Rwanoli Valley (Zaire)
Bukurungu Pass (12,550/3,825) links Bigo area to Rwimi Valley and Kisomoro road-head

Major Glaciers
Stanley Plateau covers approximately 0.22 square miles (0.35km), but from the snout of Elena Galcier over the Plateau to the snout of West Stanley Glacier unbroken ice stretches for over 1¼ miles (2km).
Speke Glacier covers approximately 0.16 square miles (0.25km).

Huts and Bivouacs
Seven huts, some merely bivouac shelters and most in disrepair and owned by the Mountain Club of Uganda.
Four huts, again in various stages of disrepair, are owned by the Parc National Albert authorities in Zaire.
There are numerous rock-shelters at convenient locations and it is traditional to use them

Convenient Centres
Fort Portal is a small township with hotels and some stores. There is a hotel at Kasese and a comfortable lodge as well as basic dormatory accommodation at Mweya in the Ruwenzori (late Queen Elizabeth) National Park. There is a trading store Ibanda owned by the local MCU agent

Guide-books
Guide to the Ruwenzori is published by the Mountain Club of Uganda in conjunction with Westcol (UK).
Additional information has been published in the Bulletin of the MCU, the MCK and such publications as the *Alpine Journal* and *Mountain Magazine*

Maps
DOS publish for the Uganda Surveys Department the following maps: 1:25,000, covering the complete range; 1:50,000, five sheets cover the complete range but the important central area is on one sheet; 1:25,000 special map covers the central area

Access
From Uganda the usual access is from the roadhead at Nyakalengija close to Ibanda. The MCU agent arranges porters, etc. Ibanda may be reached easily from Kampala by road or by train and bus via the railhead at Kasese. Daily flights link Kasese to Entebbe International Airport.
From Zaire the roadhead is Mutwanga, reached from Beni. There is an airfield at Bunia and a major airport at Kisangani.
The western flank of the Ruwenzori lies within the Parc National Albert and access is severely restricted.
Due to political problems at the time of writing, some or all of the above means of access may be inapplicable.

Southern Africa

The mountains of South Africa are not a single range but a whole series of ranges each with its own features and character. The major ranges occur around the rim of the high interior plateau and most lie within about 150 miles (241km) of the coast. The arid Karoo and the high-veld of the interior have relatively few major mountains, although some, such as the Magaliesberg, have become important climbing areas.

On a spring day in the year 1503 the Portuguese admiral Antonio da Saldanha climbed Table Mountain via Platklip Gorge. This first recorded ascent of a South African mountain was made to ascertain his bearings. Numerous further ascents of Table Mountain were recorded in the next few hundred years, but it was not until the nineteenth century that many other mountains were climbed here.

During the latter part of the nineteenth century, experienced climbers began arriving from overseas and became aware of the multitude of unclimbed peaks and faces. Many unrecorded ascents had been made by local farmers and surveyors, but until the remarkable ascent of Towerkop in 1885, there was little interest in rock-climbing.

Towerkop 7,225ft (2,202m) high in the Swartberg Range is crowned by a 400ft (120m) rock tower divided into eastern and western summits. The eastern summit is a difficult rock-climb, while the western summit was regarded as impossible until climbed by a nineteen year old youth, Gustav Nefdt, from the nearby village of Ladismith. He made the first ascent alone, but later repeated the climb with witnesses to prove his feat to disbelieving villagers. Experienced mountaineeers failed to repeat his success and the western peak was not climbed again until 1906 and then only by an alternative and easier line. Nefdt's original route was not repeated until 1947!

The Drakensberg Mountains (to the Zulus, 'Quathlamba', or 'Barrier of Spears'). Monk's Cowl from the summit of Arey's Pass with the cliffs of Cathkin Peak on the left and Champagne Castle on the right. The North Face of Monk's Cowl (left-hand side) has a reputation for difficult rock-climbs

News of the climbing of Towerkop helped to inspire the small group of enthusiastic climbers in Cape Town who made regular trips to Table Mountain. A well-known botanist, Dr Rudolf Marloth, suggested the formation of a mountain club and sixty gentlemen gathered to discuss the proposal at a local cafe. The first meeting of the Mountain Club took place on 4 November 1891. Further sections of the club formed in other centres and the initially separate Natal Mountain Club eventually also became a section of the Mountain Club of South Africa. With such a benevolent climate, mountaineering in South Africa has a very relaxed atmosphere.

Table Mountain, surrounded by the suburbs of Cape Town, became the home of South African mountaineering. Today it is one of the most climbed

mountains in the world and holds nearly five hundred recognized routes—most of them severe rock-climbs. Its cliffs are formed of hard grey quartzitic Table Mountain sandstone which weathers in intricate forms, making climbable the most unlikely looking crags.

Table Mountain is merely an outlier of the whole system of fold mountains of the Western Cape, known as the 'boland' (high land). The mountains stretch from the Cape northwards up the west coast, and eastwards for hundreds of miles.

The Cedarberg, 100 miles (160km) north of Cape Town, has a distinct character and remarkable features of its own, with gnarled old cedar trees and weirdly weathered sandstone formations, such as the Maltese Cross and the Wolfberg Arch. Peaks include the Tafelberg and the adjoining Spout, each with numerous fine rock routes.

East of the Cape lie several parallel ranges, including hundreds of peaks which eventually link up with the southern end of the Drakensberg. Within sight of Cape Town lies Du Toits Peak on which is found the great North-West Frontal Route (G) opened by Mike Mamacos in 1949, and Witteberg with its classic Frontal Route (E). Slightly further afield in the Hex River Mountains, skiing facilities have been developed on Waaihoek (6,400ft/1,951m) (University

Hex River Range—the Mostertshoek Twins from Waaihoek Peak in winter. The former provide opportunities for snow- and ice-climbing at this time of year, whilst Waaihoek offers skiing facilities

of Cape Town Mountain and Ski Club) and on Matroosberg (7,386ft/2,251m) (Ski Club of South Africa) while the Mostertshoek Twins (6,570ft/2,003m) provide some opportunities for snow- and ice-climbing in winter. The mountains of the Western Cape are hot and dry in summer, while rain and snow fall regularly in winter.

The Magaliesberg, named after an early African chief, Mogali, is a small range of mountains in the Transvaal rising only to 6,000ft (1,829m), scarcely 2,000ft (610m) above the surrounding highveld of the Witwatersrand. It is of significance because of its proximity to the major cities of Johannesburg and Pretoria. The deep gorges which dissect the range have fine rock-climbs although the mountains are unspectacular in appearance.

The great Drakensberg (Dragon Mountains) stretch for hundreds of miles along the eastern margins of the interior plateau, from the Eastern Cape to the Transvaal, but the highest peaks and major climbing area lie on the border between Natal and Lesotho. The great crags and pinnacles of the Drakensberg are formed of weathered basalt, rising above the sandstone of the foothills known as the 'Little Berg'. These rolling hills are covered by grasslands, green in the wet summer months and dry and cold in the winter when snow and ice appear on the peaks. Magnificent Bushman rock-paintings are a feature of many of the caves in the area. The mountains abound with wildlife, including eland, baboon and even leopard, while the rare African lammergeyer is often seen.

The earliest climbing in the Drakensberg was carried out by the Reverend A. H. Stocker, a member of the Alpine Club who, in 1888, climbed Champagne Castle (11,072ft/3,375m), Sterkhorn, and attempted Cathkin Peak. Cathkin Peak was eventually climbed in 1912 and Cathedral Peak in 1917. The basalt faces of Monk's Cowl were first climbed in 1942 (Dick Barry's first attempt on the peak ended in his death in 1938). The Bell was climbed by Hans and Elsa Wongtschowski in 1944. After many attempts the Devil's Tooth was eventually climbed in 1950. Strangely enough the highest peak in Southern Africa was not discovered until 1951—a little known summit in Lesotho called Thabana Ntlenyana (the Little Black Mountain) was found to be the highest point south of Kilimanjaro!

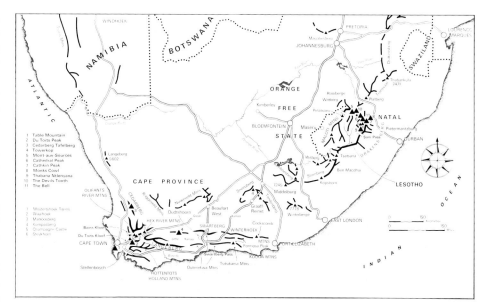

Situation: Republic of South Africa; Kingdom of Lesotho

Most Important Peaks
Table Mountain (3,566/1,087) 1503: Antonio de Saldanha. There are nearly 500 described routes today
Du Toits Peak (6,580/2,006) (first ascent unrecorded). North-west frontal route opened 1949: M. P. Mamacos and C. C. Butler
Cedarberg Tafelberg (6,465/1,971) 1896: Mann and Villoen
Towerkop (7,225/2,202) 1885: Gustav Nefdt—solo
Mont-aux-Sources (10,820/3,282) 1836: Reverend Arbousset and F. Dumas (French missionaries)
Cathedral Peak (9,856/3,004) 1917: R. G. Kingdon and D. W. Bassett-Smith
Cathkin Peak (10,390/3,167) 1912: G. T. Amphlett, Tobias, W. C. West, Father A. D. Kelly, T. Casement and Melatu
Monk's Cowl (10,611/3,234) 1942: H. Wongtschowski, J. Botha, E. Rhule and A. S. Hooper
Thabana Ntlenyana (11,425/3,482). Surveyed 1954: H. Peake and A. Bisschoff
The Devil's Tooth (9,915/3,022) 1950: D. Bell, P. Campbell and T. Scholes
The Bell (9,812/2,991) 1944: H. and E. Wongtschowski

Some Important Passes
Du Toits Kloof (3,432/1,046) opened in 1949, this major road-pass is the main access to the Du Toits Kloof Mountains and links Paarl and Worcester
Bains Kloof (3,825/1,166) this road-pass, completed in 1853 by the famous road engineer Andrew Geddes Bain, provides access to surrounding mountains and links Wellington just north of Paarl to the Breede River Valley, north of Worcester
Swartberg Pass (5,174/1,577) this remarkable road-pass crosses the Groot Swartberg and descends by spectacular hairpins to the Karoo
Sani Pass (9,439/2,877) the highest road-pass in Southern Africa, this crosses the southern Drakensberg. The 'mountain road' leading across Lesotho via Mokhotlong finally emerges from the Maluti Mountains by the Moteng Pass to Butha Buthe. This formidably rough road is used for the 'Roof of Africa Rally'
Drakensberg Passes—there are no road-passes through the Natal Drakensberg into Lesotho, but many foot- and horse-passes are used by mountaineers

Convenient Centre
Cape Town has several stores retailing mountaineering equipment and the headquarters of the Mountain Club of South Africa are also here (Hatfield Street)

Huts
The MCSA owns a number of mountain huts and shelters and there are skiing huts at Matroosberg, Waaihoek and several places in the Drakensberg and Maluti Mountains

Access
Cape Town, Durban and Johannesburg have international airports and provide access to the Western Cape Mountains, the Drakensberg and the Magaliesberg respectively. Many mountain areas are administered by the Forestry Department and permits are required for access. Most peaks can be climbed from a road, but in the Drakensberg a base camp is usually required

Maps
Excellent 1:50,000 sheets of the South African Trigonometrical Survey cover most areas and the Forestry Department publishes maps of certain wilderness areas and hiking trails

Guide-books
The *Table Mountain Guide* describes easy climbs on Table Mountain, while *Climbs on Table Mountain* lists the remainder, with references to full descriptions in the *Journal of the Mountain Club of South Africa*. Major routes in the Drakensberg are listed in *The Drakensberg of Natal* by Doyle Liebenberg who is President of the Mountain Club of South Africa

North America and the Arctic

The Bugaboos lie in the Northern Purcell Range in the south-east corner of British Columbia. We look across the Bugaboo Glacier towards the granite spire of Snowpatch (10,050ft/3,063m). Resisting many attempts, Snowpatch Spire was unclimbed until 1940, at which time it was described as North America's number one climbing problem. The first ascent took a line on its south-east side—approximately the right-hand skyline. Seen here is the impressive South-West Face

Opposite: Sculpted by desert winds, the Fisher Towers of Utah, improbable fingers of crumbling sandstone, rise from the Colorado Plateau, 17 miles north east of Moab. The tallest, seen here, is the Titan, 900ft (274m) high. It was first climbed in 1962 following a route close to the right skyline; since then the sunlit face has also been climbed

Greenland

Most of Greenland, the largest island in the world and one-quarter of the size of the United States, lies north of the Arctic Circle. It stretches from Cape Morris Jesup, only 440 miles (700km) from the North Pole and the world's most northerly land, southward 1,250 miles (2,000km) to Cape Farewell—as far south as Scotland's Shetland Isles. Although a great desert of ice covers 82 per cent of its surface, a narrow strip of green encircles much of its coastline during the short summer months. Flowers bloom, reindeer, musk ox, sheep and even a few cattle graze in endless daylight and a population of some 48,000

Greenlanders—of pure Eskimo, Danish or mixed race—go about their business which is usually connected with fishing or hunting. Most live on the South-West coast which is relatively ice-free and where the capital, Godthaab, with its population of nearly 9,000, has year-round access to the open sea. Not so the South-East coast where even in summer the pack-ice limits a sea approach to only two or three months in late summer.

Small wonder perhaps that Greenland's magnificent mountains, which ring the edges of the ice-cap and in many cases rise straight from the long fjords that cut deep into the coast, were

slow to attract the attention of mountaineers: sea journeys were long and landings often frustrated. With modern air travel, however, Greenland has become the goal of a host of small expeditions and it is fair to say that parts are now perhaps the best known 'unexplored' mountain area in the world. Climbers are attracted by a bewildering number of peaks, relatively stable summer weather and twenty-four-hour daylight. Against this must be set the short season and the difficulties of travel, both along the coast and inland where the glaciers are often in poor summer condition.

Most northerly of Greenland's mountains are the Roosevelt Range in Peary Land. Only with complex logistic support is it possible to operate in this region, and the British Joint Services Expedition of 1969, who first climbed here, used full air-lift back-up. They found a series of small steep alpine peaks strung together by long sharp ridges and, using skis for approach, they climbed twenty-one summits fairly easily, although harder climbs were possible.

The mountainous area of Queen Louise Land, separated from the sea by a formidable 22-mile wide glacier, was one of the last major areas of the east coast to be explored. During another Joint Services Expedition here in 1951–4 the highest peak, Gefionstinde, was climbed, most of the way by dog sledge.

'. . . A Mountaineer's dream come true—the Arctic Riviera . . .' thus have the Staunings Alps of Scoresby Land been described. In this complex area, some 60 × 30 miles (96 × 48km), serried ranks of sharp and impressive peaks, hung with steep faces, fine buttresses and pinnacled *arêtes*, rise from innumerable glaciers, some of considerable size—some seventy summits exceed 8,000ft (2,400m). The rock is usually excellent granite of many colours and

Access to the Watkins Mountains is more difficult and few expeditions have climbed here, although they were among the first mountains to be surveyed from the air. Massive and ice-covered, with exposed cliffs of horizontal strata, they hold some interesting and difficult snow- and ice-routes. Several very high, unsurveyed and unclimbed peaks exist in the south east of the area.

North of Angmagssalik, Mount Forel—possibly the second highest mountain in Greenland—lies on the edge of the ice-cap and is separated from the coast by an extensive and little-known area of mountains and glaciers,

climbs on rock, ice and mixed ground, of all standards and up to 6,000ft (1,800m) in length, have been made by the constant stream of expeditions from many nations which have climbed here since the early 1950s. The Staunings compare well with the European Alps to which they are similar in scale and appearance, but the climbing season is short—for practical purposes only July and August. Glacier travel and route-finding through ice-falls and over high passes can be interesting—or troublesome—and skis are often useful, especially in July. While today virgin summits are rare, most peaks will have had only one ascent. Unfortunately, as access involves the use of an airstrip maintained primarily for mining use, the Greenland authorities are currently hesitant in allowing climbers to visit the Staunings.

called Schweizerland. Many of its peaks are spectacular, with fine clean-cut rock-ridges and much steep ice and a host of them rise above 7,500ft (2,250m). Especially notable among the peaks is

Above: **A camp in the upper basin of the Lang Glacier, Staunings Alps. On the skyline (right) are the peaks of the Diadem, with (extreme right) Downing Fjeld**

Left: **East Greenland—Ingolfsfjeld (7,323ft/2,232m). Since it was first reconnoitred in 1968, this peak has attracted a number of expeditions. The first ascent by a Croatian expedition followed the East Ridge, partly visible in this picture to the left of the summit**

Greenland

Pharoh (9,800ft/2,987m) a fine pyramid of rock and ice which gave a very steep and serious 2,000ft (609m) ice-route on its West Face during its first ascent in 1968. Other splendid peaks include Pointe de Harpon (8,970ft/2,734m) and De Quervains Bjerg (8,850ft/2,697m). Perhaps mention should be made of the chisel-shaped rock peak of Ingolfsfjeld (7,323ft/2,232m) above the head of the Kangerdlugssuatsiaq Fjord 90 miles (155km) up the coast from Angmag-ssalik. Its first ascent by a Croatian party in 1971, by the difficult East Ridge, was a fine achievement, but the second, by the British who forced the 5,000ft (1,500m) South Face with sixty-three pitches in 1975, is the hardest climb yet to be made in Greenland. But travelling conditions here are difficult, the ice changes year by year, and several expeditions making for Mount Forel have had great difficulty breaking through this maze of mountain and glacier.

Behind Cape Farewell, in the far south, lies a fine region of attractive alpine country with a sub-arctic climate and a relatively long climbing season. Though access is difficult several expe-ditions have been active here. Some of the peaks have ice-summits—including the highest one, Point, 7,360ft (2,243m)—but the region is charact-erized by an abundance of incredible rock spires, towers and *aiguilles* of excellent granite and gneiss which resemble the Paine and Fitzroy peaks of Patagonia. Notable are the difficult Cathedral (6,988ft/2,130m) and Minster (6,594ft/2,010m) which were climbed by an Irish team in 1971, and the great palisade of the Apostelens Tom-melfinger which gave an eight-day climb to a French team in 1975, via its specta-cular South Pillar.

Upon the accessible west coast several expeditions have climbed in the area of the Sukkertoppen Ice-Cap, a small com-pletely independent ice-cap of only (!) 1,000 square miles (1,609 sq km). Of the jumble of icy peaks which lie to the west and south of Sukkertoppen, the highest is Mount Atter.

Another concentration of interesting mountains lies around the Umanak Fjord. Punta Italia is probably the high-est peak in West Greenland and, close to it, Qioqe (6,100ft/1,859m) gives a superb 5,000ft (1,524m) West Ridge, a difficult climb on perfect rock. Uper-nivik Island, said to be the most beauti-ful in Greenland, lies in the Fjord: measuring only 15 × 12 miles (24 × 19km), it contains more than seventy-five sharp rock- and ice-peaks of real alpine character and the several expe-ditions to pioneer here have been largely Italian or from St Andrews University, although Bill Tilman climbed here in 1961. The highest peak is Great White Tower 6,854ft (2,089m), first climbed in 1950.

Further up the coast, on Melville Bay, the striking little Devil's Thumb, a famous landmark for the Dundee whalers of long ago, gave Tom Longstaff a difficult climb in 1934, and is just another Greenland '*bonne-bouche*'. There are many other such prizes, but enterprising mountaineers must be pre-pared to use skis and sledges, inflatables and kayaks to reach them. The accessible peaks are now well known but hundreds of virgin summits await those able to overcome the access problems of the more remote coasts.

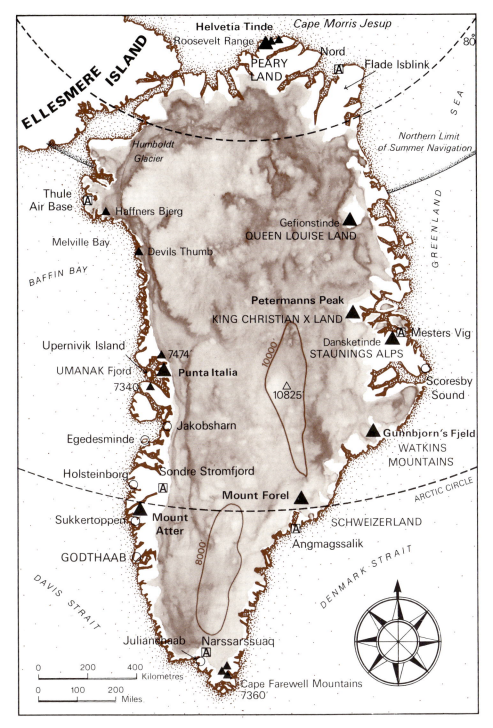

Left: **Attilaborgen, the most impressive mountain at the head of the Sefstroms Glacier, seen here from the Sefstromstinde, looking west across the glacier towards the Greenland Ice-Cap**

Situation: A province of the Kingdom of Denmark, in the North Atlantic off the North American continent

Important Mountains

1 Gunnbjorn's Fjeld (12,139/3,700)—Watkins Mountains—1935: L. R. Wager and party
Mount Forel (11,024/3,360)—Schweizerland—1938: André Roch and party
Ejnar Mikkelsen Fjeld (10,699/3,261)—Watkins Mountains—1970: A. Ross and party
Petermanns Peak (9,646/2,940)—King Christian X Land—1929: A Courtauld and party
Dansketinde (9,613/2,930)—Staunings Alps—1954: J. Haller and W. Diehl
Hjornespids (9,383/2,960)—Staunings Alps—1960: M. Slesser and I. McNaught-Davis
Gefionstinde (c8,800/2,680)—Queen Louise

Land—1952: F. R. Brooke and party
Punta Italia (7,578/2,310)—Qioqe Peninsular, Umanak Fjord—1960: Piero Ghiglione and party
Ingolfsfjeld (7,323/2,232) 1971: A Yugoslav Expedition
Mount Atter (7,185/2,190)—Sukkertoppen Ice-Cap—1956: M. W. Holland and party
Helvetia Tinde (6,300/1,920)—Roosevelt Range—1969: Brude Reid and party

Glaciers

The Greenland Ice-Cap, the second largest ice-sheet in the world, covers 66,500 square miles (107,018 sq km), is some 1,550 miles (2,500km) in length and contains approximately 12 per cent of the world's land-ice. There are, in addition, some 29,500 square miles (47,500 sq km) of separate 'glaciers' and the Humboldt Glacier, which is 60 miles (96km) wide, is considered the largest in the Northern Hemisphere

Convenient Centres

Mountaineering in Greenland is entirely expeditionary

Guide-books

Staunings Alps—Greenland, an expedition guide, which deals only with the mountains of Scoresby Land and neighbouring Nathorsts Land is published by Gastons/Westcol (UK).

Greenland by polar explorer Mike Banks is published by David & Charles (Newton Abbot) and is a useful source book. The history of ice-cap exploration is covered, but little mountaineering

Montagne di Groenlandia by Mario Fautin covers all mountain activity up to 1968 very comprehensively.

Useful notes in *Mountain Magazine* and *Alpine Journal*

Maps

The Danish Geodetic Institute publishes map sheets of scales 1:250,000, and a few at 1:25,000, covering much of the more accessible coastal regions. Reliability in difficult areas is not always good. American military maps (AMS) are fair at the 1:250,000 scale and there is the 1:1,000,000 World Aeronautical Chart.

Gastons/Westcol publish a two-sheet special mountain map of the Staunings Alps at 1:100,000 scale. Various expeditions have published the results of their own surveys, notably in the *Alpine Journal*

Access

Scheduled international flights operate into Sondre Stromfjord or Thule, from Copenhagen and elsewhere or from Iceland into Narssarssuak. From Sondre Stromfjord there are local services to Narssarssuak, Angmagssalik and Mestersvig while a USAF flight to Thule may sometimes be available. Many communities on the West Coast are linked by Greenlandair helicopter. Helicopters may be chartered at great expense from Angmagssalik or Mestersvig. Many expeditions arrive by chartered aircraft from Iceland. New STOL airstrips are being built at Godthaab, Jakobshavn, Holsteinborg and elsewhere for a service which will radiate from Sondre Stromfjord.

Major settlements can expect a ship once a month if the ice permits and regular boats serve the East Coast from July to September. There are regular sailings from Denmark to the West Coast. Launches can usually be hired locally for coastal transportation.

All expeditions require formal permission well in advance from the Danish Ministry for Greenland who also have stringent insurance requirements to cover possible search and rescue

Baffin Island

For 700 miles (1,120km) the north-east coast of Baffin Island faces Greenland across the Davis Strait. Deeply indented by a myriad fjords, the coast is backed by a tangle of mountains holding sizeable glaciers and several considerable ice-caps. This mountainous backbone, some 50 miles (80km) wide, falls westwards to a plain dotted with lakes and muskeg, the typical tundra of this part of arctic Canada.

John Davis navigated this coast, eventually landing on it, in 1585. However, the whalers who followed had other priorities and both the Eskimo inhabitants and the interior remained unknown for a further three centuries, until anthropologists and surveyors commenced serious explorations. The first real mountaineering took place in 1934 when Tom Longstaff, and other members of Sir James Wordie's crew, climbed several peaks in the Eglinton Fjord area. Among the team was Pat Baird, now considered the authority on Baffin's mountains, who returned in 1953 to lead a major scientific expedition which also made several important climbs, among them the first ascents of the island's two highest peaks. Their activities, and those of almost all subsequent expeditions, have centred on the Pangnirtung Pass at the edge of the Penny Ice-Cap. The Ice-Cap fills much of the interior of the Cumberland Peninsula, an area similar in size to Scotland which sits astride the Arctic Circle at the far south-east extremity of Baffin's mountain spine. Meanwhile Baffin's other mountains are

little known; vast areas have yet to be visited and hundreds of peaks remain virgin. A few climbs have also been made elsewhere on the Cumberland Peninsula, notably at the head of Kingnate Fjord and in the hinterland of Cape Dyer where the peaks assume more 'alpine' shapes than those of the Pangnirtung area. Landmarks here are Mounts Raleigh and Gilbert, named by Davis in 1585 and climbed nearly four hundred years later. Up the coast, besides Eglinton Fjord, expeditions have visited Clyde Inlet and Swiss Bay where Baird has reported peaks around 6,000ft (1,830m) and boasting huge rock walls.

The Pangnirtung Pass, about 1,200ft (360m) above the sea, and the Weasel and Owl Valleys leading to it, cut a deep U-shaped trough right across the Cumberland Peninsula. On either side the truncated buttresses and spurs of upstanding peaks rise some 5,000ft (1,520m) or more above the valley floor. Long glacier tongues reach down between them, providing highways between further avenues of peaks, or to the Penny Ice-Cap to the west.

Typically these ice-carved mountains are spectacular in form. There are towers and spires of naked rock, massive ice-crowned bastions and shapely pyramids of rock and ice. Great rock walls and prows, sheer or overhanging, are the special characteristic of the region. Rarely loose, the rock itself is a rough and compact granite which provides superb climbing, both on the easier lines as well as on the difficult 'big walls'. The

climbing season is short: most of the rock should be clear of snow by mid June, but the autumn snows return in late August. During this period four weeks of fair weather might reasonably be expected. Early in the season, of course, daylight is unlimited.

Most parties establish a base camp in the main valley, usually beside Summit Lake, placing subsidiary camps beneath chosen peaks; but travel, both to, and above, base camp, can prove tiresome. Unstable moraines, unpleasant muskeg and difficult river crossings make the 25-mile (40km) long Weasel Valley heavy going, and the Owl Valley, slightly longer, only marginally less so. Even crossing the valleys from side to side can be a major operation. Skis or snowshoes can be essential early in the season on glaciers which may later be awash with slush and meltwater. Mosquitoes also can make life uncomfortable.

Few of the summits so far climbed have presented much difficulty with their easiest way, and some of these alpine-style routes have been extremely good, for instance, the beautiful ice-*arêtes* of Tête Blanche and majestic Odin, the latter probably the most beautiful mountain in the region. Rather harder first ascents have been by 'mixed' routes, notable being the long many-towered West Ridge of Mount Volpedo and the splendid ¾-mile West Ridge of Mount Loki, with its several difficult rock steps. From the north Loki has been described as '. . .a steeple, its point gently bent over by the wind'. The outstanding peak,

Curious, flat-topped Mount Asgard is the finest peak in the Pangnirtung Pass area. Seen here from the north with its awesome West Face in profile (right). The East Face (left) was climbed in 1972 by a British party

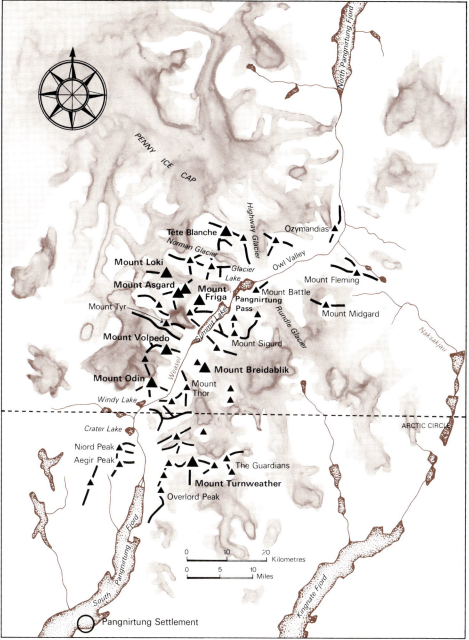

Situation: Dominion of Canada—North West Territories; Franklin District

Cumberland Peninsula
1 Tête Blanche (7,074/2,156) 1953: Hans Weber, J. Marmet-Rothlisberger
2 Mount Odin (or Mount Queen Elizabeth) (7,014/2,138) 1953: same party with Pat Baird and F. Schwarzenbach
Mount Friga (6,650/2,027) 1961: T. Goodfellow and Cambridge party
Mount Asgard (6,598/2,011) 1953: Hans Weber, J. Marmet-Rothlisberger and F. Schwarzenbach
Mount Volpedo (6,560/2,000) 1972: Bruno Barabino and party
Mount Breidablik (6,500/1,980) 1971: Guy Lee and Phil Koch?
Mount Loki (6,300/1,920) 1965: Mike MacMallum, Don Morton, Bob Paul, Pat Baird
Mount Turnweather (6,035/1,839) 1963: G. Weetman, S. Paterson, F. Largiader and Reverend Sidney Wilkinson
Mount Raleigh (6,000/1,829) 1962: Bill Tilman and party

Eglinton Fjord Area
Pioneer Peak (5,500/1,692) 1934: Tom Longstaff and Sir John Hanhan
Longstaff Tower (4,000/1,219) 1934: Tom Longstaff and Sir John Hanhan

Major Glaciers
Penny Ice-Cap—approx 2,500 square miles (4,023sq km)—summit at 8,500ft (2,590m)
Barnes Ice-Cap—approx 1,400 square miles (2,253sq km), some 75 miles (120km) long
Bylot Island Ice-Cap—of similar size

Huts
Parks Canada have a hut at Summit Lake and shelters at the head of Pangnirtung Fjord and at the north-east end of Owl Valley

Guide-books
None, but reports have been published in many journals, especially the CAJ, AAJ and AJ; *Mountain World* 1954 and 1964, and *Big Wall Climbing* by Doug Scott (Kaye & Ward, London, 1974) contain useful chapters

Maps
The area is covered by the official Canadian Survey, scale 1,250,000, published by Surveys and Mapping Branch of the Department of Mines and Technical Surveys, who will also supply aerial photographs

Convenient Centres
Pangnirtung Settlement boasts an hotel, a supermarket, a camp site and the HQ of the Pangnirtung National Park.
Broughton Island is an Eskimo settlement and DEW line station and boasts a store.
There are various other settlements (and DEW line stations) on the coast, for instance Cape Dyer and Clyde Inlet

Access
Pangnirtung air strip is reached by air services from Montreal via Frobisher Bay. Skidoo, sledges or motor canoes can be hired from Pangnirtung for onward travel to the fjord head, depending on the state of the fjord ice. Similar access from Broughton Island, southward up North Pangnirtung Fjord. As the area adjacent to the Owl and Weasel Valleys is now a National Park, certain restrictions will be in force and Parks Canada will supply details

however, is Mount Asgard whose twin summits are matching, flat-topped, cylindrical rock-towers. From the saddle between them, reached over snow-covered slabs, the higher north summit is gained by 400ft (120m) of steep and stiff climbing. The 4,000ft (1,220m) East Pillar, climbed in 1972 by Doug Scott's party, is probably the hardest 'big wall' climb yet made in Baffin (5.8/A1). An easier line was made the previous year on the South Buttress of the lower peak. Other major rock-climbs are the Great Prow of Mount Breidablik and the East Face of Mount Killibuck, where 3,000ft (900m) of pleasant slabs are topped by a difficult 1,000ft (300m) headwall. Both were climbed in 1971. The three pillars of the huge West Face of Mount Overlord, climbed in 1975 and '76 by Scott and Hennek, provide excellent, hard free-climbing. Many similar great challenges in the area await determined rock-climbers, among them the smooth curling overhang of Mount Friga's 2,000ft (610m) Buttress, and the Eiger-like West Face of Mount Thor rising straight from the Weasel Valley. And further afield the scope is as enormous as the access is difficult.

In 1973 the area between the north and south Pangnirtung Fjords was declared a national park. Tourism was to be developed and various facilities were planned to cope with the expected visitors. Mountaineers who know Baffin Island are concerned about the effect this will have on the fragile arctic wilderness.

Tetons

The spiky, horn-like peaks of the Tetons, among the most alpine mountains in the contiguous USA, rise on the Wyoming–Idaho border, some 30 miles (48km) west of the Continental Divide. Both flanks drain to the headwaters of the great Snake River, flowing 900 miles (1,450km) towards the Columbia and the distant Pacific. Measuring only some 40 × 14 miles (60 × 20km), the Tetons are a compact range formed by glacial erosion, during repeated ice ages, of an uplifted 'block mountain' of basically pre-Cambrian rock. Several very small glaciers remain, apparently stable after at least a century of retreat, while the rock that forms the peaks—a mixture of gneiss, schists and granitic intrusions—is firm and has proved excellent to climb on. Summer lasts from mid-June to mid-September, with the best weather in July and early August. Then come thunderstorms and a spell of severe weather is usual at the end of the month.

On the east the major summits rise abruptly some 6,000ft (1,800m) and more from the river flats, the sage brush, the groves of spruce, aspen and cottonwood and the chain of deep lakes that carpet the wide basin of Jackson Hole. Westward the slopes fall less steeply to the forest and farmland of Pierre's Hole. On either side the line of jagged summits, scattered with snow patches through high summer, dominates the landscape and provides one of the most magnificent mountain prospects in the country.

Probably unseen by white men until 1807, the three central peaks—Grand, Middle and South Teton—became landmarks to the explorers and trappers of the early nineteenth century who dubbed them 'Les Trois Tetons'—'the three breasts'. Controversy surrounds the first ascent of the Grand; ascents claimed by surveyors in 1872 and credited to a military party in 1893 are unsubstantiated, but that of 1898 is conclusive. Now known as the Owen Spaulding Route, by modern standards an easy technical climb, it is today the much frequented *voie normale*. There were no further climbs for twenty years, until the superintendent of the nearby Yellowstone National Park invited well-known climbers to pioneer in the range as part of his

The Grand Teton blocks the head of Teton Canyon above the Valley of Pierre's Hole to the west of the Teton Range. To the right is Middle Teton, while Mount Owen is in cloud to the left. It is late October, soon after the first heavy snows of the winter

campaign for the creation of a Teton National Park. On both counts he was successful. A park was established in 1929 and subsequently enlarged in 1950 to cover 465 square miles. Meanwhile all the major peaks had been climbed by 1931, and the ensuing decade saw the Tetons become, for a while, the crucible of American technical climbing.

Today there are more than twenty different climbs, some difficult and some straightforward, on the many ridges and faces of the Grand Teton which is the centre of climbing activity in the range. Of the seven ridges the popular Exum—the most westerly of the three southern ridges—and the 4,000ft-long (1,220m) pinnacled East Ridge are justly famous, while the superb North Ridge is one of the great American classics. The North

Face, climbed in 1936 by Jack Durrance and the Petzoldt brothers—one of whom, Paul, had started guiding in the Tetons in 1924—still enjoys a considerable reputation. A fine line up a great fang-shaped rock wall, crossing two small snow-fields—it is 2,800ft (850m) in height and not excessively difficult. The steep West Face is a less aesthetic line and rather harder and, at the date of its first ascent in 1940, by Jack Durrance and Henry Coulter, was considered the most demanding climb in North America. A modern classic, and rare in the USA because it is a summer ice-climb, is the Black Ice Couloir which slices up under the West Face. Its ascent in 1961 was a milestone in American alpinism.

There is, of course, much climbing

among the other peaks of the range. Mount Owen, with its sweeping snow-fields and serrated rock-ribs, is the most difficult major summit and was the last to be climbed, probably because it appears unobtrusive from afar and is relatively inaccessible. The party that climbed it included some of the most notable American climbers of the day and the most ubiquitous of Teton pioneers: Fryxell and Smith were the first rangers in the new Teton Park.

Mount Owen's North-East Snow field is one of the few snow-climbs in the range. Graceful Teewinot boasts hard rock routes on its fine North-West Face, and a worthy traverse onwards to Mount Owen. Mount Moran, massive and majestic, holds the classic 'CMC Route' on its East Face, an intimidating line which

proves to be straightforward on closer acquaintance. The long and elegant South Buttress is one of the many hard routes made in the early '60s by climbers such as Leigh Ortenberger, Dave Dornau, Barry Corbet, Willie Unsoeld, Yvon Chouinard and others, at a time when the range again became a focal point of American alpinism. A few years later, winter ascents of the Teton climbs were being made, pre-eminent among the winter pioneers being the Lowe 'Clan' from Utah who claimed both the North Face and the combined Black Ice Couloir/West Face of the Grand. This latter is accepted today as the most serious alpine climb in the 'Lower 48'.

Today there is more to the Tetons than just the climbs—there is something of the atmosphere of the European Alps.

The range reflects much of the history and development of American mountaineering and the achievements of many of its greatest exponents. The mountains are accessible, the climbing is well-documented and is concentrated in a relatively small area with Jackson as the nearest approach to a North American Chamonix and all that that entails! As an added attraction the range is especially rich in wildlife, and bear, moose and elk are among the creatures often seen by climbers. It is small wonder that the Grand Teton is the most popular summit in North America.

Situation: United States of America—States of Wyoming and, marginally, Idaho

Major Peaks
1 Grand Teton (13,766/4,196) 1898: Reverend W. Owen, F. Spaulding, J. Shive and F. Peterson
2 Mount Owen (12,928/3,940) 1930: R. Underhill, K. Henderson, F. Fryxell and P. Smith
3 Middle Teton (12,804/3,903) 1923: A. Ellingwood and Miss E. Davis—but certainly reached by Red Indians years before
4 Mount Moran (12,605/3,842) 1922: L. Hardy, B. Rich and B. McNulty
5 South Teton (12,514/3,814) 1923: A. Ellingwood and Miss E. Davis
6 Teewinot (12,325/3,757) 1929: F. Fryxell and P. Smith
7 Cloudveil Dome (12,026/3,666) 1931: F. Fryxell and A. Hilding

Important Passes
Paintbrush Divide (c. 10,650/3,245) links Cascade Canyon to Paintbrush Canyon.
Hurricane Pass (c. 10,500/3,200) links Cascade Canyon to Alaska Basin which drains into Idaho. It is crossed by the 24 mile 'Skyline Trail' which then recrosses the divide to Death Canyon en route to Jackson Hole.

Major Glaciers
More than a dozen small glaciers and perennial ice-fields—the largest is Teton Glacier, approximately 0.75 miles long. Triple Glaciers of Mount Moran approach this size also

Guide-books
Climbers Guide to Teton Range by Leigh Ortenberger published by Sierra Club, San Francisco. *Guide to Wyoming Mountains and Wilderness Areas* by O. H. Bonney (Swallow Publishers)

Maps
The excellent UGGS. 'Grand Teton National Park' contour map at scale 1:62,500

Convenient Centre
The city of Jackson, a summer and winter sports resort, has every facility, including a professional corps des guides and climbing schools

Access
By air
Regular air services fly to Jackson from Denver, Salt Lake City, Billings and West Yellowstone. There are excellent connections to these cities from elsewhere in the U.S.
By road
Jackson is 180 miles north of Rock Springs, a town on Interstate 80, between Cheyenne and Salt Lake City, or 87 miles east of Idaho Falls on Interstate 15.

All climbers are expected to 'book out' and observe the usual formalities at National Park HQ at Moose or at Jenny Lake Ranger Station. The current regulations are not restrictive or irksome and many of the rangers themselves are climbers

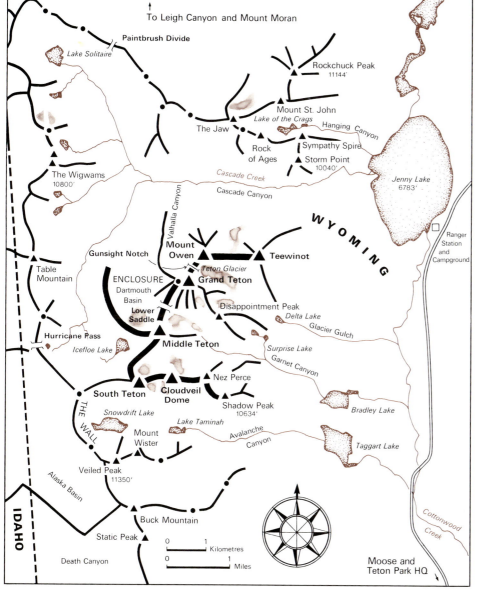

A famous view of the Tetons from the east across the Snake River. On the right is the depression of Cascade Canyon and, right to left, the summits of Teewinot, the Grand, Middle Teton, South Teton, and Nez Perce, Mount Wister and, far left, Buck Mountain

95

In the Ruwenzori of Uganda: looking towards McConnell's Prong from Lake Kitandara

Merely a 150ft (46m) gendarme on the North-West Ridge of Weismann (15,157ft/4,620m), the highest summit of Mount Luigi di Savoia, McConnell's Prong is the major feature in the southward view from this beautiful little green lake over 13,000ft (3,962m) up among the 'Mountains of the Moon'. It was climbed in 1971 by Ian Howell and Phil Snyder who took five hours to fight their way a little over one mile through the dense helichrysum undergrowth to its foot. Their route, up the eastern – or left-hand – side of the pinnacle, led up a chimney to a greasy groove which they had to surmount using combined tactics. Higher up, straightforward aid-climbing was necessary and they graded the climb 'V A1'.

Overleaf top: **California Sierra: Mount Russell**

A formidable-looking rock pile from all directions, Mount Russell (14,086ft/ 4,293m) was one of the last of the major Sierran peaks to be climbed; as late as 1926. It lies just to the north of Mount Whitney.

In this picture Gary Colliver is standing on the moraine that holds Iceberg Lake just below the North-East Face of Whitney which is up on the left. It is June and the lake, at 12,640ft/(3,853m), is still covered with green ice. It must be one of the highest tarns in the Sierra.

The Sierra are wonderful mountains with a real feeling of remote wilderness that is lacking today in the more spectacular Alps. This is 'Big Country' and everything one expects of the American West.

Overleaf bottom: **Interior Ranges of British Columbia – in the Bugaboos: Snowpatch Spire from the north**

This picture was taken on the descent down the 'voie normale' of Bugaboo Spire from the prominent shoulder on the South Ridge. On the left the sheer West Face of Snowpatch (10,050ft/3,063m) rises from the snow plateau of the Upper Vowell Glacier which falls to the Bugaboo Glacier and its unseen ice-fall. The East Ridge of Pidgeon Spire, its lower section rejoicing under the title of The Pidgeontoe, rises on the right. In the distance are Howser Peak and Marmolata – rather less interesting features.

The Bugaboo Group are without doubt the best known mountains in British Columbia, a province chockful of mountains. The peaks are mostly easily accessible from the extremely comfortable Conrad Kain Hut, which we found to be run by two charming girl Rangers of the BC Parks Service, and the climbing has a distinctly alpine aura about it, much more so than elsewhere I have been in North America. Bill March and I selected the highly recommended East Arête of Bugaboo Spire as our first route in the area and we found it quite difficult – especially as it snowed hard most of the way up! The climbing is comparable to the famous Bugeleisen, or Flat Iron, in the Swiss Bregaglia although rather steeper. Only when we reached the summit did the clouds roll back and we saw the impressive spires around us for the first time.

We were not lucky with the weather: the July pattern seemed to be clear mornings, clouding up to snow by mid-afternoon. We were able to take advantage of this and climb as one does in the Alps, making the most of a pre-dawn start, climbing swiftly on a route which we knew we could complete in time, reaching the hut again before the weather broke. Thus we traversed Snowpatch Spire and Pidgeon Spire. Unfortunately few other parties seemed prepared to adopt this standard alpine routine and nothing else was achieved while we were there.

Several fine American and Canadian climbers have been active in the Bugaboos and some exceedingly fine routes have been made. We were suprised that climbs of such quality are not better known in Europe for they compare well with the great classic rock-routes in the Alps and their pioneers deserve the same recognition that we give to the Comicis, the Cassins and the Allains in Europe!

Previous page: **Mount Robson – the highest peak in the Canadian Rockies – seen from the north across Berg Lake**

The right skyline is the rarely climbed Emperor Ridge, probably the most aesthetic line on the mountains, with, below it, the steep ribs of the Emperor Face, its ascent finally accomplished in 1978. The left skyline is the Fuhrer Ridge with, left again, the outlying peaks of the Helmet (11,200ft/3,414m) and Mount Waffl (9,500ft/2,896m). Immediately below the summit is the 2,600ft (792m) ice-wall of the North Face from which the Berg Glacier pours down into the lake, breaking off as small icebergs (the remnants of several are seen in the water).

It was early morning when I took this picture: we had bivouacked comfortably on the lake shore and the morning was cool and crisp and smelt of pines. We had arrived, tired and despondent, at the same spot just thirty-eight hours before after a 12-mile (19km) hike from the roadhead. The two climbs we fancied, the Emperor Ridge or the North Face, were obviously out of condition as the frequent avalanches demonstrated. As Bill March and I brewed up, we relaid our plans: we decided to attempt the classic Kain Face route and to do it at once. We cached all our food and surplus climbing gear and set off into the evening towards the long Robson Glacier. Had we realized that the summit was still 8 miles (13km) away and that the snow was deep and soggy, we wouldn't have started. We climbed through an horrendous ice-fall in the dark and, about midnight, reached the snowy shoulder of the Dome at about 10,000ft (3,048m). Here we intended to rest for a couple of hours and brew up. But voices came through the night and we located a lonely tent whose friendly occupants invited us inside for a while. The steep Kain Face itself, immediately above the tent, proved easier going than we had dared hope and we watched the dawn from the wide ridge above it. There was some moderate climbing on the final slopes of the Roof and then we were on the small sharp summit. We were determined not to be caught in soft snow again and, three hours after leaving our new friends' tent, we were back again sharing breakfast. By mid-afternoon we had returned to Berg Lake, exhausted but very happy, and we settled early into our bivouac. This picture means quite a lot to me!

Yosemite Valley: late October; Half Dome is seen from the meadows by Ahwanhee Bridge

The California Geological Survey of 1865 wrote of Half Dome: '. . . Half Dome is a crest of granite rising to a height of 4,737ft (1,444m) above the Valley, perfectly inaccessible, and probably the only one of all the prominent points about the Yosemite which never has been, and never will be, trodden by human foot. . .' This is the great North-West Face on which there are at least four major routes, three of which, including the original 1957 route made by Robbins, Gallwas and Sherrick in five days, climb directly to the brow on the left and one – Tis-sa-ack, put up by Robbins and Peterson in '59—running up the middle of the face just left of the great shadow. The easy way, laced with steel cables, lies up the East Face well round the corner to the left.

It is rare for truly spectacular places to be actually beautiful, the very words are a contradiction in terms. But Yosemite is an exception. It is, in any case, unique.

Unfortunately, when such a precious place is bestowed with excellent 'facilities' and fine access roads, it becomes yet another in the long list of spectacles to be 'done' by the summer tourist. In high summer the valley floor is raucous with the sound of revving engines, transistors and voices, and tainted with exhaust fumes. Of course Yosemite is not alone in suffering such a fate. Anyway, at this time of year it is too hot for serious climbing and the 'old timers' – the climbers who've been around a while – and the real mountain men migrate up to Tuolumne Meadows and the high mountains where it is cool and, though no longer empty, folk hike rather than drive.

And then the holidays are over and summer ends. Autumn comes to the valley. The mornings are crisp, the meadows are silent and the colours mature and richen. Serious climbing can start again and once more Yosemite is somewhere it is good to be.

Wind River Range

Running for nearly 100 miles (160km) along the crest of the Continental Divide, deep in the heart of Wyoming, the remote Wind River Range is one of the most rugged sections of the Rocky Mountain system. Carved by glacial erosion from granite and gneiss batholiths, the narrow chain of mountains rises from a beautiful landscape of wide and open U-shaped valleys, boulder-strewn alpine meadows and a multitude of small lakes. On the range's western flanks is born the Green River, the major arm of the Colorado, while the eastern waters drain to the Bighorn and on towards the great Missouri.

The mountains themselves form two distinctive groups to the north and south, the former containing no less than eight summits of 13,500ft (4,100m) or over—among them the highest peak in Wyoming. Here too lie the U.S. Rocky Mountains' most extensive glaciers. Although they rise over 3,000ft (900m) above the lakes and meadows at their feet, these northern peaks stand back while still giving the impression of great vertical relief. Typically they present craggy and shattered faces, while glaciers and *nevé* fields hang on some eastern slopes. Gannett Peak is a distinctive snow-capped whaleback and an easy glacier and snow-climb from Wilson Meadows to the north east. A claimed first ascent by Captain Bonneville in 1833 is now considered unlikely. Controversy also surrounds the first ascent of long-crested Fremont Peak, 5 miles southward: John Fremont claimed 'the highest summit in the Rockies', and—despite some scepticism—his claim now appears authentic. Fremont is best climbed from beautiful Island Lake, in the Titcomb Valley to its west, but the ridge crest on which these mountains are strung is fairly easily crossed in many places. Winter ascents, using skis, have been made of several.

While slightly lower, mostly between 11,000 and 13,000ft (3,350–4,000m), the southern area contains some of the finest sculptured and most awesome-shaped peaks in the Rockies. Rising typically above arcing sheets of slabs, vertical walls and rough scree-slopes, these sharp summits, often linked by knife-edge *arêtes*, offer some of the best mountain rock-climbing in the United States. Some may only be reached by serious climbing but many, including the massive cliff-girt Wind River Peak, are accessible to strong hiking parties.

While Mount Hooker holds the most imposing wall in Wyoming—the 1,800ft (5,500m) North Face which gave a difficult three and a half day climb to Royal Robbins' party in 1965—it is the Cirque of the Towers that has achieved widespread fame. A ridge of some seventeen summits with names such as Watch Tower, Shark's Nose, Overhanging Tower, and Wolf's Head, most of them about 12,000ft (3,650m), clusters around Lonesome Lake, cradling small snowfields, and offer a superb selection of climbs of all standards. Particularly fine are blade-thin ridge, while the complete traverse of the *cirque*, first made in two days by Robbins, Dick McCracken and Charlie Raymond in 1965, is a classic of sustained, but not excessively difficult, climbing. Close by, the serrated crests of Warbonnet and the two Warriors extend the *cirque*. Mount Bonneville stands at the head of a further impressive *cirque* several miles north.

Once a familiar barrier to the trappers of the early nineteenth century, and the settlers who followed them, the Wind Rivers today lie almost entirely within designated Wilderness or Primitive Areas—or within the 1,500 square mile Arapaho and Shoshone Indian Reservation which reaches the main divide in the central section. Conservationists criticize both the Basque shepherds with their large flocks and the commercial 'dude' horseback parties who intrude into this otherwise unspoilt wilderness, but the area is virtually roadless and a long hike of at least 20 miles (30km) is necessary to reach the interior peaks. Despite the tremendous potential, both realized and unrealized, climbers tend to approach the range in a holiday mood—for fun climbing. Thus the Wind Rivers have contributed little to the development of American mountaineering.

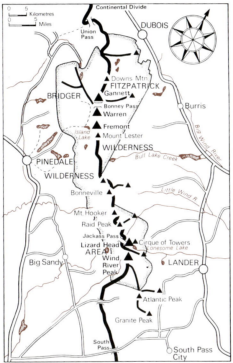

Lonesome Lake and the Cirque of the Towers. Since the late 1950s this attractive and remote area has become steadily more popular. On left Warbonnet rises over Jackass Pass, while centre are the two Warrior peaks

Situation: United States of America—State of Wyoming

Important Peaks
(Height order, height in feet and metres, date of first ascent and party of first ascent)

1 Gannett Peak (13,804/4,207) A. Tate and F. Stahlnaker in 1922
2 Fremont Peak (13,745/4,189) Lieutenant J. Fremont with Kit Carson and party, 1842? Certainly the Hayden expedition 1878
3 Mount Warren (13,722/4,182)
Wind River Peak (13,192/4,021) highest of the southern peaks
Lizard Head (12,842/3,914) in the southern area
Bonneville (12,570/3,831) 1946: H. Willits and W. Stewart
Pingora (11,884/3,622) 1940: O. H. Bonney, F. and N. Garnick

Major Glaciers
Dinwoody and Mammoth Glaciers, on S.E. and W. flanks of Gannett Peak respectively, measure about 1 × 2 miles while Gannett Glacier, N.E. of its peak, is some 1½ miles square.

Major Passes
South Pass (7,550) southern limit of the range, an historic pass on the Oregon Trail, one of the easiest across the Rockies, now traversed by
Union Pass (9,210/2,807) northern limit of the range
Bonney Pass (12,700) useful crossing east–west, immediately south of Gannett Peak

Guide-books
Guide to Wyoming Mountains and Wilderness Areas by O. L. Bonney (Swallow Publishers); *Wind River Trails* by Finnis Mitchell (Wasatch Publishers)

Maps
Most of the Range is covered by new USGS 1:24,000 maps but the S. section, including Cirque of Towers is still only covered by the One Inch sheets.
US Forest Service maps to 'Bridger National Forest' and Shoshone NF at Half Inch are useful.

Convenient Centres
None—mountaineering in the Wind Rivers is semi-expeditionary and climbers must be self-sufficient. Jackson, some 80 miles north of Pinedale, is a 'mountain' resort (Tetons) with all facilities

Access
The towns of Lander, (on US 287) to the east, or Pinedale, (on US 187) to the west, are the most convenient start points. Nearest airports are respectively Riverton or Rock Springs although Jackson may be more convenient. Gannett Peak area is best reached via the Inkwells Trail from Burris to the east, but permission is required from the Indians whose land it crosses. The alternative Glacier Trail from Dubois is 5 miles longer. From the west a trail leads to Island Lake from Elkhart Park, 11 miles north of Pinedale. The Southern Peaks, Cirque of the Towers, etc, are best reached from the west from Big Sandy Opening south of Pinedale, via a rugged trail over Jackass Pass

The West Face of Gannett Peak, the highest point in the State of Wyoming. On the left, Mount Koven; on the right, the high serrated Pinnacle Ridge which extends southwards

Colorado Rockies

The long rope of the Rocky Mountains becomes tangled where it crosses Colorado. This convolution of crest and sub-crest covers a vast area of high ground—over a thousand summits top 10,000ft (3,050m), while no less than fifty-three rise above 14,000ft (4,300m). Formed by the erosion of a metamorphic uplift, these mountains have a complicated geology. Typically rounded flanks give easy hikes over scree and boulders to most summits, while steeper flanks hold rocky *cirques*, tarns and a few tiny lingering glaciers. Below the treeline, at some 11,500ft (3,500m), the valleys are heavily forested with fir and aspen; among the wide range of fauna black bear, mountain lion, bighorn sheep and elk are to be found.

East of the Continental Divide the rivers water the rolling prairies of the Great Plains on their way to join the Missouri/Mississippi system. The Colorado is born on the western slopes, while the Rio Grande drains south east to Texas and the Gulf of Mexico.

Gold and silver orchestrated the development of Colorado from the 1859 Gold Rush until early this century. Miners penetrated the mountains, opened trails and actually ascended at least six of the 'fourteeners', as they are known to Coloradans. Their ghost towns and abandoned workings are a feature of the wilderness. But Indians had certainly preceded them, and Old Man Gun is known to have trapped eagles—for their feathers—on the summit of Longs Peak. Most of the high peaks, however, were first ascended by the federal Hayden Survey of 1873-6, or the concurrent, military Wheeler Survey. As Denver and the towns at the foot of the mountains grew, so the more accessible summits became popular. Pikes Peak, symbol of the Gold Rush ('Pikes Peak or bust!'), was insulted by a cog railway in 1890—still in operation—while guiding started on conspicuous Longs Peak in 1880. A National Park, enclosing Longs Peak and a sizeable portion of the Front Range, was established in 1915, thanks largely to the efforts of Enos Mills, a notable guide of the period.

Longs Peak is the most important mountain in Colorado and its massive square summit dominates the park. While scrambling trails lead hundreds of hikers to the top, its intimidating 1,800ft (550m) East Face, rising above dark

The North Face of Pyramid Peak (14,018/4,273), just south of the Maroon Bells above Aspen. Several routes have been made on this sandstone face and the regular route (1909) is one of the more awkward in Colorado

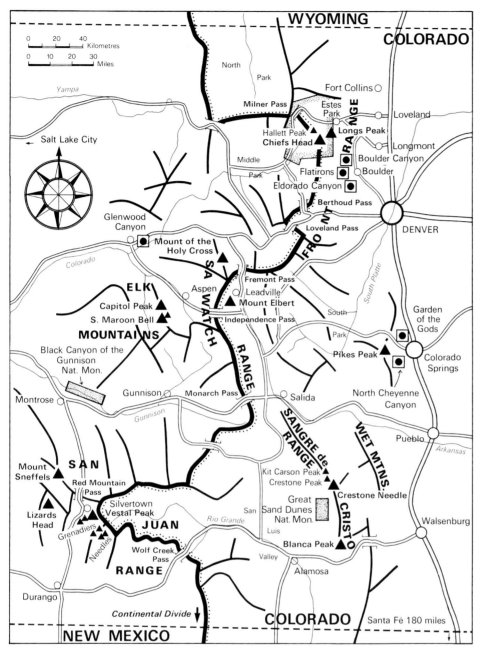

Capitol Peak, with sharp ridges of granite and good climbs on its North-West Face, is one of the harder summits.

Many consider the San Juans, a complex chain displaying a wide variety of rock, colour and mountain form, to be Colorado's finest range. Sneffels, with its gendarmed ridges, and the surrounding peaks are bold, jagged and upstanding. There are several steep climbs in the rugged Needles group, particularly on the 1,200ft (370m) East Face of Monitor, and some excellent easier ridge routes while the summits of Vestal and Arrow in the Grenadiers are the most difficult to reach in the state, barring only Lizards Head. A 400ft (120m) tower of rotten rock crowns this peak and its first ascent in 1920 was a landmark in American climbing. It is still considered quite difficult (Class 5.7).

Supposedly named 'Blood of Christ' by Spanish settlers, because of its brilliant alpenglows, the Sangre de Cristo Range contains three of Colorado's most imposing peaks—the last of the 'fourteeners' to be climbed. Steep, craggy and pinnacled, Kit Carson and the two Crestones are built of firm conglomerate and hold the most important 'high mountain' routes outside the National Park. The classic of the region, on a face a mile wide and all but 2,000ft (610m) high, is the Ellingwood Arête of Crestone Needle, first climbed in 1924 (Class 5.6). High and elegant, Blanca Peak also holds good climbs.

There is plenty of scope for new climbs, but these are high mountains; blanketed by snow from December to May, their summer weather is fickle and severe afternoon thunder storms are characteristic. Colorado's best rock-climbing has been developed on low altitude crags, the most famous of which is Eldorado Canyon where extremely high technical standards appertain. Most notable, however, is the Black Canyon of the Gunnison, an awesome chasm 20 miles long and over 2,000ft (610m) deep. Climbs, on granite and gneiss, have been made here since the 1930s and big wall routes since the early 1960s. The Painted Wall, 2,500ft (760m) high, loose, overhanging, its purple rock striped with white veins, is the big challenge. Its first ascent in 1972, by Bill Forrest and Kris Walker, took eight days and was considered the most serious climb in Colorado. A recent development is winter ice climbing on frozen waterfalls, the most famous being Bridalveil Fall near Telluride. There is certainly plenty to climb in the 'Mountain State'.

Chasm Lake, holds one of America's most renowned big walls—the Diamond. The first ascent of this smooth outward-leaning upper wall was delayed by a park authority ban, but eventually, in 1960, Dave Rearick and Bob Kamps, visitors from Yosemite, made the three-day climb. It is now a major classic and is usually free climbed in two days. Several other lines grace the Diamond and there are more climbs, some of considerable vintage, elsewhere on the East Face.

The Front Range, with its craggy mountains and nearby cities, is now well developed, and among the noteworthy 'high mountain' climbs are those on the 1,000ft (305m) North Face of Hallett Peak and the remote 1,500ft (450m) North-East Face of Chiefs Head elsewhere in the park. Southward, the rather

lower Indian group, around Arapaho Peak, contains some twenty-five rocky summits, some steep walls and several fine rock needles of which Lone Eagle (11,900ft/3,630m) is the most famous.

Colorado's three highest peaks are among the fifteen 'fourteeners' in the rounded Sawatch Range: all are simple hikes. Less interesting than it sounds is the Mount of the Holy Cross, long a legend among the Spanish Conquistadors, its North-East Face once holding a gigantic snowy cross in a sequence of couloirs and ledges. The more spectacular Elk Range contains several handsome peaks, notably the two shapely Maroon Bells whose cliffs and buttress of layered brown sandstone are well known to Aspen visitors. Their ascents are stiff scrambles, but nearby

Situation: United States of America—State of Colorado

Some Important Peaks

1 Mount Elbert (14,433/5,399) 1874: H. W. Stuckle of Hayden Survey. This is the highest peak in the Rockies, second highest in contiguous USA

4 Blanca Peak (14,338/4,370) 1874: Wheeler Survey party

15 Longs Peak (14,256/4,345) 1868: W. Byers, John Wesley Powell and party, but certainly climbed by Indians before this date

21 Crestone Needle (14,191/4,325) 1916: A. R. Ellingwood and Eleanor Davis

25 South Maroon Bell (14,156/4,315) possibly 1909: Percy Hagerman

28 Mount Sneffels (14,150/4,313) 1874: Franklin Rhoda of Hayden Survey

30 Capitol Peak (14,130/4,307) probably Hayden Survey—1870s

31 Pikes Peak (14,110/4,301) 1820: Major Stephen Long's party

53 Mount of the Holy Cross (14,005/4,269) 1873: F. V. Hayden and W. H. Jackson

Vestal Peak (13,846/4,220)

Chiefs Head (13,579/4,139)

Lizards Head (13,113/3,997) 1920: A. R. Ellingwood and Barton Hoag

Major Passes—road-passes across the Continental Divide

Milner Pass (10,758/3,279)—within Rocky Mountain National Park

Berthoud Pass (11,314/3,449)

Loveland Pass (11,992/3,655)

Fremont Pass (11,316/3,449)

Independence Pass (12,095/3,687)

Monarch Pass (11,302/3,445)

Wolf Creek Pass (10,587/3,227)

Red Mountain Pass (11,018/3,358)—an important north–south pass

Largest Glacier

Arapaho Glacier, approx 1 square mile (1.5 sq km), on east flank of Arapaho Peak

Convenient Centres

There are many ski and mountain resorts and most, if not all, facilities can be found in the nearest town: Estes Park is convenient for the Longs Peak area; Buena Vista north of Salida for the Sawatch; Aspen or Crested Butte for the Elks; Telluride or Silvertown for the San Juans, and Salida for the Crestones

Huts

There are several mountain shelters, maintained by the park authority, within the Rocky Mountain National Park. Elsewhere abandoned mine buildings and remote shacks can be useful

Access

There is a major airport at Denver with connections to most places of any size, eg, Gunnison, Montrose, Durango, Alamosa, etc. Colorado has a good road system, many passes are kept open in winter and most resorts are accessible by bus, while an old railroad, built during the mining boom and still running, is useful for approaches in the San Juans.

A large part of the mountain area lies within either the 400 square mile (644sq km) Rocky Mountain National Park, or within twelve National and several State Forests

Map

USGS publish excellent sheets 1:24,000 covering the entire Colorado Rockies

Guide-books

Guide to the Colorado Mountains, by Robert Ormes, is published by Swallow Press (Chicago)—covers the mountains but little technical climbing. Rock guides are available to the Boulder area and Rocky Mountain Park, etc.

Mount Princeton (14,197/4,327) in the Sawatch Range 15 miles N.W. of Salida is seen here from the east

Sierra Nevada

The California Sierra, the 'snowy mountains' of the Spaniards, the country of the giant sequoia and the 1849 Gold Rush, stretches for 430 miles (700km) from the fringes of the Mojave Desert to the Feather River Basin below the Southern Cascades. Carved by heavy glaciation from a massive block, uptilted to the east, Sierran topography is complicated by a series of secondary crests, remains of a more ancient range. Ten major rivers flow westward through 50 miles (60km) of heavily forested foothills, typically in deep canyons, to the broad fertile San Joaquin and Sacramento Valleys. Spectacular Yosemite is world famous, while Kings Canyon is over 7,000ft (2,100m) deep. The short eastern torrents, however, are soon swallowed by the deserts and salt pans of the Great Basin. Forming the geographical, if not the political, eastern boundary of California, the Sierra Nevada was the final hurdle on the old Overland Trail.

Known as the High Sierra, the rugged southern section is the loftiest range in the contiguous United States, scores of peaks rising above 13,000ft (4,000m), eleven of them topping 14,000ft (4,300m). There are no road passes for 170 miles (270km). Winter snowfall is normally extremely heavy and, although below the permanent snowline, the higher peaks cradle sixty tiny glaciers and snow patches linger through summer. Jagged summits rise above rocky *cirques*, a myriad tarns and high meadows famous for their spring flowers, while acres of bare white granite lend an unusual quality to the light. Muir called the High Sierra the 'Range of Light'. The steep eastern scarp, rising 10,000ft (3,050m) from the Owens Valley to the summit crests, is one of the grandest mountain walls in the hemisphere.

Members of the California Geological Survey, exploring and mapping in the 1860s, were the first real Sierran mountaineers. Most colourful of them was surveyor Clarence King, later author of the classic *Mountaineering in the Sierra Nevada*, who made many easier first ascents. King found an Indian arrow on the summit of Mount Tyndall, and more have since been discovered on other tops. John Muir, for whom the conservation of the Sierra became a life's

In the high *cirque* under the East Face of Mount Whitney. Left of Whitney are the Keeler, Day and Third Needles. Excellent rock-climbing is to be found on these pillars as well as on this impressive face of Whitney

work, made notable ascents, often alone, in the following years. It was Norman Clyde, however, who dominated Sierran mountaineering. An eccentric 'drop-out', Clyde was a fine cragsman with over one thousand ascents and some 130 'firsts' to his credit—many of them solo—between 1914 and his death at eighty-seven in 1972.

Mount Whitney, named by King after the leader of the CGS, is surrounded by five other 14,000ft summits. King attempted the ascent several times but ended up climbing Mount Langley by mistake! The summit plateau is reached by an easy and popular 10-mile (17km) trail, but the wild *cirque* below the 2,000ft (610m) East Face and its adjoining Keeler and Day Needles is one of the most magnificent in the country and contains several classic technical rock-routes. Beautiful Mount Russell, with its narrow serrated *arêtes*, and Lone Pine Peak, below the crest to the east, also hold fine and difficult climbs.

Westward, the remote subsidiary crests of the Kings-Kern and Great Western Divides give interesting mountaineering. Here, toothed and volcanic, Black Kaweah is the Sierra's most forbidding peak, while beautiful Angels Wings has been described as an 'alpine El Capitan' and gave a four-day 1,800ft (550m) route to Allen Steck's party in 1967. Most alpine of the Sierras are the Palisades whose jagged 8-mile (13km)

crest holds the six remaining 14,000ft summits: characteristically steep on both flanks, most demand some mountaineering skill. Thunderbolt, with its very difficult summit monolith, was the last major peak to be climbed. A wealth of fine technical climbing, besides a couple of straightforward ice-couloirs, makes the area a popular one.

Among the most popular hiking terrains are the beautiful regions around Evolution Basin and the Mono Recesses. Above the former, Mount Mendel holds California's two most spectacular ice-couloirs on its North Face, while the latter region contains sixteen peaks above 13,000ft (3,962m). Massive Mount Humphreys, between the two, is one of the Sierra's more difficult peaks and a major mountaineering attraction.

Although composed of dark and shattered metamorphic rock, there is fine climbing among the seventeen clustered needles of the Minarets. Each bears the name of its first ascender and Steck's 1963 route on the south face of Clyde Minaret (Class 5.8) is a Sierra classic. None were climbed until 1923. Northwards, near the Tioga Pass, Tuolumne Meadows is where jaded Yosemite climbers come for 'rest and recuperation' among the eleven granite domes, of which Fairview is the largest and most spectacular. Nearby, the elegant spire of Cathedral Peak was the first difficult climb in the Sierra and its attractive

South-East Buttress (Class 5.4) is a 1940s classic. The most northerly group of interest is the Sawtooth Ridge, a cluster of clean white granite peaks with good climbing and easy access.

The number of summits in the High Sierra is daunting, but nearly every peak has easy ways to the top and the splendid rough granite and stable weather make the range a happy hunting ground for climbers of all abilities. Access is rarely physically difficult and an excellent trail system, including the 211-mile (340km) John Muir Trail from Yosemite to Whitney, make the mountains a popular escape for outdoor Californians. Among the exotic creatures with whom they share the back country are black bear and the rarely seen coyote, bighorn sheep and mountain lion. In winter the terrain is ideal for nordic-style ski-touring and there is good winter climbing, particularly along the long eastern escarpment.

The fine pinnacles and narrow *arêtes* of the Sawtooth group form part of the northeastern boundary of the Yosemite National Park. This picture is taken from the north east and the peaks, from left to right, are: **Matterhorn Peak (12,264ft/3,738m), Dragtooth, Doodad – followed by Col de Doodad, the lowest point in the ridge. Then come the Teeth, Sawblade, Cleaver Peak and Blacksmith Peak on the far right**

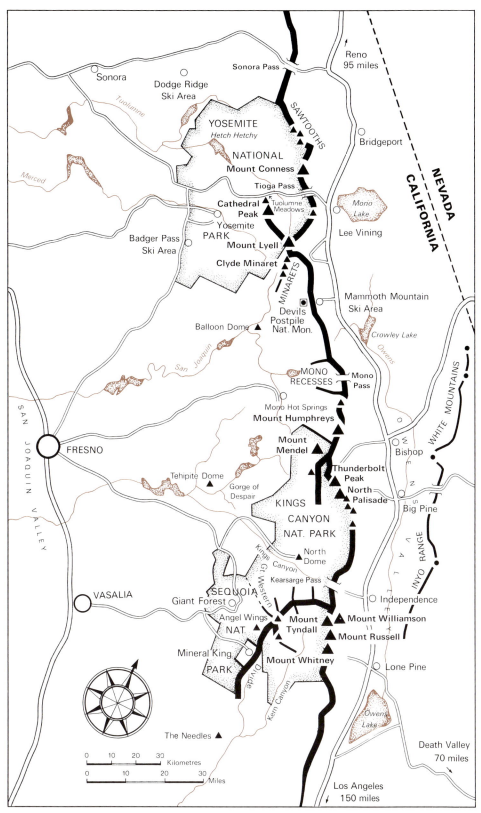

Situation: United States of America—State of California

Most Important Peaks

1 Mount Whitney (14,494/4,418) 1873: A. Johnson, C. Begole and J. Lucas—the highest point in contiguous USA

2 Mount Williamson (14,384/4,384) 1884: W. L. Hunter and C. Mulholland

3 North Palisade (14,242/4,341) 1903: J. LeConte, J. Moffitt, J. Hutchinson

5 Mount Russell (14,086/4,293) 1926: Norman Clyde—solo

9 Mount Tyndall (14,018/4,273) 1864: Clarence King and Richard Cotter

12 Thunderbolt Peak (14,000/4,267) 1931: Norman Clyde, Robert Underhill, Jules Eichorn and party

Mount Humphreys (13,986/4,263) 1904: J. and E. Hutchinson

Mount Mendel (13,691/4,173) first ascent unknown

Mount Lyell (13,114/3,998) 1871: John Tileston—the highest point in Yosemite National Park

Mount Conness (12,590/3,837) 1866: Clarence King and James Gardiner

Clyde Minaret (12,281/3,743) 1928: Norman Clyde—solo

Cathedral Peak (10,940/3,335) 1869: John Muir—solo

Major Passes

Kearsarge Pass (11,823/3,604) good packhorse trail linking Owens Valley to South Fork Kings river

Mono Pass (12,100/3,688) good trail, one of the easiest crossings in Sierra linking Owens Valley to Mono Creek and Mono Recesses region

Tiogax Pass (9,941/3,030) only road-pass within High Sierra, closed in winter. Yosemite Park Gate at crest of pass

Sonora Pass (9,626/2,934) far northern limit of High Sierra, road-pass closed in winter

Largest Glacier

Palisade Glacier in north-east flanks of North Palisade, approximately 1 square mile (2.5sq km). The Mount Lyell/Maclure glacier approaches this size

Convenient Centres

Most climbs necessitate camps or bivouacs but Yosemite Village and the small towns of the Owens Valley make useful supply points where motels, stores, restaurants and even mountain-equipment retailers may be found. There is a well-known climbing school based in the Palisades above Big Pine

Huts

There are emergency shelters on Muir Pass and on the summit of Mount Whitney

Access

The whole High Sierra lies under either Park or Forest service jurisdiction.

There are international airports at San Francisco and Los Angeles and Reno and local airports at Fresno and Modesto, besides smaller fields at Bishop and Lone Pine.

Main road access from the west is from Route 99 in the San Joaquin Valley, and from the east off US 395 in the Owens Valley. As a connection Tioga Pass is useful only in summer

Maps

USGS: excellent sheets of 1:62,500 scale cover the whole High Sierra region in thirty-four sheets

Guide-books

Climbers' Guide to the High Sierra, by Steve Roper, published by the Sierra Club (San Francisco)

Also reports in *AAJ, Sierra Club Bulletin, Ascent, Summit* and *other journals*

Yosemite

The Valley, as Yosemite is known, is a canyon, some 7 miles (11km) long and at relatively low altitude, cutting deep into the high country well to the west of the Sierra crest. Its important place in the context of world mountaineering is justified by the magnificent cliffs that line it. Some lead to summits, either of isolated pinnacles or of features such as 'Half Dome', but many, including the famous El Capitan, are just huge crags culminating in the rocky, forested ground of the canyon's rim. Here, with no objective dangers and in predictable weather, and usually only a short way from the lush meadows and redolent pines of the valley floor, philosophies and techniques have developed which have profoundly influenced the world climbing scene. Yosemite has become, arguably, the world's foremost rock-climbing centre.

Carved by water and ice through a series of exfoliation domes in the tilted granite block of the Sierra, the Valley was occupied some 10,000 years ago by a deep lake, since filled by silts and gravels. A series of high and beautiful waterfalls pours from the cliffs and in several places spectacular hiking trails follow re-entrants or pine-covered terraces from the valley to the back country above. The granite itself is compact and smoother than the eroded rock of the higher mountains. Its features are vertical—cracks, chimneys, *dièdres* and flakes abound, while overhangs are rare. Climbing is typically fierce and sustained. There is a paucity of routes that are both pleasant and easy; those that exist tend to be earthy and forested.

Yosemite was not seen by white men until 1833 and the first tourists, eager to view its natural wonders, arrived soon after settler vigilantes had trailed Indian raiders back to their secret lair in 1851. The Valley was created a National Park in 1890, largely due to the efforts of John Muir who had explored, scrambled and ascended the more easily accessible summits early on, as indeed had Clarence King and others. It was not until the early 1930s that technical rock-climbing started.

The awesome prow of El Capitan, 3,000ft (900m) of soaring sun-soaked rock, is the most arresting feature of the lower Valley. It first ascent, using siege tactics and almost continuous aid, up the fine line of the Nose, took forty-seven days spread over seventeen months. Today the Nose enjoys an international reputation and often parties queue to attempt it: with much free-climbing four days is now average time. More than twenty other 'big wall' routes grace 'El Cap', among them Warren Harding's Wall of the Early Morning Light which in 1970 aroused so much controversy with its three hundred bolt placings and twenty-six consecutive bivouacs. Salathé Wall, however, pioneered by Tom Frost, Chuck Pratt and Royal Robbins in 1961, with thirty-four pitches of delightful free and spectacular aid-climbing, is one of America's great classics.

Lost Arrow is a delicate needle high on the spray-veiled wall beside Upper Yosemite Fall. Although previously reached by tyrolean traverse, its ascent by John Salathé, in 1947, was a landmark in American climbing. Salathé, an emigré Swiss blacksmith, had invented the hard steel pitons which made the continuous five-day climb practicable. The following decade saw further technical developments specifically tailored to Yosemite conditions. Tiny chrome-molybdenum knife-blade pitons, wide-angle pegs and nylon webbing were introduced, and the then revolutionary 'Yosemite Technique' was perfected.

Half Dome broods above the valley's head, its bald brow sliced smooth by its great northern face. The first ascent of this forbidding wall—in five days in 1957—was made possible by the new developments and the boldness they engendered. It was the first Grade VI on the continent and is today a classic, although there are now a dozen other routes on this distinctive peak.

Glacier Point is famous for its Apron, some 1,200ft (360m) of sweeping slabs below a rearing headwall. Here friction-climbing has been taken to its extreme and the polished rock is laced with a network of delicate routes. Most of them end, high above the ground, at a remote rappel point on a tiny feature.

A succession of great rocks rise from the shadowed woods of Yosemite's southern wall: the Middle Cathedral is one of the Valley's most beautiful formations in the texturing of its fine North-East Face—where there is superb and mostly

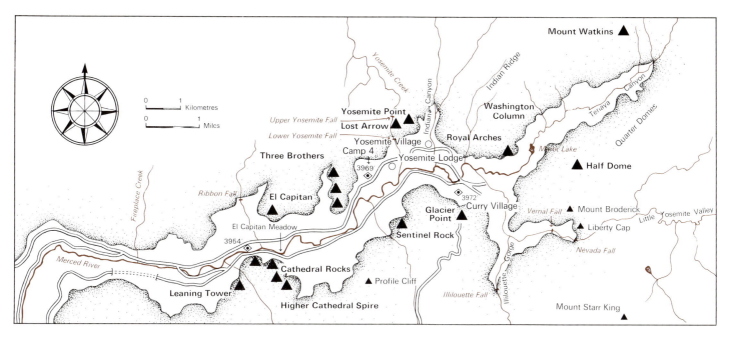

free face-climbing—and close by are the nested pinnacles of the impressive Cathedral Spires. Yosemite's third great classic climb, however, lies on the dark tombstone of Sentinel Rock. The Steck-Salathé route, originally a five-day ascent, is now climbed virtually free, but many modern climbers still require a bivouac, although it has been climbed in under three hours!

Recent years have seen a marked rise in the limits of free-climbing and a crop of short and strenuous routes on the smaller crags has resulted. There are now well over five hundred recorded climbs on Yosemite's many cliffs.

Ethics, too, have changed in twenty years. Many major routes are climbed 'clean', or soloed, and bolts are eschewed, but the old rule, that pegs placed are removed after use, has rebounded. Terribly damaged cracks on popular climbs have made the use of nuts *de rigeur*, and Yosemite fashions dictate fashions elsewhere.

Many climbers are disdainful about Yosemite, about the mass tourist influx of the summer months, the cars, the noise, the people, the trash—and the bears this attracts. But rock-climbing is so popular that a typical summer weekend sees hundreds of roped climbers in action in the Valley. When Yosemite is very hot the 'old hands' spend the summer elsewhere, and return for the fall which, together with the late spring, is the best climbing season, when the Valley is deserted. One of them, Yvon Chouinard, writes, 'Yosemite climbing tends to be difficult rather than enjoyable . . . but it possesses you with a passion that keeps bringing you back.'

Situation: United States of America, State of California

Major Features and Classic Climbs
El Capitan (vertical height 2,900/885) 'The Nose' 1958: Warren Harding, Wayne Merry, George Whitmore
Lost Arrow (1,400/430) 'Lost Arrow Chimney' 1947: John Salathé, Anton Nelson
Yosemite Point (1,200/365) 'Yosemite Point Buttress' 1952: Allen Steck, Bob Swift
Royal Arches (1,200/365) '1936 Route' 1936: Ken Adam, Morgan Harris, W. K. Davis
Washington Column (750/230) 'South Face' 1964: Layton Kor, Chris Fredericks
Mount Watkins (2,000/610) 'South Face' 1964: Yvon Chouinard, Warren Harding, Chuck Pratt
Half Dome (2,000/610) 'North-West Face' 1957: Royal Robbins, Jerry Gallwas, Mike Sherrick
Glacier Point (1,500/460) 'The Oasis via Coonyard Pinnacle'. To Coonyard Pinnacle: 1962: Bill Amborn, Joe McKeown, Rich Calderwood. To Oasis 1960: Layton Kor, Yvon Chouinard
Sentinel Rock (2,000/610) 'Steck-Salathé Route' 1950: Allen Steck, John Salathé
Higher Cathedral Spire (250/75) 'South-West Face' 1934: Jules Eichorn, Bestor Robinson, Dick Leonard
Cathedral Rocks (2,000/610) 'North Buttress' 1954: Warren Harding, Frank Tarver, Craig Holden, John Whitmer
Leaning Tower (1,100/335) 'West Face' 1961: Warren Harding, Glen Denny, Al MacDonald

Centres and Access
Yosemite Valley lies in the heart of the 900-plus square mile (93,000sq km) Yosemite National Park. Entry is by toll through one of several official gates and camping is restricted to recognized camp sites. The Valley can be approached only by road. The nearest town is Merced, in the California Central Valley. Yosemite is 84 miles (135km) from Merced and Mariposa 190 miles (306km) from the San Francisco East Bar area. There are local airports at Fresno, Modesto and Merced and an international airport at San Francisco with direct flights to Europe.

Registration for climbing is not now compulsory but there are registration facilities at the Visitor Centre in Yosemite Village.

Yosemite Village houses not only park HQ, grocery supermarkets, gift shops and art galleries but also a climbing store, a post office and a bank

Huts
Accommodation is that which might be found in any tourist mecca. There are expensive hotels, tourist chalets and camp grounds. Climbers camp at Sunnyside Campground or bivouac on the climbs which require it

Maps
USGS excellent special sheet 'Yosemite Valley' scale 1:24,000

Guide-book
Climber's Guide to Yosemite Valley by Steve Roper, published by the Sierra Club. Numerous magazine and journal articles keep the scene up to date, notably in *Mountain, Summit, Ascent,* and the *American Alpine Journal*

Opposite: **El Capitan dominates this view eastward up Yosemite Valley. On the right are the backs of the Cathedral Rocks near Bridal Veil Fall and at the head of the valley, in the distance, stand Mount Watkins and Half Dome**

Cascades

The Cascade Mountains are the interior range of the Pacific north west, continuing the barrier of the Sierra Nevada—the western wall of the Great Basin—across Oregon and Washington to fade out on the Frazer River into the Coast Mountains of British Columbia. Two very different mountain types characterize the Cascades. Best known perhaps are the line of ten major and several minor volcanoes, some extinct but four still displaying signs of activity, that march 570 miles (900km) northward from Mount Lassen in northern California to Mount Baker, only 15 miles (24km) from the Canadian border. 'Regular' mountains of rather lower altitude lie between, and, to the east of, these volcanoes. Apart from the two extremities where the western drainage is direct to the Pacific, both flanks of the Cascades feed the Columbia River or its tributaries.

The coastal areas of Oregon and Washington were settled in the 1840s and the prominent snow-capped volcanoes were ascended early on. Chief among them is Mount Rainier, named in 1892, after a British admiral, by Captain George Vancouver RN and known to the Indians as Tahoma. This majestic mountain—the most glaciated in the contiguous United States—soars in complete isolation more than 9,000ft (2,700m) above the surrounding forested highlands and its shapely ice-cap, floating above the horizon, dominates the view from the populous shores of Puget Sound 60 miles (100km) distant. Since 1899 the hub of a 375 square mile National Park, Rainier holds a fine series of ice-routes of all standards, but climbing is closely regulated by the park authorities: certain restrictions have, in the past, caused much resentment among mountaineers. A guide service was originated as long ago as the 1890s and today well organized guiding and a climbing school make tourist ascents from the south, where there are several easy glacier routes, highly popular. The current '*voie normale*' is the Ingraham Glacier, climbed with an alpine-style pre-dawn start from Camp Muir hut at 10,000ft (3,050m).

But there are some forty different routes on Rainier and, to the experienced alpinist, the steeper and more remote

The Central Cascades, Alpine Lakes area: the view from the summit of Mount Hinman towards the northern flanks of Mount Rainier whose summit floats above the clouds. The Willis Wall is well seen right below the summit

north and west flanks offer a series of fine ice-routes of a kind unique south of Canada. Two miles across at the base, the great ice triangle of the Mowich Face is 4,000ft (1,220m) high. First climbed in 1957 by a team including Fred Beckey and Tom Hornbein, it now contains several classic ice-lines. Ptarmigan Ridge bounds the face to the north: a long mixed climb pioneered in 1935, it is still not considered easy. Close beside lies the rather steeper rib of Liberty Ridge, first climbed the same year and forming the right flank of the forbidding hollow of the north face proper—the Willis Wall.

This 4,000ft (1,220m) high tangle of broken ribs, ice and horizontal bands of poor rock is topped by a menacing 300ft (90m) *sérac* band. Charlie Bell's first ascent of this major challenge—solo—in 1961 was not believed by local climbers until further ascents of the Wall proved it was not as desperate as it looked. A winter ascent was made in 1970. The Curtis Ridge on its left, a fine mixed route of 1957 vintage, divides the wall from the long and straightforward Winthrop Glacier.

Of the other Cascade volcanoes most hold an easy regular route: Mount St Helens, its summit reached by several hundred hikers on a good summer weekend, is Washington's most popular mountain. However, the easiest lines on Mount Jefferson and on the spectacular basalt plugs of Mount Washington

(7,802ft/2,378m) and North Sister (10,085ft/3,074m) do require serious scrambling. Other routes are more interesting and there are some exciting and unusual ice-climbs on most of these beautiful and easily accessible volcanoes.

In contrast the so-called 'North Cascades' of Washington—the north-central area much of which is now contained in a National Park—are a complex of several hundred sharp rock peaks rarely topping 9,000ft (2,750m) but whose height differential, summit above base, often exceeds that of the far higher peaks of California or Colorado. Typically forming narrow ridge crests flanked by rocky walls and hung with ice-fields, these mountains, the most alpine in the 'Lower 48', often rise above extensive glaciers. Much of the climbing is of exceptional quality. There are problems however: characteristically the weather is notorious—heavy rain and low cloud are common—and the valleys are often choked with impenetrable bush.

Exploration here was delayed until the early 1930s. Many peaks have no easy routes and the line of first ascent was dictated more by expediency of approach than by ease of climbing! The region was virtually unknown, except to local climbers, until the 1950s. Outstanding among North Cascade pioneers is the ubiquitous Fred Beckey, a member of the first ascent party on Forbidden Peak in 1940, at the age of sixteen, and still active in 1978. Notable mountains

include remote Slesse Peak, actually just in Canada, whose formidable North-East Buttress gave Beckey's party a three-day climb in 1963, and ruggedly handsome Mount Stuart with its North-East Face of fine granite above the little hanging Ice Cliff Glacier. The impressive gneiss fangs of the Picket Groups' twin *cirques* are hard to reach and the wildest and least explored mountains of the Cascades. Mounts Challenger, Fury, Terror, McMillan Spires, and others, resemble the peaks of the Swiss Bregaglia and Alex Bertulis made a ten-day traverse of the group—some 9 miles' climbing—in 1963. Unusual in its easy access from the new Cross-State Highway is Liberty Bell whose 1,200ft (366m) granite East Face gives four-day 'big wall' routes in Yosemite style, and whose surrounding molar-like towers include Concord, Lexington and Early Winter Spires and hold climbs of all standards. Frank Smythe once described the small yet imposing Index Peaks in the Alpine Lakes Area as 'the little Alps of Washington'. Surprisingly the fine climbing on these steep fangs is an easy drive from Seattle.

In winter there is heavy snowfall in the North Cascades, particularly on the west side of the crest. Snow-shoeing and ski-touring trips can be good and some winter climbing is done, but winter ascents of the major big routes have yet to come.

The three summits of Mount Index, prominent from the Stevens Pass Highway, Washington

Situation: United States of America—States of Washington, Oregon and California; Canada—Province of British Columbia

Most Important Peaks
Volcanic
1 Mount Rainier (14,408/4,392) probably 1870: Hazard Stevens and P. B. van Trump
2 Mount Shasta (14,162/4,317) 1854?
3 Mount Adams (12,307/3,751) 1854: B. F. Shaw, E. J. Allen, A. G. Aiken and A. J. Burqe
4 Mount Hood (11,225/3,421) 1857: H. L. Pittock, L. Chittenden, W. Cornell and Reverend T. A. Wood. Highest mountain in Oregon
5 Mount Baker (10,703/3,262) 1868: E. T. Coleman, T. Stratton, J. Tenant and D. Ogilvey
6 Mount Jefferson (10,570/3,222) 1888:
Lassen peak (10,457/3,187): southernmost Cascade summit
Mount St Helens (9,677/2,950) 1853: Thomas Dryer and party

Non-volcanic
1 Bonanza Peak (9,511/2,899) 1937: J. Leuthold, C. & B. James
2 Mount Stuart (9,470/2,886) 1873: A. McPherson and party
Mount Fury (8,292/2,527) 1938: V. Josendal and party—highest picket summit
Slesse Peak (7,970/2,429) 1927: F. H. Parkes, S. Henderson and N. Winram
Liberty Bell (7,500/2,286) 1946: Fred Beckey, C. Welsh and J. O'Neil
Mount Index (5,979/1,822) 1950: Fred Beckey and Pete Schoening

Major Passes
Washington Pass (5,477/1,669) crossed by new north Cross-State Highway (also crosses Rainy Pass—4,850ft) linking Belingham and Skagit Valley on west to Okanogan and Columbia River valleys on east. Pass is open only May to November
Stevens Pass (4,061/1,238) crossed by Highway US 2, links north Pugen Sound area to Wenatchee on Columbia River
Snoqualamie Pass (3,010/917) crossed by Interstate 90, links Seattle to Yakima
Chinook Pass (5,440/1,658) road-pass linking Tacoma and Yakima
White Pass (4,500/1,372) road-pass linking southwest Washington to Yakima

Major Glaciers
Emmons Glacier on Mount Rainer, approximately 6 miles long and 1.7 miles wide and descending to 5,000ft, is the largest glacier in the 'Lower 48' States. Mount Rainier's system of twenty-eight glaciers contains 48 square miles of ice. Mount Baker's glacier system, including the Roosevelt and Coleman glaciers, totals 31 square miles

Huts and Bivouacs
There are several climbing huts on Mount Rainier operated by the Mount Rainier National Park, but camps and bivouacs are usual elsewhere

Guide-books
Climbing History and Routes of Mount Rainier, by Dee Molenaar; *North Cascades,* by Miller (published by The Mountaineers, Seattle); *South Cascades,* by Sterling and Spring (published by The Mountaineers, Seattle); *Cascade Alpine Guide,* by Fred Beckey (published by The Mountaineers, Seattle); *Challenge of the North Cascades,* by Fred Beckey (published by The Mountaineers, Seattle); *Challenge of Mount Rainier,* by Dee Molenaar (published by The Mountaineers, Seattle), and many other books and guides published by The Mountaineers.
Also *A Climber's Guide to Oregon,* by N. A. Dodge

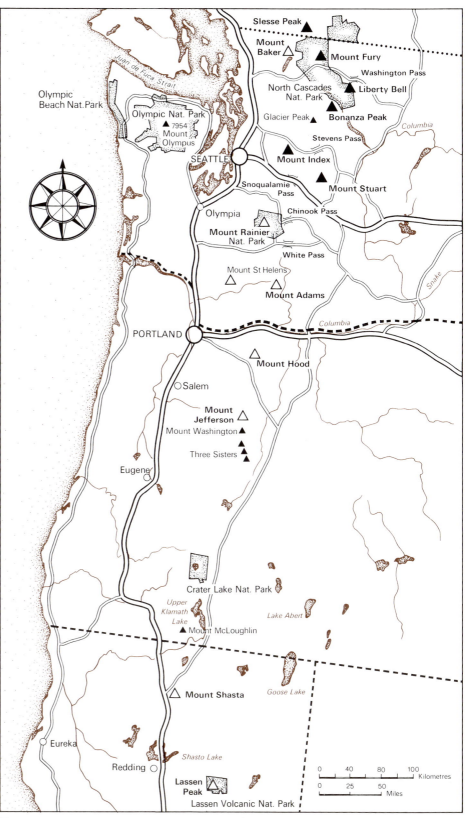

Maps
There is a special USGS series of Mount Rainier National Park maps at scale 1:24,000 and also the USGS 1:62,500 (1in. to 1 mile) map of the park on a single sheet.
Elsewhere standard coverage on USGS 1:62,500 scale

Convenient Centres
Except on many of the volcanic peaks, where there is usually a 'lodge' at the road-head below the *voie normale*, most mountaineering is not 'centred'. Seattle and Portland, however, are convenient to the mountains, and are major cities with every facility

Access
Seattle has a major international airport with direct flights to Europe. All US cities and most towns of any size have airports with scheduled internal services. As elsewhere in the USA, cars may be rented almost everywhere, and aircraft chartered freely at many airfields. Both Mount Rainier and an important segment of the North Cascades are National Parks and certain access restrictions and regulations are enforced

Canadian Rockies

Forming an almost continuous mountain wall for 450 miles (720km), the Canadian Rockies stretch north west from the 49th Parallel—the US border. A comparatively narrow range, the high ground rarely more than 50 miles (80km) across, the Rockies mark the Continental Divide. At first the watershed is between the rivers of the Great Plains and the Pacific. But the Columbia Ice-Field is a rare triocenic watershed and the Athabasca River, which flows north from it, ends its long journey in the Arctic Ocean. A further grouping of worthy, yet little-known, peaks centred on the Lloyd George Massif some 300 miles (480km) further north, yet not forming part of the Divide, is considered to be the final outpost of the Rockies.

For the traveller bowling westward across the rolling Alberta prairies, the sudden first sight of the Rockies is sensational. From about 40 miles distant the abrupt saw-blade of peaks, hundreds of them, extends from horizon to horizon. Built of uplifted sedimentary rocks, often limestones and shales, these mountains have been heavily glaciated and still contain a very considerable amount of ice. Typically the mountains are spectacular and steep, sometimes massive, sometimes forming great towers or shark-fins, the rock always markedly stratified. More than fifty rise above 11,000ft (3,350m). Turbulent rivers course through broad U-shaped valleys, thickly carpeted with coniferous forest. Beautiful lakes of impossible colours abound, some, such as Maligne Lake, Marvel Lake, Moraine Lake and Lake Louise are of wide fame. Wildlife is plentiful and includes moose, caribou, mountain goat, wolf and bear. Dangerous grizzlies, predatory mosquitoes, impenetrable forest, unfordable rivers and inclement weather are problems the Rocky mountaineer must live with. But the more accessible regions are a mecca for tourists and over half the main area of the range is contained within National or Provincial Parks. The 150-mile (240km) Banff-Jasper Highway, opened in 1940, which traverses the three contiguous valleys of the Bow, North Saskatchewan and Athabasca Rivers, under the east flank of the Continental Divide, is one of the world's most scenic mountain roads.

Early mountaineering in the Rockies was facilitated by the Canadian Pacific Railway, but even then long expeditions with pack horse teams were usually necessary from the railhead. The first important climbs were made around the turn of the century during the several visits of Norman Collie and his Alpine Club Parties who discovered the Columbia Ice-Field in 1898, and fellow member Sir James Outram with his guides. Notable pioneering was carried out too by members of Boston's Appalachian Club. These intrepid pioneers laid the foundations of the sport of mountaineering in North America.

The monarch of the Rockies is awesome Mount Robson, a peak of world stature. Isolated westward of the main chain, its aloof summit and gigantic shoulders rise 10,000ft (3,000m) above the Frazer River and seem to fill the sky. The route of first ascent, after six years of attempts, was the Kain Face, now one of the continent's classic climbs. It is a long and complex ice-route of Himalayan rather than alpine style, serious but not technically difficult by modern standards. Unwilling to descend this intimidating face, Conrad Kain led his party down the unknown southern flank of the mountain—now the *voie normale*—thus also completing the first traverse. A professional guide, Kain was the greatest pioneer of the age. There are three other ridges, including the famous Emperor Ridge, and an elegant 2,600ft (800m) North Face of steep ice, besides the 'regular' route from the south, which boasts a hut. Objective dangers, violent storms and daunting reputation combine to make Robson a most worthy prize, not claimed by many.

Another formidable peak is Alberta, the last of the Rockies' major summits to be reached. Steep and difficult from all sides, its ascent by a Japanese party with Swiss guides was a notable achievement, not repeated until 1948. The silver ice axe reputedly left on the summit by the Japanese was not found.

Perhaps the most beautiful mountain is Assiniboine, the so-called 'Matterhorn of the Rockies'. A famous sight, rising above the flowery meadows around remote Magog Lake, the peak can be climbed by several routes, classic being the narrow and icy North Ridge, a fine mixed climb of little difficulty in good conditions.

In a range where approaches are often long and arduous, the more easily reached areas have been well developed. Such are the high snow-peaks around the Columbia Ice-Field; majestic Columbia, the Twins, Kitchener and others have straightforward 'regular' routes and are often reached on skis. Athabasca and its satellite, Andromeda, tower over the ice-field's tourist complex and provide a series of fine snow-climbs of all standards, including the attractive and straightforward 'Sky Ladder' ice-face. Another popular area is that around Lake Louise, Lake O'Hara and Moraine Lake with its beautiful 'Valley of the Ten Peaks'. Here, interesting alpine climbs on rock, ice or mixed ground can be completed in a weekend from Calgary. In recent years a small band of Canadian and American alpinists have been attacking the often spectacular north faces. These are usually serious ascents of up to 4,000ft (1,200m) on difficult mixed ground with bivouacs. Typical classics are Edith Cavell and Temple, but others include Alberta, North Twin, Columbia and Hungabee. A much sought-after prize, the intimidating Emperor Face of Mount Robson, was finally climbed in 1978. This demanding 5,000ft route comprised extremely steep ice interspersed with difficult rock steps: graded 5.9/A3 it took three days. Another recent trend is the winter ascents of frozen waterfalls or water- and ice-choked gullies, sometimes multi-day climbs. Meanwhile, excellent rock-climbs have been developed on foothill crags in the easily reached Canmore area, east of Banff. Although the usual shattered limestone of the Rockies is notorious, climbers have found the quality improves with steepness, on both crag and mountain. Tremendous opportunity for new climbs still exists, not just new routes, but even, in the most remote areas, perhaps the odd minor summit?

Situation: Dominion of Canada—Provinces of Alberta and British Columbia

Some Major Peaks
1 Mount Robson (12,972/3,954) 1913: W. M. Foster, A. H. McCarthy with Conrad Kain
2 Mount Columbia (12,294/3,747) 1902: Sir James Outram with C. Kaufmann
3 North Twin (12,200/3,719) 1923: W. Ladd, J. Munroe Thorington with Conrad Kain
4 Mount Clemenceau (12,001/3,658) 1923: D. Durand, H. Hall, W. Harris, H. B. De V-Schwab
5 Mount Alberta (11,874/3,619) 1925: Yuko Maki and party with H. Fuhrer, H. Kohler and J. Weber
6 Mount Assiniboine (11,870/3,618) 1901: Sir James Outram with C. Bohren and C. Hasler
Mount Temple (11,626/3,544) 1894: S. Allen, L. Frissel and W. Wilcox
Mount Hungabee (11,457/3,492) 1903: H. C. Parker with C. and H. Kaufmann

The 'Matterhorn of the Rockies'—Mount Assiniboine seen from close beside Magog Lake to the north. The classic North Ridge falls straight towards the camera and the ACC bivi hut is below the West Face at 8,700ft (2,650m) and is reached via the steep and narrow ice-couloir that splits the headwall just right of centre

Some Major Peaks continued

Mount Athabasca (11,452/3,491) 1898: J. Norman Collie and Herman Woolley

Mount Joffre (11,316/3,449) 1919: J. W. Hickson with E. Feuz. Highest peak south of Assiniboine

Mount Edith Cavell (11,033/3,363) 1915: A. J. Gilmour and E. W. Holway

Mount Lloyd George (9,800/2,987) 1947: Frank Smythe, Noel Odell, Henry Hall, Rex Gibson, David Wessel and John Ross.

Major Passes

Crowsnest (4,451/1,357)—carries Canadian Pacific Railway and road between Lethbridge and southern British Columbia

Vermillion (5,416/1,651)—a direct road-link between Banff and southern British Columbia

Kicking Horse (5,333/1,625)—carries CPR and Trans-Canada Highway between Banff, Calgary, and Golden, Vancouver

Bow (6,878/2,096)—carries Banff-Jasper Highway (Highway 93)

Howse (5,020/1,530)—ancient fur traders' pass linking Saskatchewan River to Columbia River. Crossed only by foot-trail

Sunwapta (6,660/2,030)—carries Banff-Jasper Highway (Highway 93) across boundary between Banff and Jasper National Parks

Athabasca (5,736/1,748)—important historical passage from the Athabasca to the Columbia River—from the Great Plains to the Pacific—for voyagers and fur traders during the first half of the nineteenth century—crossed only by a foot-trail

Yellowhead (3,750/1,143)—carries Canadian National Railway and Yellowhead Highway (Highway 16) between Edmonton, Jasper and Vancouver, or northern British Columbia boundary between Jasper National Park and Mount Robson Provincial Park

Pine Creek Pass (c 3,000/915)—carries Hart Highway and CNR between northern Alberta and northern British Columbia

Major Glaciers

The Columbia Ice-Field—150 square miles (325 sq km) measures 10 miles x 15 miles

Clemenceau Ice-Field—40 square miles

Huts and Bivouacs

There are some 13 climbing huts in the range, owned variously by the Alpine Club of Canada and/or the various park authorities. The majority lie south of the Sunwapta Pass. Occasionally park cabins make useful bases in specific instances

Guide-books

Climber's Guide to the Rocky Mountains of Canada in 2 volumes is published jointly by the American and Canadian Alpine Clubs. The annual Canadian and American Alpine Journals are also very useful

Maps

The area is covered by sheets of the official 1:50,000 map published by the Department of Mines and Technical Surveys, Ottawa. Special sheets to specific areas such as Mount Robson and Mount Assiniboine are issued. There is also a special sheet 'Banff Park' to scale 1:190,080 (3 miles = 1in) while National Parks of Canada publish a special sheet 'Jasper National Park' at 1:250,000. Both these latter maps are extremely useful

Access

There are major international airports at Calgary and Edmonton, though the former is more convenient for most of the range. There are small local airstrips at Banff and Jasper. The only feasible access to the Lloyd George Range in the far north is by (float) plane chartered from Fort Nelson, reached by air or road from Edmonton or Prince George. Banff and Jasper are served by rail from Calgary and Edmonton (and major cities to east and west) respectively, while major bus lines operate from Calgary to Banff, from Banff to Jasper and from Edmonton to Jasper, etc.

Regulations in the National Parks require climbers to 'sign-out' before embarking on climbs but the attitude of the British Columbia Provincial Park Authorities—who operate both the Mount Robson and Mount Assiniboine Parks—appears to be more reasonable

Mount Athabasca (11,452ft/3,491m), on the left, and Mount Andromeda (11,300ft/3,444m), on the right rise over the snout of the Athabasca tongue of the Columbia Ice-Field. Clearly seen in this view up the Sunwapta River from the north are the standard route on the former— the North Ridge (Norman Collie and Herman Woolley, 1898) and, at the far right, the upper section of the famous Skyladder – the elegant arcing northern ice-face of Andromeda. In the left foreground can be seen a curve of the incredibly scenic Banff – Jasper Highway

Convenient Centres

The town of Banff and Jasper are excellent centres with almost every facility. Both are notable tourist resorts with all that that entails. The ACC maintain a well-equipped clubhouse for members and their guests at Canmore, close to Banff. There are numerous 'official' campsites within the National Parks and several small towns outside could be useful bases. Camps and bivouacs are usual on the mountains or their approaches

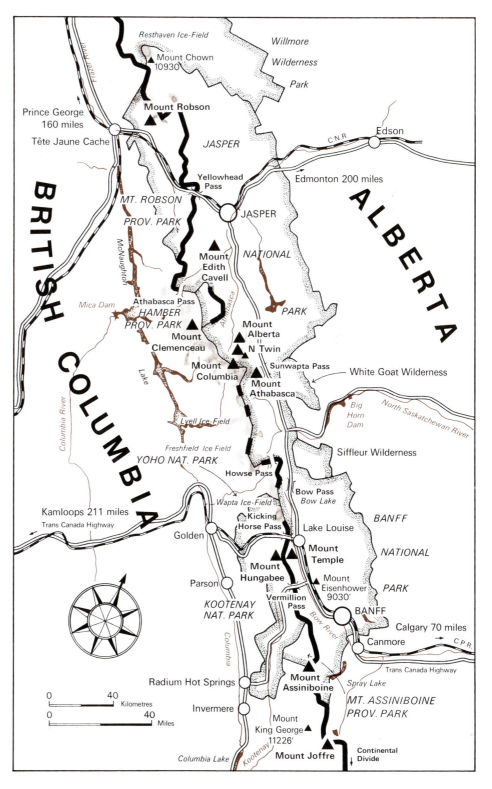

St Elias, Fairweather and Wrangell Mountains

In the far south-western corner of the Yukon, the largest mountain uplift in North America spills over the frontier into Alaska. These are the St Elias Mountains where hundreds of angular ice-hung peaks rise above the greatest glaciers on earth outside the polar regions. These mountains, close behind the Pacific shore, are subject to some of the world's worst weather, and here also towers the world's most massive summit—Mount Logan.

Mount St Elias itself, a beautiful pyramid of ice just 35 miles (56km) from the open sea, was first recorded by Vitus Bering, a Danish navigator in Russian employ, in 1741. It was left to Captain Cook, however, thirty-seven years later, to give this conspicuous mountain the name Bering had first given to the Cape. Indeed it was Cook who first used the name 'Alaska' for the 'great country' of the Aleut Indians.

Long believed to be North America's highest peak, St Elias could only be climbed once its approaches had been explored. A difficult coastal landing and a polar-style ice-cap traverse had of necessity to precede the Himalayan-scale ascent and there were to be seven expeditions before the Duke of the Abruzzi's party reached the summit by the technically straightforward North-East Ridge. It had been a difficult thirty-one day journey, but the expedition was carefully planned and superbly equipped. The mountain was not climbed again for forty-nine years, when a Harvard party, supported by air-drops, climbed the more direct, but rather harder, South-West Ridge in a thirty-day trip. Since then the long North-West Ridge and the difficult, double-corniced

East Ridge have been ascended—the latter climbed in 1972, utilizing three camps actually on the ridge itself. However, incessant bad weather and heavy snowfall ensure that few parties are successful; up to 1972 only seven of the previous thirty-three attempts made the top.

Not until the International Boundary Commission started its work in 1913 was it confirmed that an even greater mountain lay some 30 miles (50km) north east of St Elias. Named after the first director of the Geological Survey of Canada, Mount Logan's summit plateau stretches 11 miles (17km) over a succession of tops and saddles, after rising 14,000ft (4,260m) in huge cliffs and many ridges from the midst of a glacier system almost as large as Switzerland.

In 1925 the Alpine Clubs of Canada, America and Britain planned a joint expedition to attempt Logan. A chain of supply dumps was laid by dog-team during the winter and in May the 180-mile (290km) approach began. The venture was successful, the climb itself being relatively easy, but the expedition was extremely arduous and the retreat from the summit in a blizzard became an epic of survival. André Roche led the second ascent in 1950, but by then the approach was by air. Now six of the great ridges have been climbed including the spectacular 'Humming Bird' or Central South Ridge on which Allen Steck's team spent thirty days in 1965, cutting off retreat as they went, and later describing the climb as a 'six-mile-long nightmare'. It was a milestone of American mountaineering.

The Alaska-Yukon frontier is a hypothetical line joining prominent sum-

mits, among them some very interesting peaks. Notable are Mounts Hubbard and Alverstone whose huge rock- and ice-faces invite serious investigation. Close to the frontier is Mount Kennedy whose steep 6,000ft (1,830m) North Ridge gives a very difficult climb on rock, snow and ice. In 1968, the regular route was climbed by Senator Robert Kennedy. Many of the hundreds of lesser peaks are still virgin and few of the larger ones have been repeated.

Across the Skolai Pass, the peaks become the Wrangell Mountains, technically the easiest major summits in Alaska. Named after the explorer, Baron von Wrangell, who operated in the area before the Alaska Purchase of 1867, these attractive peaks have been dubbed the 'jewels of Alaska' and a dozen rise above 12,000ft (3,660m). Mounts Sandford and Wrangell are ice-covered volcanoes—the latter actually erupted within the last century and its steam now heats a research station on the summit. These mountains, together with massive Mount Blackburn, can be ascended largely on skis, but steeper and more difficult routes have been climbed.

Southward lies the compact Fairweather Range, so named—perhaps in jest—by Cook in 1778. Dramatic and rugged, these are young mountains, still rising fast, and subject to serious earth-

Mount St Elias from the north. Visible from the coast, only 35 miles (56km) away, this was the first of the American giants to be discovered and climbed by Western explorers

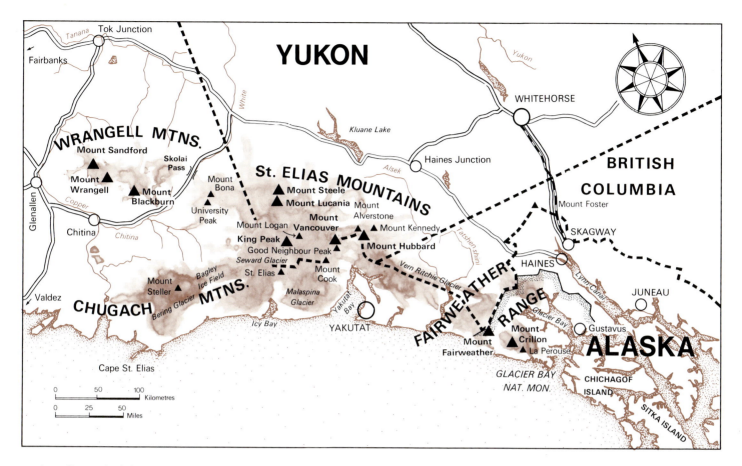

quakes. Several of the extensive glaciers which cloak the range flow into the sea which surrounds the mountains on three sides—the tidal ice of Glacier Bay is world-famous. The seven mountains above 12,000ft (3,660m) are dominated by beautiful Mount Fairweather itself whose sharp icy summit and broad shoulders rise only 14 miles (22km) from the ocean. At one time considered the most important unclimbed peak in North America, its ascent was not repeated for twenty-seven years, but there are, today, five separate routes on its ridges. The ascent of shapely Mount Crillon was not repeated until 1972, and then by the fluted ice of its West Ridge. Mount La Perouse, a serene pyramid of 10,728ft (3,270m), was first climbed by a 1952 survey party, but since then two difficult routes have been made, including the icy North-East Ridge/North Face, climbed alpine-style in 1972.

Situation: United States of America—State of Alaska; Dominion of Canada—Yukon Territory and Province of British Columbia

Most Important Peaks
1 Mount Logan (19,520/5,951) 1925: A. H. MacCarthy, H. F. Lambart, A. Carpé, W. W. Foster, N. Read and A. Taylor. The highest mountain in Canada, second in North America

2 Mount St Elias (18,008/5,489) 1897: Duke of the Abruzzi, Vittorio Sella, four Courmayeur guides, including Petigax and Macquignaz, and four others
Mount Lucania (17,147/5,226) 1937: Bradford Washburn and Robert Bates
Mount Steele (16,644/5,073) 1935: Walter Wood, Hans Fuhrer and two companions
King Peak (17,130/5,221) 1952: Elton Thayer and party
Mount Vancouver (15,820/4,922) 1949: A. Bruce-Robertson, W. Hainsworth, R. McCarter and Noel Odell
Mount Hubbard (15,015/4,577) 1951: Walter Wood's party
Mount Fairweather (15,318/4,669) 1931: Allen Carpé and Terris Moore
Mount Crillon (12,726/3,879) 1934: Bradford Washburn and H. Adams Carter
Mount Blackburn (16,390/4,996) 1912: Miss Dora Keen and G.W. Handy
Mount Sandford (16,237/4,949) 1938: Bradford Washburn and Terris Moore
Mount Wrangell (14,163/4,317) 1908: R. Dunn and W.T. Soule

Most Important Pass
Skolai Pass—links the Chitina river and the White river; an historic pass used by gold-seekers crossing from the Copper river country to the Klondike

Major Glaciers
The Malaspina Glacier covers some 1,500 square miles (2,414sq km) and is 50 miles (80km) across. The Bering Glacier, together with the Bagley Icefield, the Seward Glacier, the 80-mile (128km) long Hubbard Glacier and the Vernritche Glacier form a continuous ice-field, 235 miles (378km) in length, from behind Cape St Elias to the Alsek river

Guide-books
Part of the area is covered by *Expedition Yukon* by Marnie Fisher and there are also very useful articles in *Ascent* 1975-76 ('S.E. Alaska' by Fred Beckey) and *The Alpine Journal* 1976 and 1978 ('Shining Mountains, Nameless Valleys—Alaska and the Yukon' by Terris Moore and Kenneth Andresko). Other articles appear in *AAJ* and *CAJ* besides other magazines and journals.

Maps
USGS publish 1:250,000 and 1:63,360 sheets covering the American side of the frontier; Canada publishes 1:250,000 in NTS.

Access
Much of the Fairweather Range lies within the US Glacier Bay National Monument, and park service regulations prohibit air drops and aircraft landings within the monument boundary. Access permits must also be obtained.

A large part of the St Elias Mnts (8,500 square miles/1,368sq km) lies within the Canadian Kluane National Park and certain regulations must be complied with here also.

There are major airports at Whitehorse and Juneau—the former may also be reached by the Alaska Highway and the latter by sea from Seattle. A road connects Haines to Haines Junction on the Highway, while a railway and new road links Skagway to Whitehorse. Access to the mountains themselves is either by light aircraft landing on glaciers, lakes or sea inlets, chartered from Whitehorse, Juneau, or Glennallen (on the Glenn Highway), by sea—Yakutat is convenient for the Hubbard Glacier for instance—or on foot and skis from the Kuane Lake region on the Alaska Highway—100 miles (160km)

Alaska Range

In 1794 Captain George Vancouver RN sailed up Cook Inlet and recorded that 'stupendous mountains covered with snow' stood far to the north. It was the first historical record of Mount McKinley and the Alaska Range which, rugged and intensely glaciated, arcs around the hinterlands of the Gulf of Alaska for over 400 miles (640km). Despite McKinley's colossal stature, fewer than twenty other peaks exceed 10,000ft (3,050m) and most average between 7,000 and 9,000ft (2,000–2,750m). Those that are high are thus generally isolated and imposing. Many peaks are the result of granitic intrusions in the basic synclyne formation of the range

Mount McKinley, North America's highest mountain, reflected in a tundra pond. Native Indians call this peak Denali—'the Great One' or 'Home of the Sun'—and indeed, even in the Himalaya, there is not a mountain with a greater height difference, base to summit

and rise as sharp summits with mighty cliffs and jagged spires heavily cloaked with ice, while others are composed of poor sedimentary or metamorphic rock. The range has been described as a crucible of evil weather, forming, as it does, a natural barrier between the warm damp Pacific coast and the cold interior. It is not, however, a continuous divide: several Yukon tributaries actually rise south of the range and their valleys, or other low passes, divide it into four main massifs.

The largest and most important of these is centered on Mount McKinley, a huge yet shapely mass dwarfing the lesser summits that cluster round its feet, many of them major peaks in their own right. Its northern flanks rise 17,000ft (5,000m) in 12 miles (19km) and hold 16,000ft of snow cover. Five major ridges and a complex array of spurs and buttresses spring from its two summits and bear between their crests a myriad tortured ice-falls and five huge glaciers.

The summit boasts what is probably the most severe year-round climate on earth!

Known to the Indians as Denali— 'the Great One'—and named in 1897 for the 24th president, Mount McKinley's first ascent was claimed by the eminent explorer Dr Frederick Cook in 1906. His story was controversial at the time—it later proved spurious—and in 1910 a party of Alaskan 'sourdoughs' succeeded in reaching the North Peak, thinking it was the highest point. In what was a most remarkable exploit, they even dragged with them a 14ft flagpole. Eventually a carefully planned expedition reached the 2 mile (3km) distant and rather easier South Peak by a similar route up the Muldrow Glacier, an ascent not even attempted again for nineteen years.

Both the Muldrow Route and the now 'regular route', via the West Buttress, are easy snow-climbs of no technical difficulty, but the mountain is Himalayan in scale and high-altitude

effects on it seem to be abnormally accentuated. Bradford Washburn, intimately associated with the mountain since his own first ascent—the third—in 1942, and the pioneer of the West Buttress, writes, 'the ascent is a curious paradox. Under certain conditions it can be surprisingly easy while under others it can be fiendishly difficult . . . even the most powerful group may be forced to take a month or more by the easiest route'. Notwithstanding, the easy routes are popular: they are regularly guided and park authorities estimate that some 225 people ascended the West Buttress during 1976.

Today more than a dozen other lines have been climbed, four of them on the awesome 10,000ft (3,050m) South Face. Here the classic is the Cassin Rib, first climbed in 1961 by an Italian team, using siege tactics, over thirteen days: it is now usually climbed alpine-style and has even been soloed.

Each of the six ice-ridges, meeting on the summit plateau of stately Mount Foraker, have now been climbed, the first being the North-West. A notable landmark in Alaskan mountaineering, however, was the 1977 ascent of the South Face by George Lowe and Mike Kennedy: an horrendous climb, on rock, snow and ice, of ninety belayed pitches, it set a new standard for alpine-style ascents. Mount Hunter, with its three summits, appears rounded and serene, but is actually quite difficult and holds several routes, plus great potential, in its tremendous south-east *cirque*. Mount Huntington is one of America's most savagely beautiful mountains—a pyramid of three fluted and heavily corniced ice-*arêtes*. The North-West Ridge, Terray's original route, and the East Ridge have been climbed, as well as the West Face ('65), and the North Face ('78). All are difficult but there have been several repeat ascents. Attempted several times before the first ascent, via the West Ridge, the Moose's Tooth is a mile-long crest of ice above a steep 2,000ft (610m) south-facing granite wall. Two lines have been made on this wall, but the challenging East Face has repulsed strong attempts. Many peaks in the area, Silverthrone, for example, give straightforward snow-climbs, but the promise of hard new routes, on rock, ice or mixed ground, is great.

Discovered only recently, the small Kichatna—or Cathedral Spires—group is very remote. However, its modest height is no measure of the climbing difficulty involved, for its granite needles

are typically sheer all round, allow no easy lines and rise over 3,000ft (900m) above the surrounding glaciers. Several major rock-climbs have been made of the 'big wall' type and the region has been dubbed the 'Alaskan Patagonia'.

Eastward of McKinley, several handsome peaks rise some 7,000ft (2,000m) above another area of large glaciers. Despite difficult approaches over sometimes impossible ice-falls, Mount Hayes, Mount Hess (12,030ft/3,668m) and others have been climbed several times by various routes. Mount Deborah, however, another beautiful three-ridged ice-pyramid, enjoys a most formidable reputation. The very experienced, first-ascent party declared that the steep and severely corniced South Ridge gave them the most sensational ice-climb they had ever encountered, and for the next twenty-one years Deborah repulsed all comers. Eventually a six-man Alaskan team, having arrived by dog-sledge, traversed 2

miles over subsidiary summits to reach, and then climb, the South Ridge which, since the first ascent, had become otherwise inaccessible through ice movement. On the way they were forced to sit out an eleven-day storm in an igloo at nearly 12,00ft (3,700m). In 1977 the North-West Ridge succumbed and the intimidating North Face was climbed, the latter in a very bold fifteen-day alpine-style push. The East Ridge now remains as one of Alaska's big challenges.

In every sense these are arctic mountains and are repeatedly underestimated by 'outside' climbers. Except by air, they are almost inaccessible, for the surrounding bush and mighty rivers make overland approaches impractical. The best weather usually comes in April and May, while in June the typically unpleasant snow conditions can be avoided by climbing throughout the night, and skis or snowshoes are essential on the glaciers. Surprisingly, several important winter climbs have been made.

Alaska Range

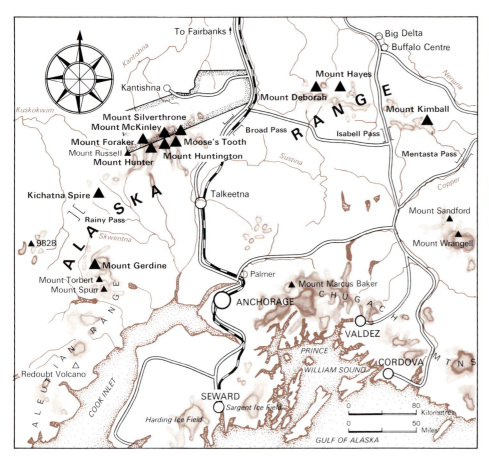

Above: **Alaska Range—view from Kahiltna Dome, looking north west towards Mount Hunter**

Opposite below: **Mount Deborah, a formidable ice-pyramid in the Hayes Range, Alaska. Twenty-one years passed between the first ascent in 1953 and the second. The North Face, seen here, was first climbed in 1977**

Below: **Mount Huntington, Alaska Range, one of America's most savagely beautiful mountains. The North-West Ridge, first climbed by a French party in 1964, is facing the camera; the West Face is on the right; on the left is the North Face, climbed in 1978 by a two-man party, alpine-style**

Situation: United States of America—State of Alaska

Major Peaks
1 Mount McKinley
South Peak (20,322/6,194) 1913: Archdeacon Hudson Stack, H. Karstens, W. Harper, R. Tatum. (Highest summit in North America)
North Peak (19,470/5,935) 1910: Pete Anderson and Bill Taylor
2 Mount Foraker (17,402/5,304) 1934: Charles Huston, T. Graham Brown and C. Waterston
3 Mount Hunter (14,573/4,442) 1954: Heinrich Harrer, Fred Beckey and Henry Meybohm
Mount Silverthrone (13,220/4,030) 1945: Bradford Washburn and party
Mount Huntington (12,240/3,731) 1964: Jacques Batkin and Sylvain Sarthou of Lionel Terray's party
Moose's Tooth (10,335/3,150) 1964: Walter Welsch, Klaus Bierl, Arnold Hasenkopf and Alfons Reichegger
Mount Hayes (13,832/4,216) 1941: Bradford Washburn and party
Mount Deborah (12,540/3,822) 1954: Heinrich Harrer, Fred Beckey and Henry Meybohm
Mount Kimball (10,350/3,155) 1969: Grace Hoeman, D. Osborne, T. Kensler, M. Sallee
Mount Gerdine (12,600/3,841)
Kichatna Spire (8,985/2,739) 1966: Art Davidson and Rick Millikan

Major Glaciers
Kahiltna Glacier—46 miles (74km) long
Muldrow Glacier—41 miles (66km) long
Ruth Glacier—38 miles (61km) long

Major Trans-range Passes
Rainy Pass (c2,500/750)—track linking Cook Inlet area to the Kuskokwim country
Broad Pass (c2,350/720)—traversed by both Alaska Railroad and the highway from Anchorage to McKinley National Park and to Fairbanks
Isabell Pass (c2,500/750)—traversed by Richardson Highway and the Alaska Pipeline from Fairbanks to Valdez
Mentasta Pass (c2,500/750)—traversed by Glenn Highway linking Anchorage to the Alaska Highway direct

Guide-books
A Tourist's Guide to Mount McKinley by Bradford Washburn (Alaska Northwest Publishing Co, Anchorage). *Alaska Mountain Guide* by J. Vin Hoeman.
Also articles in *AAJ*, *Mountain*, *Ascent* and *The Mountain World* 1956-57

Maps
The brilliant 1:50,000 map of the immediate McKinley area, some 8 miles in all directions, was published by the Swiss Foundation for Alpine Research/Museum of Science, Boston.
Quite useful maps of 1:250,000, covering all areas, are published by USGS, including special sheets of the National Park.

Convenient Centres
Mountaineering in Alaska is expeditionary only

Access
Flying is the usual method of transport to most places in air-minded Alaska and it is standard practice to charter light aircraft to fly in to suitable glaciers when approaching these mountains. Airdrops of supplies are also often arranged. Several bush pilots operate from the airfield at Talkeetna which may be reached by road, rail or air from Anchorage where there is an international airport with direct flights from the 'Lower 48' and Europe. Anchorage may also be reached by sea from Seattle.

A large portion of the McKinley group lies within the Mount McKinley National Park, established in 1917. Mountaineering in the park is strictly controlled and application for permission to do so must be submitted sixty days in advance to park headquarters. Two-way radios are supposed to be carried on major climbs—a very controversial policy which many mountaineers claim induces a false sense of security.

Aircraft may not land within the park boundaries. There are currently proposals to extend the south boundary some 25 miles (40km) southward. The park headquarters lie on the National Park Road, just off the Anchorage-Fairbanks Highway, and the road leads on some 70 miles (113km) to the region of Muldrow Glacier snout

South America

The great plateau of Roraima
(9,219ft/2,810m) surrounded by 2,000ft walls
is the original of Conan Doyle's 'Lost World',
and stands on the frontiers of Guyana,
Venezuela and Brazil. First ascended by the
jungle slopes on the far side by Sir Everard
im Thum and Mr Henry Innes Perkins in
1889, it has been ascended several times
since. The great rock prow in the picture was
forced in 1973 by Joe Brown, Mo Anthoine,
Don Whillans and Hamish MacInnes. They
took 17 days on this extremely difficult
2,000ft climb.

Peruvian Andes

The mountains of Peru, their highest point only 600 miles (965km) south of the Equator, are undoubtedly the most important summits of the whole 5,000-mile (8,046km) Andean Chain as far as the mountaineer is concerned. Peru is the goal of most of the foreign climbers who come to South America, many of them Americans for whom access is particularly easy.

Many well-travelled mountaineers consider these mountains to be the most beautiful in the world. Typically they are splendid ice-peaks with spectacular summits, their ridges encrusted with massive cornices and wild ice formations, and their fluted and often avalanche-raked flanks dropping to tangled glaciers. The high peaks are mostly granitic intrusions rising above the sedimentary rocks and shales of arid uplands, a tawny, tussocky landscape studded with little green glacial lakes and, early in the season, bright with wild flowers.

The Pacific shore is barely 60 miles (96km) from the main crest in the north of the country and short rivers flow steeply to the sea. So extreme, however, are the geophysic acrobatics hereabouts that, taking into account the offshore deeps of the Lima Trench, there is an altitude differential of 40,000ft (12,192m) in just 180 miles (290km). Across the crest, a few yards away, the glaciers feed the headwaters of the vast Amazon system to flow some 3,500 miles (5,632km) to the distant Atlantic. In southern Peru the Amazonian rain forests, less than 1,500ft (457m) above the sea, creep to within 80 miles (128km) of the eternal snows. The Peruvian Andes must truly be among the most extreme continental divides on earth.

Throughout the mountains there is constant evidence of the Incas and other, earlier, vanished civilizations, among the most impressive being the mysterious remains of Machu Picchu, 8,000ft (2,440m) up on the eastern edge of the Cordillera Vilcabamba, poised on its dizzy crags above the gorges of the Rio Urubamba. The mountain people are Indians, descendants of the Incas. Many live as high as 16,000ft (4,876m), scratching a precarious existence from their bleak potato fields and herding their flocks of llamas. In these high regions they tend to be a sullen people, and many habitually chew coca which helps to alleviate their harsh circumstances. At more favourable altitudes maize and yucca are grown, sheep are tended and folk are more forthcoming.

The main Andean crest, as it runs south into Peru, parallels the coast, never more than 100 miles inland. The first group of high mountains into which it rises is the Cordillera Blanca, closely followed by the rather less extensive Cordillera Huayhuash, before falling off into a series of minor ranges, rarely rising above 17,000ft (5,180m), although the difficult Nevado Huagaruncha rises to 18,797ft, for some 200 miles. And here a second crest, parallel to the main one and higher, rises out of rain forest to the east, having as its northern prow the Cordillera Vilcabamba. A series of high mountain groups follow; the Urubamba, the Vilcanota, the Aricoma, the Apolobamba astride the Bolivian frontier, and across it the Cordillera Rea. The main western crest meanwhile rises to the Cordillera Occidental, a group of high and extinct volcanoes of archaeological rather than mountaineering interest. Between them, the two crests cradle a high antiplano on which sits the great Lake Titicaca, its shores shared by Bolivia and Peru, just 12,505ft (3,811m) above the sea.

All these Cordillera contain high, icy, glaciated mountains. All the major peaks and almost all the minor peaks have now been ascended and the trend in recent years has been for small parties to attempt new and technically difficult climbs, or for those less ambitious to repeat existing routes, in alpine style. The days of the major expedition snatching dozens of first ascents in a few weeks are long past.

In Peru the rain comes from the east, from the hot damp Amazon forests, and the southern winter is the dry season. Generally speaking this lasts from May until well into August with the best snow conditions probably in early June and high winds springing up late in July. Storms, rarely prolonged or severe, do happen, but stable weather and clear skies are usual throughout this period. Weather in the eastern Cordillera, particularly in the Vilcabamba jutting as it does into the Amazon lowlands, tends to be less settled than in the two northern ranges.

The long white line of the Cordillera Blanca forms the eastern backdrop to the attractive valley of the Rio Santa. These are some of the peaks that surround Nevado Huantsan towards the southern end of the Cordillera, here seen from the south west near Ticapampa, a village south of Huaraz

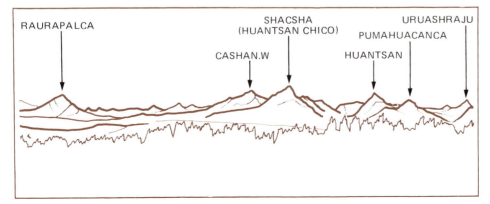

RAURAPALCA — SHACSHA (HUANTSAN CHICO) — URUASHRAJU — PUMAHUACANCA — CASHAN.W — HUANTSAN

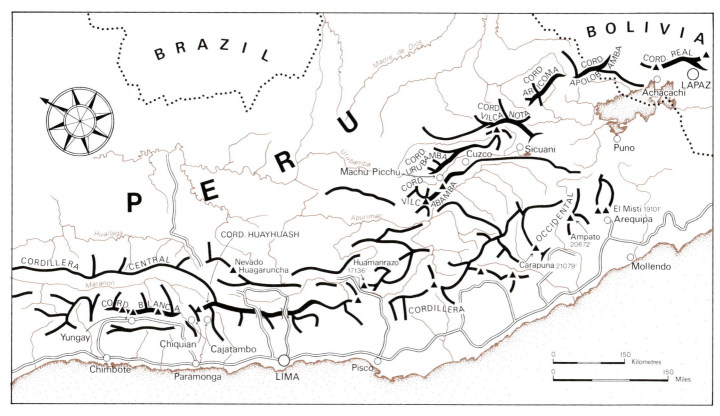

Cordillera Blanca

This is the most extensive as well as the most popular of the Peruvian cordillera. Access is easy and there is climbing at all grades. Most of the range lies within the Parque Nacional Huascaran, which was actually created two decades ago, but only recently became functional. Eleven major mountains and many more tops reach 20,000ft (6,100m), and over seventy summits rise above 18,000ft (5,490m): Huascaran is the second highest mountain in the Americas. Below the summits the glaciers are the largest in the tropics; they are steep, broken and receding and they have earned—for Huascaran in particular—an evil reputation. In 1962 a hanging glacier, breaking from its northern flank, engulfed the village of Ranrahirca, killing 6,000 people, while avalanches caused by the 1970 earthquake destroyed Yungay, Huaraz and Aija and thousands more died including all fifteen members of a Czech expedition then attempting the mountain.

Yungay and Huaraz lie in the long and attractive valley of the Rio Santa, along the western foot of the mountains. Bushy hedges, eucalyptus groves and small cornfields make an attractive foreground to the long line of white peaks and the people living in the neat villages along the valley floor are friendly. Forming the western wall of the valley is the Cordillera Negra, a series of easy snowless summits up to 16,000ft (4,880m) which give good hiking and superb views of the big mountains across the valley.

Since 1903, when an Englishman, C. R. Enoch, first crossed on the high passes over the Cordillera Blanca, mountaineers have been interested in the range, but the first major expeditions were made by large Austro-German parties in the thirties, in which Erwin Schneider was prominent, and it was they who completed the basic exploration.

As Peruvian mountains go, Huascaran is not one of the most beautiful: an ugly wedge from either end, its two summits are connected by 1½ miles of high ridge which the regular route gains at its lowest point—a huge saddle called the Garganta—from the west. It has now been climbed many times and several difficult climbs have been made. These include the South Face (Americans, 1958), the West Ridge (Canadians, 1969) and the huge, 4-mile (6km) long East Face—an ice-wall 3,000ft (914m) high, topped by a thousand-foot rock-rampart up which separate routes were forced in 1971 by an Anzac party and in 1972 by Austrians.

Five miles (8km) northwards is the Huandoy group with four distinct 20,000ft (6,100m) summits arcing round a high glacier plateau. At the extremities the south and east peaks rise as great horns of rock and ice, but it is the South Face of the former Huandoy Sur (20,918ft/6,395m) which is especially notable. This 3,000ft (914m) wall, largely of rock, defeated nearly a dozen expeditions, one led by Whillans in 1968, before Desmaison's French team, using micro-pitons and thirty-five bolts, surmounted it after thirty-seven days of siege tactics in 1976.

Chacraraju, in the same massif, is one of those long twin-summited peaks that appears a spectacular spire seen end-on and is not less impressive from either flank. As recently as 1955 the *Alpine Journal* commented that it 'will require siege or suicide, or perhaps both, if the summit is ever to be climbed'. It was climbed the next year by what Terray considered the most difficult ice-climb of his career, and such is the progress of Andinismo (the local name for Andean mountaineering) that now several independent routes have been made on this formidable mountain. Americans climbed the corniced ice- and rock-step of the North Ridge in 1964 and ascended the ice-flutings of the beautiful South Face in 1977: the French meanwhile climbed the lower East Peak in 1963.

Perhaps the most famous mountain in Peru is Alpamayo. From the north west it appears a steep and perfect pyramid of ice. From the south west it is an immaculate trapezoid of tapering ice-flutings and has been likened to a white cathedral. First attempted by a Swiss expedition in 1948, the North Summit was reached by a Franco-Belgian party in 1951: the South Summit, however, is slightly higher and the intervening 200 yards (183m) of ridge dangerously corniced. This beautiful peak has now been ascended several times, both by its ridges and the steep East Face, and it has also been traversed.

Even more spectacular is Nevado Cayesh, one of the lesser summits of the

Above: **Huascaran is seen from above the Yanganuco valley to the north east. The North Peak is on the right, the Garganta col at the centre, and the higher South Peak stands on the left**

Right: **The southern flanks of Chakraraju are hung with typically Andean ice formations: the West Peak, to the left, is the higher of the two summits**

Chinchey group where there are six tops above 19,690ft (6,000m). From the south it seems a soaring rock dagger spattered with ice bulges and too steep and dangerous to be practicable. To the west, however, Cayesh presents a large rock-face, which, though steep, gave New Zealanders Stu Allen and Steve Dawson a difficult four-day climb in 1973. The original route lay up the heavily corniced South Ridge.

Not all the large peaks are difficult, although even on the regular routes they do require familiarity with sustained snow and ice terrain. Besides Huascaran, Nevado Copa (20,351ft/6,203m) and Nevado Pisco (19,029/5,800), there are several other peaks giving easy routes which have been repeated several times. There are likely to be new routes to climb in the Cordillera Blanca for many years yet, but in the meantime the range is an ideal place to enjoy high-altitude alpine-style climbing amid some of the most spectacular mountains in the world and without the pressures of weather, logistics and politics that seem to bedevil other high ranges.

The spectacular peak of Nevado Cayesh in the Chinchey group is seen from the south. The 1973 New Zealand route runs up the face just to the right of the left-hand skyline. The South Ridge, facing the camera, was the line of the first ascent in 1960

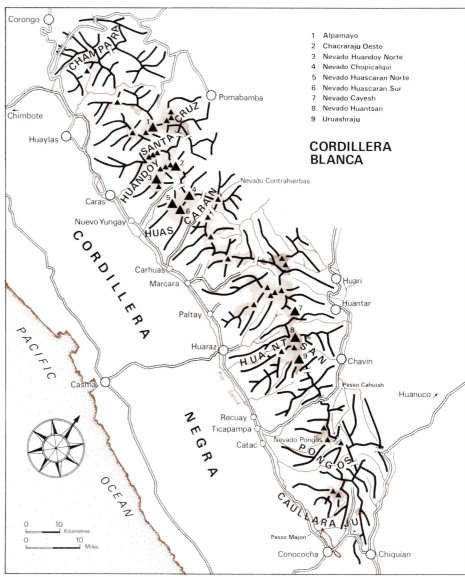

CORDILLERA BLANCA

1 Alpamayo
2 Chacraraju Oeste
3 Nevado Huandoy Norte
4 Nevado Chopicalqui
5 Nevado Huascaran Norte
6 Nevado Huascaran Sur
7 Nevado Cayesh
8 Nevado Huantsan
9 Uruashraju

Situation: Peru

Most Important Peaks

1 Nevado Huascaran Sur (22,208/6,769) 1932: H. Bernard, E. Hein, H. Hoerlin, and E. Schneider
2 Nevado Huascaran Norte (21,833/6,655) 1908: Annie Peck and G. and R. Taugwalder (?)
Nevado Huantsan (20,981/6,395) 1953: Lionel Terray, Tom de Booy, C. Egeler
Nevado Huandoy Norte (20,980/6,395) 1932: E. Hein and E. Schneider
Nevado Chopicalqui (20,817/6,345): H. Hoerlin, E. Schneider, E. Hein, and P. Borchers
Chacraraju Oeste (20,055/6,113) 1956: Lionel Terray and his six-man party
Alpamayo (19,510/5,947) 1957: G. Hauser, F. Knauss, B. Huhn and H. Wiedmann
Nevado Cayesh (18,769/5,721) 1960: L. Stewart, D. Ryan and L. Crawford
Uruashraju (18,815/5,735) 1966: Carlo Mauri and Domingos Giobbi

Maps

Alpenverin, Vienna, publish 'Nevado Huascaran', scale 1:25,000, and also, from Innsbruck, 'Cordillera Blanca', scale 1:200,000 (1964).

Instituto Geografico Militar, Lima, cover the Cordillera Blanca in seven sheets at scale 1:100,000 (1971-73).

The Swiss Foundation for Alpine Research publish 'Cordillera Blanca and Huayhuash' at scale 1:300,000

Guide-book and Bibliography

Yuraq Janka, Cordilleras Blanca and Rosco—a guide to the Peruvian Andes, Part I, by John Ricker, is published jointly by the American and Canadian Alpine Clubs, 1977; *Cordillera Blanca*, by Kinzl and Schneider; *Ascent of Alpamayo*, by Kogan and Leininger (Harrap, 1954); *The Untrodden Andes*, by C. G. Egeler and Tom de Booy (Faber, 1955)

Access

From the international airport at Lima it is a day's journey—250 miles (402km)—by road, in car, bus or rented truck, to the Rio Santa valley. The town of Huaraz (at 10,000ft/3,050m) is a convenient centre for the southern end of the range, while the smaller town of Yungay (at 8,5000ft/2,590m) is convenient for the northern end. It is possible to fly the 10 miles (16km) from Lima to Caraz north of Yungay. From either town burros may be hired to pack food and equipment into the mountains. A suitable base camp for Huascaran, for instance, can be reached on foot in one day from a roadhead at Musho (9,850ft/3,000m), above Yungay.

The Andean Society in London covers a wide range of Andean interests, including mountaineering, and arranges charter flights to Peru, among other activities

Cordillera Huayhuash/Vilcabamba/Vilcanota

CORDILLERA HUAYHUASH

This is the second highest of Peru's great ice-ranges and it lies only 35 miles (56km) south of the Cordillera Blanca to which it concedes little in height and its peaks nothing in difficulty, only in number. Six summits rise above 20,000ft (6,100m), while twenty-eight top 18,000ft (5,490m). Although the character of the landscape, the shape of the peaks and the style of the climbing are similar to those of the Blanca, it is said that the ice-formations here are even more exotic and the ice-avalanches even more numerous. A peculiarity, however, is the number of large turquoise tarns that bejewel the icy *cirques*, mirroring the great peaks around them. One such, Ninakocha at the foot of Jirishanca, is considered to be the source of the Amazon—here known as the Nupe or Rio Maranon. The range was virtually unknown until the thirties; the first climbing visit was in 1936 and the next in 1950. Since then development has been intense and, as elsewhere, the accent is now on difficult new routes. The name 'Huayhuash' is that given to an agile and clever weasel-like creature that lives hereabouts.

Yerupaja is a handsome angular peak and the second highest separate mountain in Peru. It is also known locally as El Carnicero—the Butcher. Although it has now been climbed several times it is not an easy mountain and after the epic first ascent by the South-West Ridge was not ascended again for sixteen years, despite nine attempts. Notable new lines include the West Face, climbed alpine-style in 1966 by Lief Norman Patterson and G. Peterek; the sweeping ice of the formidable 'Amazon', or North-East Face, climbed and descended in 1968 by Chris Jones and Paul Dix; and the South Face, a 5,000ft (1,520m) ice-climb made by Rab Carrington and Alan Rouse in 1977. Also in 1968 a strong New Zealand party traversed Yerupaja via the South and North Ridges. A mile away, Yerupaja Chico, often incorrectly referred to as 'El Toro', was the scene of one of Messner and Habeler's 'express' climbs, when they made the third ascent, via a new line on the South-West Face, in eight hours' climbing time.

Jirishanca is known as the 'Matterhorn of Peru'. The Spanish name means 'the Humming Bird's Beak of Ice' and it is indeed a most imposing fang, on which the rock formations seem to echo the flutings of the ice. It has been described, from another angle, however, as 'an ox horn sticking from a skull of black rock'.

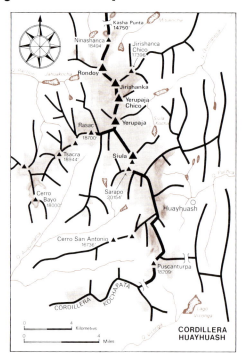

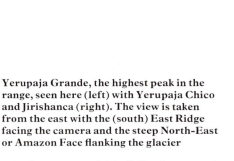

Yerupaja Grande, the highest peak in the range, seen here (left) with Yerupaja Chico and Jirishanca (right). The view is taken from the east with the (south) East Ridge facing the camera and the steep North-East or Amazon Face flanking the glacier

The first ascent of this difficult mountain was by the East buttress and, in 1969, Cassin's team climbed the sharp ice-ribs of the West Face. Neighbouring Rondoy, an ugly lumpy mountain, defeated Walter Bonatti, but was finally climbed, via the tangled ice of the North-West Face, by a relatively inexperienced party from the London School of Economics. In 1977 Rab Carrington and Alan Rouse forced the steep ice and mixed ground of the much sought-after West Face, a climb they graded ED+ and claimed was harder than Mont Blanc's Eckpfeiler Buttress.

Most Important Peaks

1 Nevado Yerupaja (21,759/6,632) 1950: D. Harra and J. Maxwell
2 Nevado Siula (20,841/6,352) 1936: E. Schneider and A. Awerzger
5 Nevado Jirishanca (20,099/6,126) 1957: T. Egger and S. Jungmeier
6 Yerupaja Chico (20,089/6,121) 1957: T. Egger and S. Jungmeier
10 Nevado Rondoy (19,301/5,883) 1963: P. Farrell, V. Walsh, P. Bebbington, C. Powell, D. Condict, G. Saddler

Access

The small towns of Chiquian, for the northern end of the range, or Cajatambo, for the southern end, are some 170 (273km) and 160 (256km) road miles from Lima respectively and accessible by bus from the capital. Base camps are some two days' march beyond

Maps

Alpenverin, Innsbruck, publish 'Cordillera de Huayhuash', scale 1:50,000.

The Swiss Foundation for Alpine Research publish 'Cordillera Blanca and Huayhuash' at scale 1:300,000.

Instituto Geografico Militar, Lima, covers the Cordillera in its 1:100,000 series

Bibliography

The Ascent of Yerupaja, by J. Sack (1954); *The Andes are Prickly*, by Malcolm Slesser (Gollancz, 1966); *Rondoy*, by Dave Wall (John Murray, 1965)

CORDILLERA VILCABAMBA

Its glaciers feeding only the Amazon, the Vilcabamba mountains jut out into the lowlands between the deep chasm of the Rio Urubamba and the Apurimac. This northern bastion of the eastern cordilleras is some 60 miles (96km) long and is split into three major massifs, although the detailed topography is confusing. First visited by Hirmam Bingham, the discoverer of Machu Picchu, in 1911, the first real climbing visit was not until 1946 when Heim unsuccessfully attempted Soray (18,964ft/5,780m): Salcantay was the first peak to be climbed. The powerful Swiss expedition of 1959 and much activity by New Zealand and Australian climbers in particular completed the first ascents of all the peaks, although there is still much scope for new routes.

Salcantay completely dominates its massif and has been climbed a number of times, probably because access from Cuzco is short and easy. The route of first ascent, the North-East Face, is fairly straightforward, but recent routes on the East, South-East and South Ridges are more challenging. It was, of course, on Salcantay that Fritz Kasparek, a member of the first successful Eigerwand team, was killed in 1954.

The Pumasillo Massif is harder to reach and very different: a series of summits of similar height, rising from a system of complex ridges, form great icy mountain walls that have been compared

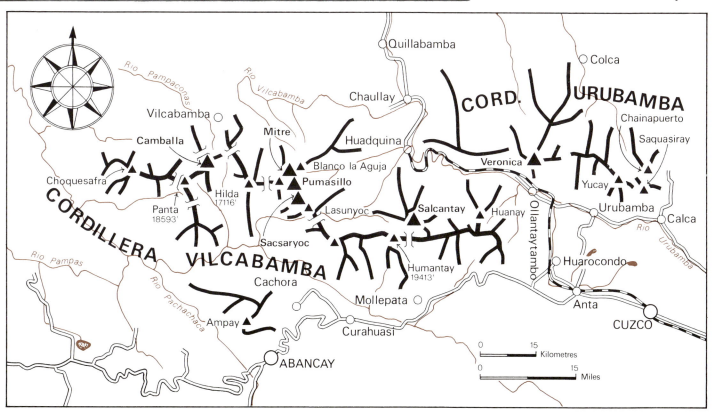

to the Lauterbrunnen Wall in the Alps. Pumasillo itself was climbed by its West Ridge, a route since repeated, and Sacsarayoc, its neighbour, turned back several attempts until the East Ridge was tried. A vertical ice-step close to the summit had to be forced by artificial means and only the lead climber was able to proceed to the top. The beautiful Mitre, with its jagged, triple-pinnacled summit, was climbed from the west while the local 'Matterhorn peak'—called Nevado Blanco la Aguja (17,790ft/5,423m), a striking black needle rising above a snowy pyramid—did not prove difficult by the North Ridge. It

is the Pumasillo Massif that has seen most of the activity in the Vilcabamba.

Somewhat lower and more remote, the Panta Massif is rarely visited, although deep valleys and rugged country lend height to its summits. Typically each peak is isolated and ascents have not been difficult. The massif was mapped in detail by the Swiss in 1959.

Some authorities consider the Cordillera Urubamba, eastwards across the deep valley of the Rio Urubamba, as an outlying region of the Cordillera Vilcabamba. It is certainly complex country and one of the few regions in Peru to offer good rock-climbing. The moun-

tains tend to rise as individual peaks, separated by deep valleys, and few present serious difficulties by their easiest lines. Veronica, also known as Nevado Waqaywilki or Padre Eterno, has been ascended several times: the easy route is from the north, but in 1973 the Poles made a good line on the North Face, and an Anglo-American party climbed the long South-West Rib, in seven days of awkward ice-climbing, in 1977. This is a region which will offer good sport to a small party without technically advanced ambitions.

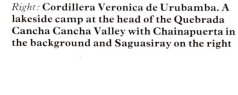

Right: **Cordillera Veronica de Urubamba. A lakeside camp at the head of the Quebrada Cancha Cancha Valley with Chainapuerta in the background and Saguasiray on the right**

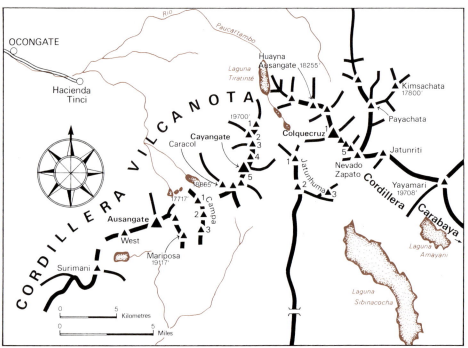

CORDILLERA VILCANOTA

This is one of the most extensive mountain groups in Peru, stretching over 100 miles (160km) south-eastwards between the Rio Vilcanota—which is in fact the upper reaches of the Urubamba—and the headwaters of the Rio Madre de Dios, a completely different Amazon tributary. For practical purposes the Cordillera Carabaya can be considered part of the Vilcanota: the whole area is extremely complex, most of the mountains rise as isolated massifs and it is difficult to draw definite boundaries. Many of the peaks are heavily glaciated, some are extremely impressive, while others are more gentle, but generally speaking they are more alpine in character than the exotic ice-formations farther north. No less than forty-two rise above 18,000ft (5,490m).

Best known are the Ausangate and

Cayangate Massifs which are easily accessible from Cuzco. Indeed, seen from that city, Ausangate has been compared to the Italian face of Mont Blanc. It is an elongated mountain on which several different routes have been made. Notable are the North-East Ridge, climbed by a Munich party in 1969, and the difficult East Face which took a French team six days to climb and descend in 1976. Beautiful Mariposa, at the southeast extremity of the massif, is a wall of ice likened to a butterfly's wing—it was climbed in 1957.

North-eastwards rises the long Cayangate chain, a row of five summits topping a long wall of fluted ice and all above 19,000ft (5,790m).

The Colquecruz—or 'Silver Cross'—Massif is the largest single group. A powerful Australian/New Zealand expedition operated in the area in 1974, made

six new routes and reached three hitherto unclimbed summits. They left only one peak in the group still virgin. Among other climbs they attempted was the traverse of the six major Colquecruz peaks—all are above 19,500ft (5,950m)—but they were defeated by dangerous cornices. This style of long-distance climbing has yet to come to the Andes.

Far to the east, rising almost from the jungles, Yayamari—the 'Father of the Little Lakes'—(19,708ft/6,007m) stands isolated, while southwards the long spur of the Nudo (Knot) de Vilcanota forms part of the enclosing watershed of Lake Titicaca. The range ends in the magnificent-looking Nudo de Cunuruna (19,180ft/5,846m). Not only is the foot of this peak easily accessible but so is its summit: its northern flank is a disappointingly easy scree-slope.

Most Important Peaks

Vilcabamba

1 Nevado Salcantay (20,574/6,271) 1952: G. Bell
and F. Ayres, D. Michael and W. Graham
Mathews, Bernard Pierre and Claude Kogan
2 Pumasillo (19,915/6,070) 1957: Harry Carslake,
John Longland
3 Sacsaryoc (19,670/5,996) 1962: P. Farrell—solo
13 Nevado Mitre (18,635/5,680) 1962: L.
Crawford, P. Farrell, H. Furndofler and V. Walsh
Camballa (18,209/5,550) 1959: Swiss Alpine Club
party

Urubamba

1 Nevado Veronica (18,865/5,750) 1956: Lionel
Terray, C. Egeler and Tom de Booy

Vilcanota

1 Ausangate (20,945/6,384) 1953: H. Harrer, H.
Steinmetz, F. Marz and J. Wellenkamp
2 Nevado Colquecruz (20,049/6,111) 1953: H.
Harrer, H. Steinmetz, F. Marz and J.
Wellenkamp
Nevado Colquepunco (19,751/6,020) 1953: Piero
Ghiglione's party
5 Cayangate V (Nevado Chimbaya) (19,718/6,010)
1966: U. Kerner, H. Oberhofer, A. Rother and K.
Winkler

Maps

Presumably these areas will eventually be covered
in the Peruvian military series. In the meantime
sketch maps may be found accompanying articles
in *AAJ*, *AJ* and *Mountain World* etc

Bibliography

Vilcabamba: *The Puma's Claw*, by Simon Clark
(Hutchinson, 1959)

Access

Both groups are reached from Cuzco, the ancient
Inca capital which can be reached from Lima by
road or air or from the port of Mollendo by rail.
Base camp sites can be reached in several days'
march from roadheads in either case, or, for the
Vilcabamba, from the railway that runs down the
Urubamba Rio from Cuzco to Chaullay

Patagonia: Fitzroy/Paine/Tierra del Fuego

Patagonia forms the final thousand miles of the continent of America; a great horn of land jutting into the tempestuous meeting-point of three of the world's great oceans. Its spine is the Andes, forming not only a convenient political frontier, but a barrier between the contrasting landscapes and climates of east and west. The Pacific littoral is narrow, an almost impenetrable wilderness, battered by continuous gales. Mountain sides cloaked with dense rain forests and wind-twisted beeches rise steeply above a maze of islands and a labyrinth of narrow fjords into which the tongues of numerous glaciers probe. The region is uninhabited save for a few canoe Indians. Broad plains, however, lie east of the mountains. Flat and arid, this is a country of wide skies and sheep with occasional townships, roads and scattered *estancia* (ranches).

The complex watershed, followed vaguely by the frontier, lies well east of the mountain crest and several of the large lakes which characterize the eastern flank drain to the Pacific. Spectacular ice-draped peaks protrude from the two long and narrow ice-caps which sit astride this mountain backbone, while some of the most dramatic rock peaks in the world are ranged along the eastern and southern flanks of the larger southern ice-cap.

Patagonia's highest summit, San Valentin, rises near the centre of the Hielo del Norte which also contains a large number of other peaks. Forty miles (60km) southwards, Cerro Aranales (11,277ft/3,437m) was first ascended by a sixteen-strong Japanese expedition in 1955, and again by Eric Shipton's four-man team during his forty-two-day north–south sledge-traverse of the ice-cap in 1963-64. A few of the other peaks have been climbed, but access is difficult and the region is rarely visited.

The Hielo Sur was first crossed by Bill

Tilman in 1953 and later Shipton made another epic north–south traverse here, taking fifty-two days, in 1960-61. One of Shipton's aims was the location of an elusive volcano, Cerro Lautaro (11,090ft/3,380m), rumoured to exist somewhere on the ice-cap: this he succeeded in doing, despite zero visibility, lured by its sulphurous smell! Twelve

A general view of the Fitzroy Group, showing, on the left, the delicate spires of Cerro Torre, Torre Egger and Cerro Stanhardt. Fitzroy is the commanding monolith on the right, with Aiguille Poincenot to its left

years later Leo Dickinson's three-man party, using parachutes as sails to assist their sledge, relocated Lautaro and ascended to its rime-rimmed crater, as well as discovering, naming and climbing another volcano, Cerro Mimosa. From the east access to this ice-cap is not so difficult and several expeditions have worked in the region, but the western flank, in particular, is still little known.

The Fitzroy group, named after an early navigator in Patagonian waters, is one of the clusters of peaks alongside the ice-cap. It is world-renowned, not only for the incredible shapes of its verglas-plastered diorite spires, but also for the remarkable rock-climbs—mostly of 'big wall' format—that have been made among them. The area was first explored in 1782 and a few minor summits were later ascended in 1916 and during the 1930s, when Agostini and then Bonacossa led Italian expeditions into the group. Several attempts were made

on the 3,500ft (1,066m) shark-fin of Fitzroy itself. Terray's success, nearly two decades later, was a milestone in world mountaineering. The French were the first to encounter the special problems presented by high-standard Patagonian climbing, problems which they solved by using ice-cave camps and fixed ropes before the final alpine-style push—now standard tactics. Since then Fitzroy has been climbed by several different routes and most of the surrounding *aiguilles* have succumbed to determined attack by various parties.

Cerro Torre, nearby, is a slender obelisk crowned with a huge rime mushroom and displays, perhaps, a rock peak's ultimate form. Its claimed first ascent, in 1959, from the north east, by Cesare Maestri and Toni Egger, is considered dubious (Egger was killed on the descent, while a delirious Maestri could recall little detail of their desperate climb). All subsequent attempts failed, including Maestri's own very controversial attempt on the south-east flank, using a compressor (driven drill)! Eventually, in 1974, Casimiro Ferrari's team made a positive ascent in classic style from the west. The Torre's 7,000ft (2,130m) East Face is still a climb for the future!

One hundred miles to the south another famous group of spectacular peaks—most of them rock towers—rise beyond rolling grassland and fine lakes, the Cordillera del Paine. Initially explored in 1882, its first small peak was climbed in 1937, but it was not until the 1950s that climbers became aware of the area's potential. The first prize to be claimed was the highest, the Paine Grande, a magnificent, yet difficult and dangerous, snow- and ice-peak. By the mid-1970s most of the major summits had been climbed, invariably after a hard struggle, by expeditions from many nations, and now attention is focusing on new routes. A notable success was the attempt made in 1974 on the 4,000ft (1,220m) East Face of the Central Tower

by a powerful South African team led by Paul Fatti. This extremely difficult climb took six weeks using siege tactics, and the Tower was then probably the world's highest vertical rock-face to have been climbed. However, just across the valley, the Fortress, first climbed by a British party in 1968, sports a huge 5,000ft (1,524m) East Face, proving that there is plenty of scope still in the Cordillera del Paine.

Strictly speaking, Tierra del Fuego is part of Patagonia and its mountains carry the Andean chain beyond the Straits of Magellan. Typically ice-encrusted and shrouded in mist, these mysterious and beautiful mountains fill a narrow peninsula, the size of Wales, from which large glaciers pour down into the sea. Monte Sarmiento is conspicuous from the Straits and was named by the early navigators. Despite even more daunting weather than that encountered further north, several expeditions have explored and climbed here. Notable have been the Italian groups of 1956 and 1966, led respectively by Alberto de Agostini and

Carlo Mauri, and Eric Shipton's Anglo-Chilean parties of 1961 and 1962, who made the first crossing of the central Cordillera Darwin. On the Argentinian side of the frontier, the town of Ushuaia lies in the rain shadow of the mountains and is a good centre for hiking in the Lapataia National Park with its beautiful forests, lakes and glaciers, and fascinating birdlife.

Patagonia has much to offer both the really serious rock-climber and the exploratory mountaineer. Scope for new routes of all kinds is vast while many peaks, especially those less accessible, are still virgin. However, atrocious weather is the greatest obstacle, so that good climbing conditions are limited to a few days each season and only some expeditions are lucky, while most are frustrated. It was Royal Robbins who once advised: 'Patagonia is exceptionally beautiful: go there to hike, go there to photograph, but if you want to climb seriously you need to be a masochist with unlimited time on your hands!'

Above: **Mount Olivia Group, Tierra del Fuego**

Left: **The Towers of Paine from the Ascencio Valley, showing the breathtaking East Faces of (left to right) the South, Central and North Towers**

Situation: Republic of Chile; Republic of Argentina

Most Important Peaks

1 Cerro San Valentin (13,314/4,058) 1952: Otto Meilung's Argentinian team
2 Cerro San Lorenzo (12,139/4,058) 1955: Agostini's expedition
Cerro Moreno (11,500/3,505) 1958: Walter Bonatti and Carlo Mauri
Cerro Lautaro (11,090/3,380) 1973: Leo Dickinson, Eric Jones, Mike Coffey
Cerro Fitzroy (11,073/3,375) 1952: Lionel Terray, Guido Magnone

Cerro Torre (10,280/3,133) perhaps 1959: Toni Egger and C. Maestri—certainly 1974: Casimiro Ferrari, M. Conti, G. Negri and D. Chiappa
Aiguille Poincenot (10,120/3,085) 1962: Don Whillans and F. Cochrane
Paine Grande (c10,600/3,230) 1958: Toni Gobbi, J. Bich, L. Carrel, etc.
The Fortress (9,400/2,865) 1968: Dave Nicol, G. Hibberd and J. Gregory
Central Tower (8,760/2,670) 1963: C. Bonington and Don Whillans
Mount Darwin (8,110/2,472) 1961: Eric Shipton, E. Garcia, F. Vivanco C. Marangunic
Mount Sarmiento (7,546/2,300) 1956: Carlo Mauri and C. Meffei

Major Glaciers

Hielo Sur—the Southern Ice-Cap—200 miles (320km) in length and some 40 miles (60km) maximum width
Hielo del Norte—the Northern Ice-Cap—some 130 miles (210km) long and of similar width

Huts

Although all mountaineering is expeditionary there is a useful base hut at Pudeto in the Paine and two shelter huts on the approaches to the Glacier Grey.

Guide-books

There are none, but the region is well documented, the classic source—in Italian—being *Andes Patagonicos* by A. de Agostini (Buenos Aires, 1945). Other valuable material is found in *Big Wall Climbing* by Doug Scott (Kaye & Ward, London 1974), *A Patagonia Handbook* (published privately by Ben Campbell-Kelly, Manchester, 1975) and the autumn 1968 'special issue' of *Mountain Craft Magazine*—predecessor of *Mountain Magazine*. Also articles in various mountaineering magazines and journals

Maps

There are useful maps in the publications above and in the *AJ*. The Argentine Automobile Club's 'Zone 8' map is reported to be very useful, while detailed maps of the Paine National Park can be obtained from the Geographical Institute in Santiago

Convenient Centres and Access

The Fitzroy region lies within the Argentinian Parque Nacional de los Glaciores and although there are no restrictions of entry, permission is required to climb and it is wise to apply in advance to park HQ in Buenos Aires.

Approach is made by sea or air to Buenos Aires from where an internal flight or a bus journey gives access to Santa Cruz or Rio Gallegos. Calafate can be reached from the latter by air or bus and trucks can be hired from there or from Santa Cruz to reach the park itself. There is a landing strip 9 miles (14km) from the park HQ at the roadhead.

The Paine Group lies within the Chilean Parque Nacional Torres del Paine (climbing permits are necessary). It is usual to approach Pudeto by bus or hired truck from the town of Punta Arenas (the world's most southerly city!) which can be reached by sea, air or road. Inflatable boats have been used to ferry men and equipment across treacherous Lago Nordenskjold.

The Argentinian section of Tierra del Fuego lies within the Lapataia National Park and is reached easily from Ushuaia on the Beagle Channel. Approach is made by regular air services or by sea

141

Australasia and the Antarctic

This is a short section. In the context of this book the mountain ranges of the Antipodes and the Far South are relatively inaccessible. New Zealand, which the average layman might well dismiss as two small grassy islands lost in the ocean and covered in sheep, is the notable exception. Even Captain Cook was surprised when first he sighted the Southern Alps: 'They are of prodigious height,' he wrote, 'the mountains and some of the valleys being wholly covered in snow'. Other travellers have likened New Zealand to a British Isles ennobled with an alpine range.

Both New Zealand islands are moun-

tainous but those of North Island are volcanic rather than alpine. In what is, in geological terms, still a relatively immature landscape, some of the volcanoes are still active. Best known is Mount Egmont (8,260ft/2,158m) whose beautiful sweeping cone so dominates the countryside in the North Island's south-west corner, although the highest is Ruapehu (9,175ft/2,796m) further east. These are gentle mountains, but they hold snow and ice and are noteworthy for

their skiing rather than for their climbing.

Alone of the mountains in the area we are considering, those of New Zealand are regularly climbed on, are covered by guide-books and detailed maps, and can be reached by fellow mountaineers from Australia, Europe or North America simply by the purchase of an airline ticket.

Although New Zealand mountaineers tended once to insularity—Peter and Alec Graham, the great guides who do-

Above: **Antarctica: Mount Wilcox is one of the fine small mountains of Graham Land, the northern end of the Antarctic Peninsula**

Top: **A dog team approaches Mount Charity (*c.*9,000ft/2,743m) in the Eternity Range of Graham Land. Access is a major problem when climbing in the Antarctic and, together with complex logistics and official discouragement, almost totally precludes mountaineering by privately organized expeditions**

Opposite above: **Ayers Rock lies in the deserts of Australia's Northern Territories some 300 miles south west of Alice Springs. There is a trail to its summit and several rock-climbs have been made surreptitiously on its steeper flanks and chimneys**

minated mountaineering here for twenty-five years, were little known abroad—they are today active among all the world's ranges. After the war men like Ed Hillary and George Lowe led New Zealand mountaineers into the limelight and younger generations have ensured their country's place among the premier mountaineering nations of the world. They are known particularly for their ice-craft.

Australia is no small island; in contrast to New Zealand it is barren, scorched and almost flat, with its small population concentrated on the fertile coast. Its mountains have been described as ' . . . so old that time has rounded them to resemble sleeping dinosaurs with here and there a skeleton showing ribs and vertebrae . . .'. The Great Dividing Range curls down behind the eastern littoral; and its highest point, Mount Kosciusko, barely exceeds 7,000ft (2,134m). Clothed largely in forest, the range is the preserve of the 'bushwhacker' rather than the mountaineer, and although there is some skiing in the Snowy Mountains surrounding Kosciusko, there are no permanent snow-fields. Peculiar rock formations rise from the inland deserts and were graced as mountains in the descriptions of the early pioneers. The famous Ayers Rock is one such.

Tasmania, however, does contain real mountains, if only of moderate height and, although guarded by fierce bush and the poor weather, the craggy peaks of this small island hold the biggest and most important climbs in Australia. The rock is excellent, usually quartzite or dolerite and climbs of between one and two thousand feet have been made on such summits as Federation Peak and Frenchman's Cap. Worthy of note, too, perhaps is the isolated 'sea-mount' of Ball's Pyramid, rising sheer to 1,843ft (562m) from the shark-infested waters of the Tasman Sea. Perhaps the greatest sea-stack in the world, several routes have now been made on its jagged rotten spire. With its many crags and cliffs, Australia has emerged as a major rock-climbing location and Australian rock-climbers have proved their skill all over the world.

New Guinea contains, after the Andes and East Africa, the third of the world's equatorial ice-caps. In 1623 the Dutch navigator Jan Carstenz remarked at the presence of the distant snows so near the equator, but it was not until 1936 that explorers managed to penetrate the thick jungles and contorted foothills to reach the glaciers. The highest peaks rise in the Indonesian territory of West Irian and excellent mountaineering has been reported from such peaks as Carstenz

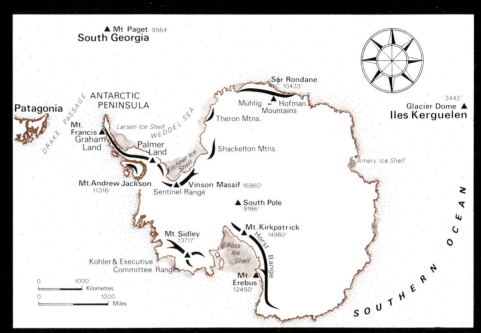

Pyramid (16,532ft/5,039m), New Guinea's highest summit and Ngga Poloe (c16,400ft/5,000m). Huge rock walls are a feature of this area. The mountainous spine extends along the length of the island into the lately Australian-administered territory of Papua, again reaching considerable height in the Bismark Range. While the great efforts to reach their mountains, made by several expeditions in recent years, have been amply repaid, access—both political and physical—is still far from easy and New Guinea's mountains will remain for a long time the preserve of only a few of the hardiest and most determined expeditionary mountaineers.

Although the Antarctic Continent is half as big again as Australia and contains extensive mountain ranges, it lies outside the scope of this book. By international agreement the continent is virtually a scientific preserve and expeditionary mountaineering in this extremely hostile environment—without the co-operation of one of the official scientific organizations, for instance the British Antarctic Survey—is well nigh impossible without very great financial resources. Although many peaks have been climbed by survey teams, moun-

taineering is not usually encouraged because of the obvious risk of accident and the consequent disruption of expensive research programmes. The continent's highest mountains are the strangely angular and sharp peaks of the Sentinel Range. Narrow ridges and steep rock walls rise well over 6,000ft (1,830m) above the surrounding ice-cap. American expeditions have been active here, with the essential assistance of the US Navy, and the highest summits—the Vinson Massif (16,860ft/5,139m) and Mount Tyree (16,290ft/4,965m), among others—have been climbed. Most accessible to 'outsiders' are the mountains of Graham Land and the Antarctic Peninsula and the islands of the South Shetland group that cluster to its west. But they must be reached through the terrible seas of the Drake Passage, and it was en route to mysterious Smith Island in the South Shetlands, with its virgin peaks some 7,000ft (2,134m) in height, that one of the greatest exploratory mountaineers of modern times, Bill Tilman, disappeared in the southern summer of 1977-78.

While the mountaineering potential of the continent is tremendous, for most mountaineers its glittering prizes will remain only dreams.

New Zealand

The astonished Captain Cook first sighted the Southern Alps in 1770. 'They are of prodigious height,' he wrote. 'The mountains and some of the valleys being wholly covered in snow . . .' The Southern Alps are the spine of mountains that runs virtually the complete 500 mile length of New Zealand's South Island, an island that has been likened to a British Isles ennobled by an alpine mountain range. Although there are fine and beautiful peaks elsewhere on this long spine, it is the culminating group of the Southern Alps some 135 miles in length and its eighteen ice-hung summits dominated by Mount Cook, that are world famous.

These are maritime mountains, a wall of high peaks rising steeply from the ocean, against which beat the prevailing north-west winds, laden with moisture, straight off the wide Tasman Sea. Precipitation is extremely high and the weather notoriously unreliable, and the Southern Alps are characterized by their heavy glaciation, probably the heaviest in the temperate regions outside the Himalaya. So great is the ice mass on the west that the fast flowing glaciers reach almost to the sea—less than 20 miles (30km) from the Divide—the ice now almost reaching the dense temperate rain forest. On the east rather longer glaciers flow less steeply to melt into broad skeiny streams feeding a series of long narrow lakes which stretch into the wide plains, less damp in the rain shadow, that roll 80 miles (130km) to the South Pacific.

The spectacular region around Mount Cook, since 1953 a National Park, and containing innumerable fine ice and mixed climbs on dozens of summits, is the mountaineering hub of the Antipodes. Access to The Hermitage at the heart of the area is easy and, despite the tourists who flock to the place, climbers are understood by the park authorities and catered for to an extent. There is here, after all, rather a long history of mountaineering.

One of the land-hungry settlers exploring the mountain fringe in the 1860s was Samuel Butler who wrote of awesome Mount Cook: 'I do not think any human will reach its top', adding responsibly, 'But I am forgetting myself admiring a mountain which is of no use to sheep.' He was soon proved wrong. In 1882 the Reverend W. S. Green and his Swiss guides all but reached the summit from the north east via the Linda Glacier, retreating only in the face of a fierce storm. The attempt stirred considerable local and foreign interest, and, in 1894, Edward Fitzgerald, an experienced exploratory alpinist, together with Matthias Zurbriggen, his Swiss guide, arrived from Europe intent on completing the ascent. They were beaten to it by a strong local party who climbed via the Hooker Glacier, the Green Saddle and the steep and loose rock of the North Ridge, a demanding and dangerous route not repeated until Cook's hundredth ascent in 1955. Fitzgerald and Zurbriggen, however, were able to claim five other major peaks and the latter made the second ascent of Cook—solo—by the now regular route, the Zurbriggen, or North-East Ridge. Green's route, finally completed in 1912, is technically the easiest, although subject to considerable avalanche danger.

Mount Cook, towering 2,000ft (610m) above most of its satellites, and no less than 8,000ft (2,400m) above its glaciers, is one of the world's great mountains.

Mount Cook: this aerial view from the south shows the great Caroline, or South-East Face, 7,500ft (2,286m) high, on the right. Facing the camera is the South Ridge, falling from Low Peak (11,787ft/3,593m), and also the South Face (in shadow) and the West Ridge. The East Ridge is the right skyline of Middle Peak (12,137ft/3,699m). High Peak is at the far end of the summit ridge. On the right, 2 miles (3km) beyond the summit, stands Mount Tasman

The traverse over the three tops of its mile-long summit ridge is a fine climb and has been combined with the peaks to north and south, Tasman and Nazomi, and the many intervening summits. Six major ridges spring from Cook's tops, holding between them four great faces: the Hooker (West) and Sheila (North-West) being predominantly ice and rock respectively, the 4,000ft (1,219m) East Face giving both ice and mixed climbing, while the Caroline (South-East) Face long held the status in New Zealand that the Eigerwand did in Europe during the 1930s. This huge 7,500ft (2,290m) ice-wall was finally climbed in 1970 without excessive difficulty, and this breakthrough, psychological as much as technical, opened other great routes hitherto also considered unjustifiable.

The relatively straightforward yet fairly serious nature of the regular routes on Cook is echoed by the standard routes on the other large peaks. Most such climbs are on ice, and rock, when it occurs, is usually poor. Height differentials are equivalent to those of the higher peaks in Europe, while gale-force winds and sudden storms pose an ever-present threat. Of the higher summits, Elie de Beaumont, which can be climbed on skis in winter, Malte Brun, where unusually sound rock holds some good climbs, and the Minarets (10,058ft/3,066m) which can also be skied, are among the few easier peaks.

Many people claim the beautiful, entirely ice-hung peak of Mount Tasman with its gracefully arcing ice-ridges is the most impressive in the Southern Alps. The long and narrow south-west *arête*, over the Silberhorn, is its easiest route and is fairly difficult. The Balfour, or West Face, is one of the most coveted of the hard modern face-climbs and access to it is long and arduous, a characteristic of most approaches west of the Divide.

145

Mount Tasman is one of the most beautiful peaks in the Southern Alps. In this view, from the east, the Silberhorn is seen to the left of the summit with the classic Silberhorn Ridge dropping steeply towards the ice-fall of the Hochstetter Glacier. The 1960 ice route on the East Face runs to the right of the central rocks while the Syme Ridge follows Tasman's right-hand crest before dropping eastward onto the Grand Plateau of the Hochstetter Glacier

Classic climbs ascend the ice of Douglas' South, and the rock Haidinger West Face: both are close above the Pioneer hut.

Zurbriggen considered Mount Sefton the most dangerous peak he had climbed and, although the rock on its ridges is notoriously bad, several of the ice-climbs on the East Face are now classic and often repeated. First climbed in 1971, the 2,000ft (610m) South Face of Mount Hicks gives very exacting mixed

climbing, the Left Hand Gullies a recent line by Bill Denz, is considered the hardest route in the Cook area.

Among the outstanding mountains beyond the Southern Alps are those of the Haast Range, 100 miles (160km) south of Cook. This is another heavily glaciated group and is very popular despite difficult access. Mount Aspiring is the highest peak, perhaps the most dramatic in New Zealand, and its perfect icy fang has been dubbed the 'Matterhorn of the South'. The classic North-East and South-West Ridges are of little difficulty while the South Face is one of the great modern ice-climbs.

Further south the mountainous block of Fjordland, deeply cut by fjords and narrow lakes, contains several ranges. The finest is the Darrans, a host of granite peaks which offer the best alpine rock-climbing in the Antipodes with routes up to 5,000ft (1,520m) in length. There are sizable glaciers and some major snow- and ice-climbs on Mount Tutoko, the highest peak, and elsewhere. Mitre Peak, a seemingly inviolate spearhead rising sheer from the fjord, dominates lovely Milford Sound, a mecca for hardy tourists and hikers. Although relatively small, it is perhaps the best known of the Darrans and its summit can be reached by an easy scramble on its hidden East Ridge. There is much potential in the area, but, except close to Milford Sound, access through dense forest and across wild rivers is extremely difficult and the rainfall is over 300in (118cm)! It is not for nothing that New Zealand climbers have earned a reputation for toughness as well as for their proficiency on steep ice.

Situation: New Zealand—South Island

Most Important Peaks

1 Mount Cook (12,349/3,764) 1894: Tom Fyfe, George Graham, Jack Clarke
2 Mount Tasman (11,475/3,498) 1895: E. A. Fitzgerald, Jack Clarke with Matthias Zurbriggen
6 Mount Hicks (10,443/3,183) 1906: Reverend H. E. Newton, R. S. Low and Alex Graham
7 Malte Brun (10,421/3,176) 1894: Tom Fyfe—solo
10 Mount Sefton (10,359/3,157) 1895: E. A. Fitzgerald, Matthias Zurbriggen
12 Mount Elie de Beaumont (10,200/3,109) 1906: H. Sillem and Peter Graham
13 Mount Douglas (10,107/3,081) 1907: E. Teichelmann, Reverend H. E. Newton and Alex Graham

Haast Range

Mount Aspiring (9,959/3,036) 1909: Jack Clarke, Alex Graham and B. Head
Mount Earnshaw (9,250/2,819) 1914: H. F. Wright and J. Robertson

Darrans

Mount Tutoko (9,042/2,756) 1919: Peter Graham and Samuel Turner
Mitre Peak (5,560/1,695)

Major Passes

Arthurs Pass (3,022/921) usually taken as the northern limit of the Southern Alps. Crossed by main road and railway linking Christchurch to Greymouth and the West Coast
Haast Pass (1,716/523)—the southern limit of the

Southern Alps, crossed by the main highway linking the Otago and south east to Westland

Major Glaciers

Tasman Glacier is over 18 miles (29km) long and the Murchison and Godley Glaciers are each about 11 miles (18km) long.

The Fox and the Franz Joseph Glaciers, while only 8 miles (13km) long, are remarkable in that they flow from approximately 10,000ft (3,050m) to nearly 700ft (213m)

Convenient Centres

The chief centre for the Southern Alps is The Hermitage (2,500/760), nowadays a roadhead complex of hotels, motels, hostels and tourist facilities. Here also is situated the headquarters of the Mount Cook National Park. There is also a campground and there are hotels near the snouts of the Fox and Franz Joseph Glaciers, west of the Divide

Huts

There are more than twenty huts in the Mount Cook Westland National Parks mostly owned by the Parks Service

Access

Virtually all of the Mount Cook region is contained within the 173,000 acre Mount Cook National Park. Elsewhere important mountain areas are contained in the larger Mount Aspiring and Fjordland National Parks. Small parks in other mountain areas are the Arthurs Pass National Park and the Nelson Lakes National Park. National Park regulations are minimal.

There is an international airport at Christchurch and Mount Cook Airlines runs a regular service between Christchurch, Mount Cook and Queenstown. There are also regular services in to Milford Sound. Otherwise access is by road and a good bus service connects Christchurch to the Mount Cook Hermitage

Guide Books

One volume by Mavis Davidson covers Mount Cook and a further volume covers Mount Aspiring

Maps

Maps are available at one-inch scale

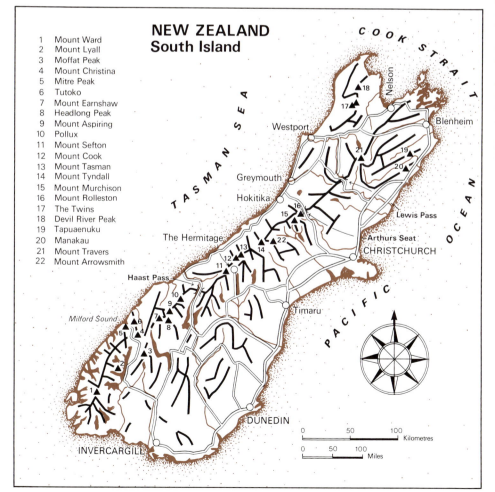

NEW ZEALAND South Island

1 Mount Ward
2 Mount Lyall
3 Moffat Peak
4 Mount Christina
5 Mitre Peak
6 Tutoko
7 Mount Earnshaw
8 Headlong Peak
9 Mount Aspiring
10 Pollux
11 Mount Sefton
12 Mount Cook
13 Mount Tasman
14 Mount Tyndall
15 Mount Murchison
16 Mount Rolleston
17 The Twins
18 Devil River Peak
19 Tapuaenuku
20 Manakau
21 Mount Travers
22 Mount Arrowsmith

Asia

Turkey—camp beneath the northern flank of Geliasin (13,674ft/4,168m) the highest summit of Resko in the Cilo Dag mountains of Kurdistan in the far south-east. The North Face rises nearly 4,000 feet above the glacier. There is excellent climbing in this lush and beautiful region

Turkestan

The Persians called it 'The Roof of the World'—this complex of high and icy mountains standing athwart the ancient trade-routes to China. Rising from the frontiers of Russia, China, Pakistan and Afghanistan, the Pamirs are, in fact, the knot from which radiate the great mountain chains of Asia—the Hindu Kush, the Himalaya, the Karakorum, the Kun Lun and the Tien Shan. Because they separate Russian and Chinese Turkestan, and because both ranges are normally reached from Russia, it is convenient to consider the Pamirs and the Tien Shan together in one chapter.

The Pamirs

The Pamirs occupy a bleak area, some 200 miles square (320 km sq), round the headwaters of the Oxus and form the watershed between the Sea of Aral and the Takla Makan desert. Strictly speaking a 'pamir' is a broad mountain valley, and a series of such pamirs, trending west to east, divide the mountains into roughly parallel groups. Several of these pamirs contain narrow lakes, one of which—Oz Zorkul—is famed as the principal source of the Oxus. Heavy snowfall on the high mountains nourishes huge glaciers, but the pamirs themselves are desolate and arid, peopled only by wandering Kirgiz nomads with their flocks. Only in the north west has irrigation brought cultivation. Abundant wildlife includes the elusive snow leopard, wolf, bear and *ovis poli*—a large mountain sheep named after Marco Polo who first described them on his journey through the Pamirs, following the silk-road, in 1273.

Both Russian and British explorers probed the region during the late nineteenth century, while playing the 'Great Game'. Today's frontiers were drawn by the 1896 Boundary Commission which created the 'Wakhan Corridor' as a buffer zone between the two empires. The very highest Pamir peaks, rising from the easternmost group, remained in Sinkiang, and little is known of them since Shipton, Tilman and Gyalzen Sherpa all but reached the summit of Muztagh Ata in 1947. Earlier explorers Sven Hedin and Sir Aurel Stein had attempted this conspicuous peak in 1894 and 1900. The Qungur massif is an icy dome but subsidiary peaks to the north west are spectacular and sharp, rising above verdant pastures and forested slopes.

Most of the Pamir peaks lie in Russia and first to be climbed was Lenin; despite its impressive North Face, a rounded and unattractive mountain. Rising steeply above the Alay valley it is easily accessible and its summit is certainly the most frequented of any big mountain in

the world. Most of the numerous routes are easy and in recent years the Russians have organized international climbing meets in the area.

Pik Communism, some 60 miles (96km) away, is rather less accessible. Massive and craggy, it bears a network of

over fifteen climbs reminiscent of the Alps and remarkable for a giant of Himalayan proportions. The 'Georgian Couloir' route of 1955, from the south west, was climbed by a British party in 1962 who found it long and tedious but not difficult. They took ten days to the summit from a base camp at 8,000ft (2,440m) 30 miles (48km) distant. There are some difficult routes on the formidable South Face, but the rock is poor.

Among the surrounding high peaks the British party also climbed Pik Patriot and Pik Garmo. It was while descending the latter that the well-known climbers Wilfred Noyce and Robin Smith were killed.

Great traverses are a feature of Russian mountaineering and in 1969 a notable one was made crossing Piks Garmo, Patriot, Russia, Communism and Pamir—over 10 miles (16km), continuously above 20,000ft (6,100m).

There are yet more high groups to the south where, close to the Afghan border, Piks Karl Marx and Engels have given good climbs and traverses. There would seem to be plenty of scope for both easy and difficult climbing if western alpinists were allowed free access to the Pamirs.

Tien Shan

For travellers on the old silk-road from Turfan to Kashgar—some 700 miles (1,126km) along the fringes of the great Takla Makan desert—the long crest of the Tien Shan formed a continuous backdrop of snowy summits across the northern horizon. The highest peaks are concentrated in a small area near the middle of this long chain, whose name in Chinese means the Celestial Mountains. Eastwards they stretch deep into China, still well glaciated and with summits rising to 19,000ft (5,800m), while westwards they break into several lower parallel groups. Their rivers are doomed; not one ever reaches the ocean, for they are swallowed up either by the deserts to the south, the salty lakes of Kazakhstan or the Aral Sea.

Although rising from extremely arid country, the mountains receive heavy snowfalls and frequent storms. As a result the slopes below the snowline are clothed with flowery meadows and fine forests of juniper and spruce, while massive glaciers gather on the upper slopes. Long and tedious approaches and savage gorges guard entry to the high central peaks and Khan Tengri is nearly 100 miles (160km) from human habitation. For many years this gigantic icy pyramid—'Prince of Spirits' in Khirgiz—was thought to be the highest point in the range. It was eventually climbed by a straightforward snow-route on the 3,000ft (914m) West Ridge. Among more recent routes on this imposing peak are the superb South-West or 'Marble' Buttress, climbed in 1964, and the long traverse from Pik Saladin over Pik Shater, both of them 6,000m (19,700ft) peaks, completed in 1968.

It was not suspected until 1932 that an even higher summit might exist deeper into the range and not until 1946, when at last the 'Marble Wall'—Marmornaya Stena—was climbed, that its location was finally confirmed. After several attempts Pik Pobeda—'Victory Peak'—was climbed by a thirteen-man summit party via the great North-East Spur, using a succession of snow-caves to sit out the frequent storms. The second highest mountain in the USSR, Pobeda is a massive dome, not unlike Mont Blanc when seen from the north. Like the other high peaks, it is liberally hung with ice, but the rock is typically poor and slaty. The most settled weather is in late August and September, but by then it is already cold and unconsolidated snow is an ever-present hazard.

The smaller western peaks are jagged, icy and alpine in character and rise to their highest point in Pik Talgar (16,460ft/5,017m) above the city of Alma Ata. Access to this beautiful region is not difficult; there are many fine summits above 12,000ft and Russian climbers are very active hereabouts. A notable summit is Free Korea Peak (15,750ft/4,800m) on which new routes were made in 1976 by a strong party of American climbers on an exchange visit. The steep 3,000ft (914m) northern ice-face was climbed solo in four and a half hours by Henry Barber, a style of climbing not permitted to Russian mountaineers.

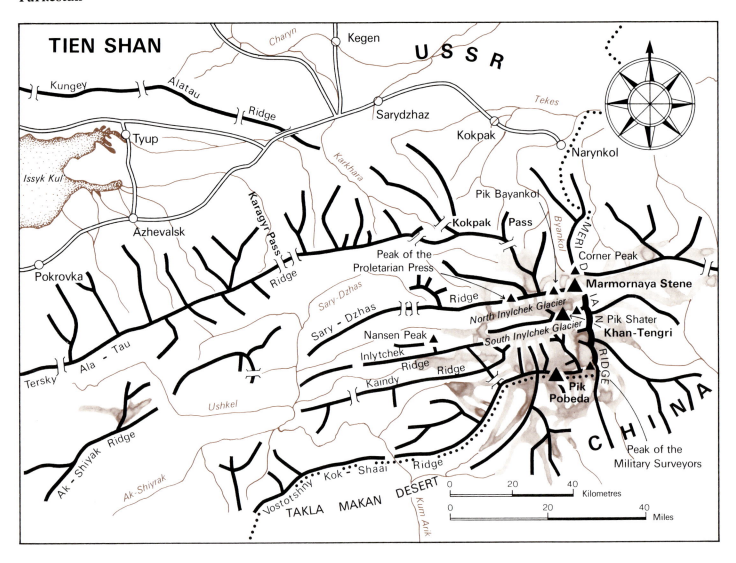

TIEN SHAN

Kungey

Alatau

Ridge

Charyn

Kegen

USSR

Tekes

Tyup

Issyk Kul

Sarydzhaz

Kokpak

Narynkol

Karkhara

Azhevalsk

Pik Bayankol

Kokpak **Pass**

Byankol

Corner Peak

Karagyr Pass

Pokrovka

Peak of the Proletarian Press

Marmornaya Stene

Ridge

Ridge

Sary - Dzhas

North Inylchek Glacier

Pik Shater

Khan-Tengri

Sary - Dzhas

Nansen Peak

South Inylchek Glacier

Ala - Tau

Inlytchek

Ridge

Ridge

Tersky

Kaindy

Ridge

Pik Pobeda

CHINA

Ushkel

Ak - Shiyak Ridge

Ak-Shiyrak

Kok - Shaai

Ridge

Peak of the Military Surveyors

Vostotshny

TAKLA MAKAN DESERT

Kum Arik

| 0 | 20 | 40 | Kilometres |

| 0 | 20 | 40 | Miles |

Distant Qungar (Kungur Tagh) in the Kashgar Range, seen from the North-East Spur of Pik Lenin

Situation: USSR—Tadzhik, Kirgiz and Kazakhstan SSR's; China—Sinkiang Autonomous Region; Afghanistan—marginally in Wakhan

Major Peaks

Soviet Pamirs
1 Peak of Communism (lately Pik Stalin) (24,551/7,483) 1933: Vitali Abalakov, solo
2 Pik Lenin (23,406/7,134) 1928: K. Wien, E. Allwein, E. Schneider
3 Pik Evgenia Korzhenevskaya (23,310/7,105) 1953: A. Ugarov and party
Pik Revolution (22,924/6,987) 1954: A. Ugarov and party
Pik MarshaL Zhukov (lately Moscow-Peking) (22,480/6,852)
Pik Karl Marx (22,068/6,726) 1946: Vitali Abalakov, A. Sikorenko and Y. Ivanov
Pik Garmo (21,637/6,595)

Chinese Pamirs—the 'Kashgar' or Muztagh Ata' Range
1 Qungur II (Kungur Tagh) (25,325/7,719)
2 Qungur I (Kungur Tjube Tagh) (24,919/7,595) 1956: K. Kuzmins Sino-Russian expedition
3 Muztagh Ata (24,758/7,546) 1956: three members of E. A. Beletsky's Sino-Russian expedition
4 Chakragil (22,071/6,727)

Tien Shan

1 Pik Pobeda (24,407/7,439) 1956: Vitali Abalakov's large party

2 Khan-Tengri (22,949/6,995) 1931: M. T. Pogrebetsky's expedition

Marmornaya Stena (21,051/6,416) 1946: A. Letavet's expedition

Some Major Glaciers

Fedchenko Glacier (Russian Pamirs) about 45 miles (72km) in length and its system, with tributaries, covers some 600 square miles (965sq km)

Great Inylchek Glacier (Tien Shan) is over 37 miles (60km) long and there are other glaciers of similar length in the Tien Shan

Some Important Passes

Pamirs

Sary Tash (c11,000/3,350) crossed by a modern motor road of sorts and is the high point between the Alay Valley and the Kashgar Valley. The frontier between Russia and Sinkiang lies well down on the east side

Neza Tash or Shindi Pass (14,920/4,548) crosses the high frontier between the Russian Oksur valley and the village of Tash Kurghan in Sinkiang

Wakhjir Pass (15,600/4,755) links the 'Little Pamir' valley of Wakhan to the Taghdumbash Pamir of Sinkiang—an old trail

Mintaka Pass (15,450/4,709) (see Karakorum chapter) links Hunza valley of Pakistan to the Taghdumbash Pamir of Sinkiang and is crossed by a modern motorable road

Tien Shan

Torugart Pass (c12,000/3,660) situated at the western end of the chain and is crossed by a modern road of sorts and links Frunze in the USSR with Kashgar in Sinkiang

Guide-books, Bibliography and Maps

The only obtainable map to the Pamirs is the Czechoslovak WA 1:500,000 *kammkarte*.

A brief resumé of routes on Pik Communism, illustrated with a series of 'topos' and a *kammkarte*, is published in *AJ* 1973.

A *kammkarte* of the Pik Lenin region is published in *AJ* 1968.

Several articles may be found in *AJ* and *Mountain World* (Swiss Foundation for Alpine Research, Allen and Unwin) 60-61 66-67

Access

To climb in the USSR it is first necessary to acquire an official invitation of some kind (see Caucasus chapter). Climbing is strictly regimented and rules govern what may be climbed, when and by whom.

The Tien Shan may be reached by flying from Moscow to either Alma Arta or Frunze and thereafter travelling by road. Nowadays it is usual to approach the high mountain glaciers of the central region by helicopter from the nearest roadhead, thus avoiding over 50 miles (80km) of difficult approaches.

In the Pamirs Pik Lenin is usually reached by flying from Moscow to Osch from where a road journey of some 150 miles (240km) leads to the Alay valley. One flies to Dushanbe for onward travel to the Pik Communism region. In the latter case helicopters are often used to ferry climbers and equipment to a base camp on the Garmo Glacier or elsewhere, thus avoiding long and tedious marches

Hindu Kush

Springing south west from the Pamir 'knot', the Hindu Kush walls the wide Punjab from the deserts of Turkestan, parting the waters of the Oxus from the Indus. It was, until recent times, the divide between the empires of Asia Minor and the historic civilizations of India. When Alexander crossed the range in 328 BC his Greek soldiers dubbed it Parapamisus—'the mountains over which no eagle can fly'—but its present name is Persian. According to Afghan tradition it means 'Hindu killer' because so many Indian slaves perished in its snows. Certainly both Genghis Khan and Tamerlane travelled its passes. More probably 'Kush' is a corruption of 'Kuh' meaning simply 'mountain'.

As a mountain range the Hindu Kush is considered to extend from the Wakhjir Pass, at the junction of the Pamirs and the Karakorum, to the Khwak Pass, north of Kabul—as the crow flies nearly 300 miles (480km). Beyond, to the south west, the mountains shrink and, losing their glaciers and alpine character, fan out into central Afghanistan. It is an arid range where searing summer heat alternates with bitterly cold and snowbound winters. Dusty brown valleys are ringed by hills rising towards the eternal snows: a major feature of the landscape is the absence of any forest or alpine zone. This harsh landscape is relieved only by irrigation: groves of poplars and plane trees, green fields and orchards of apples, apricots and mulberries surround every small village. The region is inhabited by fiercely independent tribes, and those on the Pakistani side of the frontier were mostly semi-autonomous in the days of the Raj. Some areas are almost isolated, and in the valleys of Nuristan for instance, supposedly peopled by descendants of Alexander's stragglers, an ancient pagan religion has persisted in a country otherwise entirely Muslim.

Except to a few courageous explorers travelling in disguise, the 'pundit' surveyors and other operatives in the 'Great Game', the Hindu Kush was unknown and forbidden territory to Europeans. Even after the second Afghan War, in 1880, when the British commenced to map the country, any access was fraught with danger. Surveyors ascended several minor summits and, in the 1920s and '30s, even attempted Tirich Mir and Istor-o-Nal, but serious mountaineering did not start until the 1950s when the Norwegians reached the top of the highest peak. Then came a flood of expeditions, large and small, of many nationalities. With other high Asian ra-

nges often closed for political reasons, the Hindu Kush had much to offer. Hundreds of fine peaks, though not always of good rock—usually settled weather throughout the summer, minimal bureaucratic hurdles (as they go), and easy access particularly overland, enabled small parties, often climbing alpine-style, to challenge large mountains on a low budget. In recent years, however, things have changed. Too many climbers, too much tourism and natural greed have, at the time of writing, conspired to make climbing in more popular areas of the Hindu Kush extremely expensive. No doubt the wheel will eventually turn full circle.

The Hindu Kush divides neatly into three separate regions. The eastern extends from the Wakhjir Pass some 200 miles (320km) to the Dorah Pass, with the Pakistani-Afghan frontier following its crest. At first the mountains separate the desolate Whakan from Hunza and, rising to about 18,000ft (5,480m), are rounded and generally uninteresting. Long rocky spurs leading down into Hunza do, however, offer some mountaineering potential, besides cradling the long Batura Glacier. After 50 miles (80km) a major ridge breaks southwards to become the Hindu Raj (see below) and the main chain now divides the Whakan from the narrow Chitral valley. After the Baroghil Pass the crest rises, culminating in a cluster of high snow-peaks reminiscent of the western Karakorum. Here are found some twenty '7000 metre' (22,970ft) summits and a host of mountains only slightly smaller. The region is heavily glaciated, but most ice lies on the eastern flanks where a complex of subsidiary ridges bears many of the higher peaks. Most of them are not particularly difficult to climb—technically—and nearly all hold several routes. Tirich Mir, a series of rocky, ice-hung pyramids, dominates the area. A notable climb was the ascent of Tirich North (23,150ft/7,056m) by the North Spur—a 6,000ft (1,830m) route on ice and good granite—made by Kurt Diemberger's three-man party in 1965. Handsome Noshaq, too, has several tops along its almost horizontal snow-crest and a steep, craggy 3,000ft (914m) North Face. The mountain was climbed on skis in 1970 by an Austrian team who enjoyed a descent run of nearly 10,000ft (3,050m), and seven years later by Dina Serbova, a Czech lady who made a solo journey all the way from Kabul to the summit!

Beyond the Dorah Pass, the western

Hindu Kush lies entirely in Afghanistan. Long subsidiary ridges running north and south from its contorted crest carry many of the more important summits which are rather lower than those of Chitral. This is an ideal area for alpine-style climbing on routes of all standards. In 1973 Pete Boardman's four-man party climbed Kuh-e-Mondi—a peak not unlike the Grandes Jorasses and the highest in Nuristan—by one of the two huge rock buttresses on its 5,000ft (1,524m) North Face. This was a four-and-a-half-day alpine-style climb which they graded ED. There is a straightforward route on the East Ridge and many other good lines on this mountain; the expedition also climbed five sur-

rounding peaks by more regular one-day routes. This is now no longer a virgin area, but there is scope for new and demanding climbs.

The third region, the Hindu Raj, lies entirely in Pakistan. Strictly speaking it is not part of the Hindu Kush, but, as it is the other major 'trans-Indus' chain, most authorities consider the two together. For 150 miles (240km) it parallels the Hindu Kush, forming the eastern rampart of the Chitral valley and throwing down its own important spurs into Swat and Kohistan. The valley of Swat is especially beautiful, containing both forests and the ruins of the fortress of Undegram, razed by Alexander, besides supporting a large population. Kohistan faces the Nanga Parbat massif across the Indus. The Hindu Raj mountains are high, shapely and icy and, although Longstaff had drawn attention to their potential in 1916, climbers did not visit them until some forty years later. Conspicuous Buni Zom was long considered the highest peak and not until the late 1960s were impressive Koyo Zom and the two sharp Thui peaks identified. Solitary Thui II is said to be the most beautiful mountain in either the Hindu Kush or the Hindu Raj and was finally climbed only in 1978 after three previous British attempts. However, it is only one of many challenges to be found in this rewarding, but still comparatively little-known, chain.

Noshaq—little was known of this handsome peak before 1960 when it was climbed by both Japanese and Polish parties. Since then it has been visited often and climbed by a variety of routes; in the summer of 1977 it was soloed by a Czech lady climber

Hindu Kush

Nuristan—the twin peaks of Kuh-e-Morusq and Kuh-e-Marchor, from high on Berast Shara

Peaks and glaciers of the Hindu Raj, seen here from the north east across the Yarkhun Valley from the slopes of the Hindu Kush near the Boroghil Pass. Koyo Zom is the dominating peak in the centre; to its right is Thui I; on the left is the Chatiboi Glacier; on the right the Koyo Glacier. Pechus hot springs are seen in the immediate centre foreground

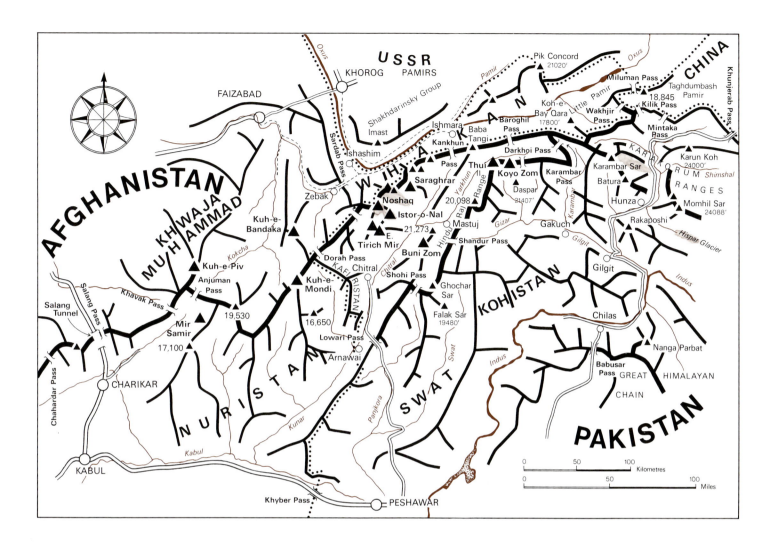

Situation: Afghanistan and the Republic of Pakistan

Most Important Peaks

1 Tirich Mir (25,263/7,700) 1950: Arne Naess, P. Kvernberg, H. Berg and Tony Streather—a Norwegian expedition
Tirich Mir East (25,236/7,692) 1964: R. Hoibakk and A. Opdal—a Norweigan expedition
2 Noshaq (24,581/7,492) 1960: Professor Sakato's Japanese expedition
3 Istor-o-Nal (24,271/7,398) 1955: possibly J. E. Murphey and T. A. Mutch (USA). Certainly 1969: J. M. Anglada's Spanish expedition
4 Saraghrar (24,110/7,349) 1959: Fosco Maraini's Italian expedition
Kuh-e-Bandaka (22,450/6,843) 1960: W. von Hansemann, D. Hasse, S. Heine, H. Winkler
Kuh-e-Mondi (20,500/6,248) 1962: S. Ziegler's German expedition
Mir Samir (19,879/6,059) 1959: Harald Biller's German expedition
Kuh-e-Piv (19,016/5,796) 1963: A. von Hillebrand's German expedition

Hindu Raj

Koyo Zom (22,603/6,889) 1968: Dr Stamm's Austrian expedition
Buni Zom (21,493/6,551) 1957: W. K. Berry and C. H. Tyndale-Biscoe (NZ)
Thui II (21,404/6,524) 1978: N. Tritton, C. Griffiths and C. Lloyd

Major Glaciers

Both the Udren-Darban, or Atrak, System and the Upper Tirich System are about 17 miles (27km) long

Most Important Passes

Wakhjir Pass (16,152/4,923) and Kilik Pass (15,600/4,755) together mark the eastern limit of the Hindu Kush, the first the boundary with the Pamirs, the second with the Karakorum. Both cross into China, the former from Afghanistan's Wakhan, the latter from Pakistan's Hunza. Both are crossed by ancient trails
Karambar Pass (15,830/4,824) this separates the Hindu Raj from the Hindu Kush. An old trail links the head of Chitral's Yarkhun river to the Karambar river of Gilgit
Baroghil Pass (12,457/3,797) an old crossing of the main Hindu Kush from Chitral to Wakhan
Dorah Pass (14,940/4,554) a direct crossing of the main Hindu Kush, it marks the boundary between east and west Hindu Kush
Khavak Pass (11,640/3,548) the western limit of the 'alpine' Hindu Kush; an ancient track crossed by Alexander and Tamerlane
Darkhoi Pass (15,013/4,576) an important crossing of the Hindu Raj
Shandur Pass (12,210/3,722) a useful crossing of Hindu Raj from Ghizar river of Gilgit to Chitral
Lowari Pass (10,000/3,050) this traverses the tail end of the Hindu Raj—the only motor road into Chitral from Pakistan. Hair-raising!

Guide-books and Bibliography

Himalayan Odyssey by Trevor Braham (George Allen & Unwin, 1974) and *The Himalaya* by Nigel Nicolson (Time-Life Books, 1975).

Also the *Alpine Journal* and the *Himalaya Journal*. The *AJ* for November 1966 (No 313) and the privately published report of the 1967 Midlands Hindu Kush expedition are both useful

Maps

The Japanese ITY *kammkarte* maps to scale 1:1300,000 and 1:200,000 are now difficult to obtain. Various localized maps are published in relevant issues of *AJ, HJ*, etc

Access

Permission is required for expeditionary mountaineering in both Pakistan and Afghanistan.

Kabul may be reached fairly easily overland from Europe and special vehicles are not necessary. The northern flank of the western Hindu Kush can be approached quite closely by overland vehicles

The Pakistani flank, Chitral, may also be approached by road as far as Chitral town and thereafter jeeps may be hired for closer approach to the mountains.

There is an international airport at Rawalpindi (Islamabad) and regular flights, weather permitting, from Peshawar into Chitral

Karakorum

Karakorum—the name comes from the ancient and important pass at the far north-eastern extremity of this complex chain of mountains. It means, in Turkish, 'Black Rubble'—an unfortunate misnomer for one of the most glittering and icy ranges on earth.

Strictly speaking this is a trans-Himalayan range, parallel to—yet not part of—the main Himalayan crest whose far western end, the Punjab Himalaya, lies south across the Indus. For some 250 miles (400km) the Karakorum forms the geographic and political frontier between the Indian subcontinent and Central Asia, stretching into the heart of the great mountain knot where Russia, China, Afghanistan and Pakistan meet on the Little Pamir. These are truly mountains beyond mountains. Karakorum waters drain either south to the Indus or northwards to the Yarkand, to be lost in the arid wastes of Sinkiang.

Rising above the largest glaciers in the temperate zones are long avenues of peaks, hundreds of them, only the higher or more eye-catching named or climbed. Nineteen tower above 25,000ft (7,600m) while the six that top 26,000ft (8,000m) cluster within 15 miles (24km) at the head of the Baltoro Glacier. Swift and enormous uplift—apparently some

5,000ft (1,520m) since the last ice age and still taking place—has given the Karakorum peaks their typically sharp and bold forms, forms unlike those of the main Himalaya. Many of the great angular and icy peaks are limestone, but around them cluster a proliferation of towers and spires hewn from granite and gneiss, many of them major peaks in their own right.

The valleys are dry and arid semi-desert with an average rainfall of less than 10in (25cm) a year, for the monsoon is spent before it reaches here. But at greater altitude the winter snowfall is high and irrigation from the summer rivers, flush with melt-water, nurtures oases green with barley and poplar and apricot groves. The natives, hardy and independent by nature, are mostly

Over five miles (8km) high, its ridges hung with tumbling ice, K2, the world's second highest mountain, rears above the Godwin-Austen Glacier. The South Face is seen here from Concordia with the East Shoulder and the Abruzzi Spur on the right, and the West Ridge on the left skyline. The Angelus (22,490ft/6,857m) is the lovely snow peak on left

on the climbing for itself.

K2, the second highest mountain in the world, towers in apparent isolation 12,000ft (3,650m) above Concordia, the wide glacier sanctuary at the head of the Baltoro. Its true height is uncertain for the 1974 Pakistan Survey computed it at 28,741ft (8,760m), only two rope lengths less than Everest, and nearly 500ft (150m) higher than that generally accepted. Its great angular pyramid of rock and ice throws down six steep ridges or spurs, only that on the south east, known as the Abruzzi Spur since the Duke reached 22,000ft (6,700m) on it in 1909, seeming to offer a reasonably straightforward line. It is in fact the line of most of the ten attempts on K2 and was climbed by both the Italians in 1954 and the huge Japanese party of 1977. As early as 1902 Eckenstein and Crowley made a bold attempt on the difficult North-East Ridge which later only narrowly beat the gallant Poles in 1976. In 1975 the large American expedition reached only 22,000ft (6,700m) on the North-West Ridge but returned in 1978 to succeed on the North East Ridge. K2's Northern Flank is said to be 'appalling'.

A beautiful cone of ice and rock masked by its more conspicuous neighbours, Hidden Peak was the scene of a major breakthrough in high-altitude mountaineering in 1975. Reinhold Messner and Peter Habeler made the second ascent by the virgin and difficult North-West Face, climbing alpine-style with three bivouacs. It was a bold concept on a very big mountain and sets a style for the future. The original route, several miles in length, was from the south.

Broad Peak is the enormous triple-headed 'Breithorn of the Baltoro' while the three Gasherbrums close by seem from afar to block the head of the glacier. Gasherbrum means 'shining wall' and this refers to the 10,000ft (3,050m) pale limestone walls of the great trapeze-shaped Gasherbrum IV, a difficult climb. Gasherbrum III is a savage rock peak and Gasherbrum II a sharp-edged pyramid.

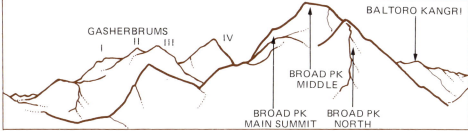

Baltis, a basically Caucasian people who speak an archaic Tibetan dialect. But in Hunza, in the far north west, the inhabitants are Aryan and the fair hair of many is said to trace their descent to the soldiers of Alexander the Great who once passed this way. With a long tradition of quarrelling and raiding, it was not until 1892 that Pax Britannica came to the Karakorum.

The mountaineering history of the region is, of necessity, closely connected with its exploration and survey and with the 'Great Game'. The story is rich and fascinating and only a few of its more important figures can be mentioned here. It starts with the journeys of Godwin-Austen and his colleagues in the Survey of India of the 1860s. Younghusband, having crossed the Gobi Desert, traversed the forgotten Muztagh Pass, from the north, in 1887, and later explored the approaches to K2. Martin Conway led the first climbing expedition to the Baltoro, Hispar and Biafo Glaciers in 1892, followed by the Americans, Dr and Mrs Workman, who made seven major Karakorum journeys between 1898 and 1912, making a number of minor ascents. In 1908 the ubiquitous Duke of the Abruzzi made a comprehensive reconnaissance of K2, mapped the complete Baltoro head, and almost reached the summit of Chogolisa (25,110ft/7,650m). The same year Longstaff's party located and explored the mysterious Siachen Glacier. There were still major gaps to be filled in by Kenneth Mason, the Duke of Spoleto, Eric Shipton and others in the 1920s and '30s. Meanwhile expeditions by many nationalities were already concentrating

Karakorum

Lower down the Baltoro, Masherbrum and the Muztagh Tower are especially notable. The former appears from the north as a great rock tooth rising from a steep cone of ice and is one of the most striking of the Karakorum peaks. In 1938 Hodgkin and Harrison got high on the mountain from the south east and narrowly survived a fierce storm, while in 1957 Whillans and Walmsley were forced back only 300ft (90m) from the summit by terrible snow conditions. The eventual ascent seems to have been more gruelling than difficult. The climbs on the seemingly impossible rock obelisk of the Muztagh Tower were an earlier breakthrough in lightweight expeditioning. Made famous by Vittorio Sella's picture, taken on the 1908 Abruzzi expedition, the peak had fascinated climbers for forty years. A few days after the four-man British team reached the summit by the North-West Ridge, a four-man French party succeeded from the south east. Neither climb proved desperately difficult.

Other famous landmarks along the lower Baltoro include the Trango Towers, of which the most elegant, the 20,500ft (6,250m) Nameless Tower, was climbed by a British team in 1976, after 4,000ft (1,220m) of extremely difficult rock-climbing. Others are Paiju Peak (21,653ft/6,602m), a tiered tower of ice and red granite, climbed the same year by a Pakistani-American party, and the gothic and wing-shaped Grand Cathedral (19,245ft/5,866m) which succumbed to the Italians in 1975.

Generally lower than the peaks above the other four great Karakorum glaciers, the Biafo peaks are less well known but equally challenging. Rows of complicated rock peaks hold walls and ridges of uncompromising steepness and promise to be prime targets for 'big wall' style climbs in the near future. Especially formidable are the row of Latok Peaks and the difficult Ogre, scene of Doug Scott's epic descent, with both legs broken, after its first ascent in 1977.

Beyond mysterious 30 square mile (48sq km) Snow Lake the Hispar Glacier leads down towards the Hunza river. Here are several large snow and ice peaks, less upstanding, but no less impressive than the Baltoro giants.

Disteghil Sar bears a massive jumble

Gasherbrum IV and Hidden Peak, from the top of the Trango Towers

of ice on its wide southern flank while Kunyang Kish is a savage and dangerous icy hulk. Beautiful Trivor (25,330ft/7,720m) was climbed by Wilfred Noyce in 1960.

Nearly 19,000ft (5,800m) above the Hunza river stands the bastion of Rakaposhi. A conspicuous pyramid dominating the Gilgit area, it was a major prize for Banks's team who climbed the lengthy and snowy South-West Ridge. The long crest extending south east is known as the Lesser Karakorum, a name with little meaning in this context, as the crest contains other major peaks. The Malubiting Group (Malubiting West—24,451ft/7,453m) contains several and Haramosh, its long ridges lording the great bend of the Indus and the scene of the 1957 tragedy so well documented in *Last Blue Mountain*, is another.

Grouped along the Siachen Glacier and the Nubra River, the mountains of the Eastern Karakorum are almost impossible to reach for political reasons at the time of writing. Saltoro Kangri (25,400ft/7,740m), actually attempted by the Workmans in 1912, was climbed by a Japanese party in 1962, and is the highest in the region. There are several peaks here over 24,000ft (7,300m) and still virgin.

Much has been done in the Karakorum, but much still remains to be done. There are new and extremely demanding routes aplenty on the great mountains and opportunities for challenging climbs in the modern idiom on a myriad small and usually virgin peaks. And, for the hardy mountain traveller, the Karakorum offers perhaps the most spectacular trekking in the world.

Above: **Muztagh Tower, often likened to the Matterhorn, seen here from the south east, looking up the Younghusband (Biange) Glacier. The South-East Ridge (climbed by the French in 1956) is on the right; the British first ascent that same year followed the North-West Ridge**

Opposite above: **Hispar Karakorum. The unclimbed North-West Face of Kunyang Kish, taken from the lower slopes of Disteghil Sar. The North Ridge is on the left; the West Ridge on the right; the Khiang Glacier in the foreground**

Right: **Gothic granite of the Lower Baltoro. The view from Urdukas looking due west down the Baltoro Glacier. Shapely Paiju is on the left, and to the right of centre lies the rock pinnacle of Uli Biaho. The Trango Towers massif is on the extreme right**

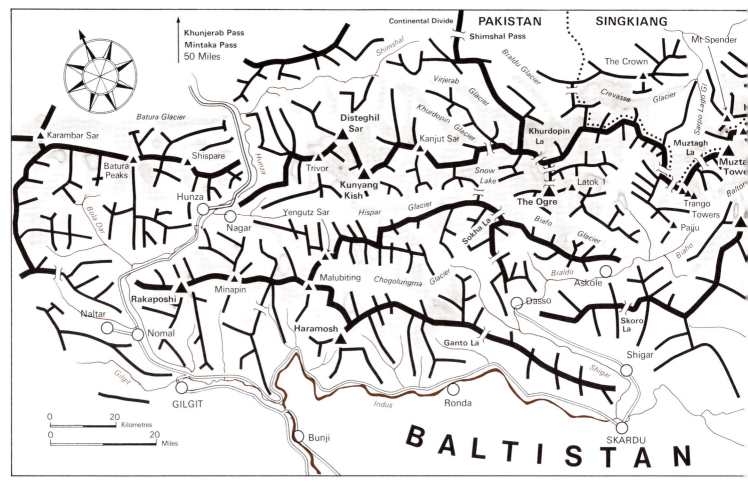

General view of Rakaposhi and the Biro Glacier from the west. The South-West Spur and Ridge, climbed by Mike Banks and Tom Patey in 1958, takes the right-hand skyline (continuing out of the picture)

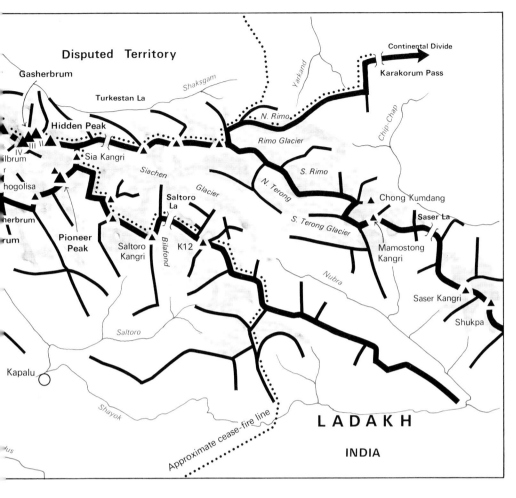

Disputed Territory

Gasherbrum
Turkestan La
Shaksgam
Hidden Peak
N. Rimo
Sia Kangri
Rimo Glacier
IV III
Ibrum
Siachen
Glacier
N. Terong
S. Rimo
hogolisa
Saltoro
La
Chong Kumdang
herbrum
Pioneer
Peak
Saltoro
Kangri
Bilafond
K12
S. Terong Glacier
Saser La
Mamostong
Kangri
Nubra
Saser Kangri
Saltoro
Shukpa
Kapalu
Shayok
Yarkand
Chip-Chap
Continental Divide
Karakorum Pass
Approximate cease-fire line

LADAKH
INDIA

Major Glaciers
The Hispar-Biafo System measures 62 miles (100km) snout to snout over the Hispar Pass. The Siachen Glacier is 44 miles (70km) long while both Baltoro and Batura are some 35 miles (56km) long

Major Passes
Mintaka La (15,450/4,709) an old trade route into Central Asia linking Gilgit to Kashgar, over the Pakistani-Chinese frontier watershed
Khunjerab La (16,187/4,934) crossed by the new Pakistani-Chinese Karakorum military road
Shimshal La (15,535/4,735) an old trade route over the watershed linking Hunza to the Shaksgam and Yarkand rivers of Sinkiang
Muztagh La (17,782/5,420) a glacier pass, an old trade route long abandoned because of glacier changes between the Baltoro and Shaksgam over the frontier watershed. Since replaced by the 'New' Muztagh La at the head of the Panmah Glacier, which is impassable by animals
Saltoro La (18,200/5,547) an old glacier-pass linking the lower Shayok river of Baltistan with the Siachen Glacier basin
Saser La (17,480/5,328) an old and important trade route linking Baltistan and the lower Shayok as well as Ladakh with the Upper Shayok and the Karakorum Pass
Karakorum Pass (18,605/5,671) an historic caravan road into Central Asia, linking Kashmir to Sinkiang. Said to have been crossed by Genghis Khan. Crosses the Chinese frontier and the continental watershed and is taken as the Eastern limit of the Karakorum Range

Reference Books
Important sources are *Abode of Snow*, by Kenneth Mason (Hart-Davis, London 1955); *In the Throne Room of the Mountain Gods*, by Galen Rowell (Sierra Club, San Francisco 1977); *Karakorum: the ascent of Gasherbrum IV*, by Frosco Maraini (Viking Press, New York 1961).

Also numerous articles in *Mountain Magazine*, *AJ*, *HJ*, etc

Maps
Swiss Foundation for Alpine Research 1:750,000 *kammkarte* 1952/1970 covers the complete range and its southern approaches; RGS 1:253,000 contoured map covers the Hispar-Biafo Region. The definitive map is the Polish 1:250,000 *kammkarte* compiled by Jerzy Wala and the Klub Wysokogorski. While difficult to obtain it is continually updated

Access
The area has always been politically and, in some parts, militarily sensitive, having been a meeting point of the Indian Raj, Russia and China. The Baltoro region was closed to all visitors from 1961 to 1974. All visitors and expeditions require formal permission from the Pakistani authorities. Today it is usual to fly from Rawalpindi to Gilgit or Skardu. Both places can be reached by the new Karakorum road linking Pakistan to Sinkiang via Hunza. Regular bus services ply the road and jeeps may be hired.

Rawalpindi is reached by air from international airports at Lahore or Karachi.

There are proposals for the establishment of a National Park in the K2 region

---

Situation: Northern Kashmir, largely in the Republic of Pakistan, but small areas are administered by China and India. Some traditional frontiers to the north east with Sinkiang were redrawn with China in 1963, while some to the south east with Ladakh are part of the Kashmir Ceasefire Line

Most Important Peaks
2 K2—Mount Godwin-Austen (28,253/8,612) 1954: A. Compagnoni and L. Lacedelli of Desio's Italian expedition

14 Hidden Peak—Gasherbrum I (26,470/8,068) 1958: Pete Schoening and Andy Kauffman of Clinch's American expedition

15 Broad Peak (26,400/8,047) 1957: M. Schmuch, Herman Buhl, F. Wintersteller and Kurt Diemberger of Schmuck's Austrian expedition

17 Gasherbrum II (26,360/8,035) 1956: S. Larch, F. Moravec and H. Willenpart of Moravec's Austrian expedition

19 Gasherbrum III (26,090/7,952) 1975: Alison Chadwick, Wanda Rutkiewicz, Janusz Onyszkiewicz and K. Zdzitowiecki of Rutkiewicz's Polish expedition

21 Gasherbrum IV (26,000/7,925) 1958: Walter Bonatti and Carlo Mauri of Cassin's Italian expedition

25 Disteghil Sar (25,838/7,885) 1960: G. Starker, D. Marchart of Stefan's expedition

28 Kunyang Kish (25,760/7,852) 1971: A. Zawada, A. Heinrich, J. Stryczynski and R. Szafirski of Zawada's Polish expedition

30 Masherbrum (25,660/7,821) 1960: George Bell and Willi Unsoeld of Clinch's American-Pakistani expedition

36 Rakaposhi (25,550/7,788) 1958: Mike Banks and Tom Patey of Banks's Anglo-Pakistani expedition

87 Haramosh (24,299/7,406) 1958: H. Roiss, F. Mandl and S. Pauer of Roiss's Austrian expedition

116 The Ogre—Baintha Brakk—(23,900/7,285) 1977: Doug Scott and C. Bonington. A British expedition

119 Muztagh Tower (23,860/7,273) 1956: John Hartog, Joe Brown, Tom Patey and Ian McNaught Davis of Hartog's British expedition

219 Pioneer Peak (22,867/6,970) 1892: Martin Conway, Charles Bruce, Matthias Zurbriggen and two Gurkhas of Conway's British expedition

Langtang Lirung from the west: Langtang Himal, Nepal

It had been a long day. We left our camp below the West Paldor Glacier soon
after dawn and found the high ridge of the Tiru Danda, along the crest of which our
trail led south, still plastered in new snow. It was tough going for the porters and for
long sections the Sherpas and I had to cut steps and help them along. And then, just
as the snow gave way to steep grassy downland, the mist came rolling in and
visibility fell to zero. Navigation was difficult, none of the Sherpas had been that
way before, and I had to think hard to recall exactly which of the network of
shepherds' paths we had taken three years ago in the sunshine and with all Nepal at
our feet. Every boulder, every looming tussock seemed familiar. By late afternoon
there were rents in the mist and, resting against green banks studded with edelweiss
and gentian, we caught glimpses of glittering ice-walls to the north, the furrowed
flanks of Pabil and Lapsang Karbo. But we could not stop for long: we must find
water and a place to camp before dusk.

It was already dusk when the mist dissolved above the narrow cleft of the Pansing
Bhanjyang Pass and Pemba's nose led us unerringly to a little alp hung on the steep
flanks of the ridge above the forest where a tinkling stream and a ruined stone-
roofed byre built between two gnarled cedars promised us a comfortable night.

About 25 miles (40km) east the alpenglow was already dying on the icy brow of
the Lirung (23,769ft/7,245m), rising above the creeping night to dominate the
horizon. The Lirung had been with us for three weeks and we had seen it from all
angles, but it was never more lovely than now. The pink became purple then steel
grey and the day was dead. High over Langtang rode the silver moon. Night had
come. 'Cha Sahib!' a shout came from the byre. 'Cha ready! Velly good cha!'

Overleaf: In the Jugal Himal, Nepal: looking north east up the Linshing Glacier towards Dorje Lakpa

Cloud streams from the summit of Dorje Lakpa 1 (22,930ft/6,989m) with the
fang of Dorje Lakpa 11 (21,380ft/6,517m) rising to its right. Leftwards, Gurkarpo
Ri (22,552ft/6,878m) appears over an icy col at the head of one fork of the Linshing
Glacier. This peak actually stands on the Tibetan border over the watershed into
Langtang and is some 8 miles (13km) distant. On the far left fluted ridges and steep
hillsides rise to Kanshurm (19,940ft/6,078m) and the other small peaks of the
Linshing Group, the most north-westerly of Jugal's mountains.

The first European to visit this region was Tilman, in 1949, when he crossed a
high glacier pass southward from Langtang with his porters and descended into the
Balephi Valley on his way back to civilization. Although several expeditions had
visited the eastern valley of Jugal—attempting Dorje Lakpa, Lonpo Gang and other
large peaks—it seems that few people know much about the northern valley, which
is awkward to penetrate, and the actual location of Tilman's Pass had been lost.

One of our objectives when we went into the Jugal was to relocate Tilman's Pass.
At first it seemed that it might be the col at the head of the Linshing Glacier in this
picture, but although it looks easy to reach, such is not the case. The going is
extremely tedious, a dangerous ice-fall descending from Kanshurm must be crossed
and we felt that the route was hardly suitable for the loaded porters who had
accompanied Tilman. Eventually we located the pass, a rather unlikely looking
notch between steep rock walls at the head of the Balephi Glacier which flows out of
sight across the bottom of this picture. It was choked by a steep little ice-fall which
we cunningly avoided by using a series of rock-ledges and, with our own porters
loaded, we were able to reach a beautiful glacier descending below the imposing
eastern ramparts of Fluted Peak towards Langshisa in Langtang.

This is the stuff of Himalyan exploration: there is more to it than just climbing
mountains, and Ian Howell and I were as thrilled to find and cross Tilman's Pass as
we have been to reach the summit of many a fine peak.

In the Langtang Himal, Nepal: the West Face of Gangchempo or Fluted Peak

How one sees beautiful Fluted Peak (20,954ft/6,387m), looking up the Langtang glen from near the Gyallshan Gompa, or monastery. The mountain dominates this part of Langtang and is one of the few summits visible until one reaches the upper glen or climbs up the hillsides to north or south. Only then are the other ice-hung peaks that wall the glen seen in their true magnificence.

Tilman's 1949 party was the first of several who attempted Gangchempo over the years. It looks a difficult mountain, but close inspection reveals several possible routes, the easiest lying between the two southern ridges and appearing quite straightforward yet hidden from almost all directions. This is the line supposedly taken by the two climbers who, rumour has it, reached the summit in the early 1970s.

Ama Dablam and Thangboche Monastery, Khumbu Himal

Apart from Everest, Ama Dablam (22,494ft/6,856m) is probably Khumbu's best-known peak. It is seen here rising 6 miles (10km) to the north of the famous Thangboche Monastery in what is now a classic mountain view. The route by which it was first climbed in 1961 lies close to the right-hand skyline.

The usual route to Everest passes by the monastery and descends through the woods beyond to reach the Imja Khola at the valley bottom en route to Pangboche and Pheriche. Most passersby camp in the meadow beside the monastery and the area is now so popular that the National Park authority has built a small lodge, quite tastefully designed, to alleviate pressure on the site and to avoid further despoilation of the fragile environment.

I once met an American monk here and asked him what pressures had led him to join the monastic community. 'Why, man!' he replied. 'When ah'd done me three combat tours in 'Nam, ah' thought ah' git me t'someplace real quiet!' I hope recent trends have not disillusioned him!

Himalaya

Everest approach route. Kusum Kanguru
(left) and Gonglha (right), both rising
steeply above the east bank of the Dudh Kosi
river, forming the watershed between the
Dudh Kosi and the Hinku Dronka valleys

Nanga Parbat

As the western bastion of the Great Himalayan Chain, the location, the character and the history of Nanga Parbat justify for it a special place in the annals of mountaineering. An isolated massif, composed largely of gneiss and hung with huge glaciers, it rises 23,000ft (7,000m) above the arid valleys of the Indus and Astor which curl round its feet. it is, wrote Trevor Braham 'not a single mountain but a dazzling white structure standing on a purple plinth and containing several peaks'. In Sanskrit its name means 'naked mountain' but a more fitting title is that used by the natives of its western flanks—Diamir—meaning 'King of the Mountains'. The most westerly 'eight thousander', it is one of the grandest peaks of the Himalaya.

It also bears a strange aura of malevolence. In the mid-nineteenth century a huge rock-slide from Nanga Parbat dammed the Indus, creating a large lake. The tremendous flood later released when the dam broke swept away an entire Sikh army, besides causing terrible havoc far down to the plains. In eighty-three years no less than thirty-six men, seventeen of them Sherpas, have died during the twenty-two attempts on the summit which only fourteen men have reached on five successful expeditions. A tragic mountain indeed.

Nanga Parbat is a massif rather than an individual peak. Its main characteristics are its long crest, high for over 15 miles (24km), and the three vast faces which fall from it. The Rakhiot Flank, a mass of tumbling ice-cliffs 11,000ft (3,350m) high is crowned not by the summit, but by the subsidiary peaks of the Silver Crags, North and South, and the névé of the Silver Plateau. Somewhat narrower, the Diamir Face is of similar height, and a tangle of rocky ribs and sérac-choked gulleys rise to a collar of steep ice-fields around the rocky summit of Nanga Parbat itself. Falling fully 14,800ft (4,500m) below the summit the Rupal Flank is probably the highest precipice in the world and both the summit of this and Rakhiot Peak throw down major buttresses into a steep desert of rock and ice.

Nanga Parbat from the north: the Rakhiot Face with (skyline, left) the South-East and North-East Peaks (the Silver Crags) and between them the Silbersattel. On the right is the North Summit from where the ridge continues back to the Main Summit, hidden from view

The Rupal or South Face of Nanga Parbat rises 14,900ft (4,500m) above the Rupal Valley and is considered to be the highest mountain face in the world. It was first climbed in 1970 by the South Tyrolean brothers Reinhold and Gunther Messner, and later by two other members of the same expedition. The route follows the spur system in the centre of the picture

The first attempt was led by Albert Mummery—the foremost mountaineer of his day—three years after the region was pacified, in 1892. His companions, Geoffrey Hastings and Norman Collie, were extremely experienced alpinists and they were joined from India by Charles Bruce with two experienced Gurkhas. After making a reconnaissance of the Rupal Flank, they crossed the Mazeno Pass to the Diamir Face which Mummery, together with one of the Gurkhas, proceeded to climb to almost 21,000ft (6,400m) by a difficult rock-rib leading straight up the centre— Mummery retreating only when his companion became sick. Deciding now to examine the Rakhiot Flank, the party set off towards the Indus, leaving Mummery and the two Gurkhas to attempt a direct route over a conspicuous col (20,350ft/6,200m) between Nanga Parbat II and Ganalo Peak. They disappeared—probably avalanched on the dangerous ground below the col. Fifteen years afterwards Bruce wrote, 'I wonder if Nanga Parbat will ever be climbed—it is probably as difficult a mountain as there is to tackle'.

It was to be thirty-seven years before the next attempt when a modest German expedition, led by Willy Merkl, explored a route on the Rakhiot Face. The climbers found a circuitous route up to the main ridge north east of Rakhiot Peak which they bypassed to establish a Camp VII at 22,800ft (7,000m) on the ridge beyond, before the monsoon forced a retreat. A long and desperately vulnerable route, some 8½ miles (14km) from Base Camp to summit, and menaced by avalanche on the lower reaches, it seemed, however, technically straightforward.

The Germans returned again in 1934, but logistic problems and indecisive leadership frittered away good weather. The lead climbers reached the foot of the north-east summit (25,750ft/7,850m) and could probably have reached the top that day, but decided to await a joint ascent with their friends on the morrow. Unfortunately the monsoon struck that night, and nine days of blizzard followed. When the weather eased, three climbers, including the great Willo Welzenbach and Merkl himself, together with six courageous Sherpas, were dead in the snow beyond Rakhiot Peak.

Three years later the Germans tried again, but Camp IV, below Rakhiot Peak, was overwhelmed in the night by an avalanche. Seven climbers and nine Sherpas died. The next expedition (1938) achieved nothing while the 1939 expedition only made a reconnaissance of the Diamir Face.

The first serious, if controversial, attempt after the war was successful. Dr Herrligkoffer, Merkl's non-climbing stepbrother, organized an Austro-German expedition which established Camp V at 22,640ft (6,900m) on the North-East Ridge between Rakhiot Peak and the Silbersattel. From here Herman Buhl, in an incredible forty-hour solo push, reached the summit over 4 miles (7km) away and returned safely, having bivouacked in his shirt sleeves.

Despite several recent attempts by other nationalities, Nanga Parbat does seem an Austro-German 'preserve' and since 1953 Herrligkoffer has organized a further seven expeditions to the mountain. That of 1962 was successful on the Diamir Flank, taking a difficult line up ice-couloirs and rock-ribs to the left of Mummery's Rib. Only four camps were placed, but a winch was needed to keep supplies flowing. Toni Kinshofer, Anderl Mannhardt and Siegfried Low reached the summit, but Low was killed on the descent.

Herrligkoffer's 1970 expedition attacked the Rupal Flank by the South-South-East Pillar. The South Tyrolese brothers, Reinhold and Gunter Messner, reached the summit from Camp V (24,200ft/7,380m) comparing the final mixed ground to the North Face of the Matterhorn. Gunter was unwell and, having no rope, they felt unable to descend this difficult ground, so they descended the Diamir Face via Mummery's Rib, a remarkable feat of mountaineering. Ironically, Gunter was killed by an ice avalanche on the easy glacier below the face. Not only was the conduct of the expedition considered controversial, but the outcome was extremely acrimonious.

A Czechoslovak party repeated Buhl's Rakhiot route in 1971, while an Austrian team of only four climbers all reached the summit by the South-West Ridge, gained from the far left 'of the Rupal Flank, in 1976. They made two bivouacs above a Camp IV at 24,600ft (7,500m). This now seems to be the safest, quickest and easiest route on the mountain.

In 1978 Messner climbed Nanga Parbat again, this time entirely on his own. Leaving only a lonely liaison officer at his Base Camp, he reached the summit in three and a half days via a new line on the Diamir face. The whole incredible adventure lasted only twelve days! It must rank as one of the greatest Himalaya feats.

Situation: Pakistan—Kashmir—Punjab section, Great Himalaya

Most Important Peaks
12 Nanga Parbat (26,658/8,125) 1953: Herman Buhl—solo
North-East Summit (25,953/7,910) 1971: members of Czechoslovak expedition
Nanga Parbat II or North Peak (25,643/7,816)
Silberzacken (Silver Crag) North (24,925/7,597)
Silberzacken South (24,704/7,530) 1971: members of Czechoslovak expedition
186 Rakhiot Peak (23,210/7,074) 1932: P. Aschenbrenner and H. Kunigk
260 Chongra I (22,390/6,824)
410 Ganalo (21,673/6,606) West Summit 1939: Peter Aufschnaiter and Ludwig Chicken
464 Chongra West (IV) 20,480/6,242) 1939: members of German expedition

Major Passes
Mazeno Pass (17,640/5,377) a tiresome but easy pass around the south-west side of the Nanga Parbat massif, used both by local tribesmen and mountaineers. It links Astor and the Rupal Nullah to the Diamir basin and Chilas on the Indus.

The mass of high ground from which Nanga Parbat rises is demarcated from surrounding areas of the Punjab Himalaya by two famous and historical passes which carry motorable tracks Babusar Pass (13,690/4,173) carries the old frontier road from Abbottabad to Chilas, which continues on to Gilgit.
Bursil Pass (13,775/4,199) the direct link from the Vale of Kashmir to Astor, this is an old trade route from India to Sinkiang

Access
Nanga Parbat lies close to the Kashmir Ceasefire Line and as such is in a politically and militarily sensitive area. In any case expeditions to the mountains of Pakistan require official permission and are strictly controlled.

Approaches are usually made from Gilgit which is normally reached by air from Rawalpindi. This one-hour flight has been called the most spectacular and hazardous in the world, and during it the aircraft passes close beside Nanga Parbat. From Gilgit jeep roads are followed southwards to Talichi and beyond, but final access is on foot. Donkeys, horses and porters can be hired locally. It is about two days' march from the Indus to Rakhiot Base Camp in the beautiful 'Marchenwiese' meadow at about 10,800ft (3,300m). Astor can be reached by jeep from Talichi.

The monsoon breaks in this area in the first week of July

Maps
Survey of India 1:100,000 2 sheets (1934); Nanga Parbat Gruppe 1:50,000 compiled by the 1934 German expedition (1936). These maps are no longer freely available but the following modern maps are useful if of limited scale:
American AMS military aerial survey 1:250,000 'Gilgit-Nanga Parbat'; Swiss Foundation for Alpine Research 1:750,000 'Karakorum-Nanga Parbat' (1952 and 1970)

Important Publications and References
The Siege of Nanga Parbat (1856-1953) by Paul Bauer (1956); *Nanga Parbat* by Karl Herrligkoffer (Elek 1954); *Das Buch von Nanga Parbat 1895-1953* by G.O. Dyhrenfurth (1954).
Numerous articles in *Mountain World, Mountain Magazine, Alpinismus, Himalayan Journal, Alpine Journal, etc*

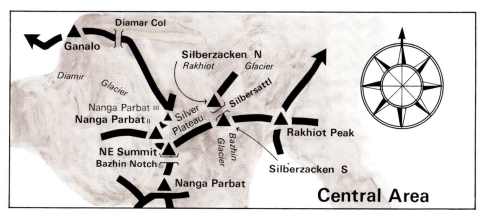

Central Area

Punjab

Sickle Moon in the Kishtwar Himal, seen here from the East, was first climbed in 1975 by an Indian Border Police expedition

This is a convenient title for the great block of mountainous country that forms the backdrop to the plains of the Punjab. Stretching 150 miles (241km) to the deep valley of the Upper Indus, its extremities are marked by the Sutlej river and, over 300 miles (480km) to the north west, by that final bastion of the main Himalayan chain, Nanga Parbat. Now lying in Pakistan, north of the Kashmir Cease-fire Line, Nanga Parbat is covered elsewhere. This chapter deals with the Indian section of the Punjab Himalaya that continues from Kashmir through the old state of Jammu into Himachal Pradesh.

Several parallel mountain crests may be discerned. The main watershed is, of course, the Great Himalaya, and here it forms the divide between the Upper and Lower Indus. Between Nanga Parbat and Nun Kun it hardly tops 19,000ft (5,790m), while, beyond that massif, the culminating point of our area, the peaks of Kishtwar, Lahul and Spiti are nowhere large.

Alongside, to the south west, are the broken chains of the Pir Panjal and the Dahaula Dhar. The former walls the lovely Vale of Kashmir, famous for its lakes, mosques and Mogul palaces and a noted tourist resort. Once the bed of an ancient lake, it has been well described as 'an emerald set in pearls'. Eastwards the Pir Panjal forms the fine little mountains of Kulu. All this is verdant country, the most 'European' stretch of the Himalaya. Valley orchards, flower-filled meadows and woods of pine and birch remind the alpinist of familiar scenes.

Paralleling the Himalayan watershed

to the north lies the arid Zaskar Range and the 'moonscape' of the remote and one-time autonomous state of Ladakh, astride the Indus. Sometimes known as 'Little Tibet', from the religion, culture and landscape both share, it is a high desert region where snow-tipped mountains rise above barren valleys and terraced green oases surround the scattered villages and monasteries. The Zaskar and the parallel Ladakh Range, north of the Indus, contain few large peaks but Sasir Kangri (25,170ft/7,672m), the far south-eastern pillar of the mighty Karakorum, rises only 50 miles (80km) north of Leh, Ladakh's capital

West of Nun Kun there are many attractive small summits of alpine character, between 16,000 and 19,000ft (4,880-5,800m), easily accessible from Srinagar. Bruce, with Eckenstein and Conway, was climbing here in 1892 and later the area became very popular, especially when the Aircrew Mountain Centre was established at Gulmarg—now the home of the Ski Club of India—during World War II. A notable peak is the sharp and impressively stratified tri-angle of Kolahoi (17,799ft/5,425m), climbed by Ernest Neve and Kenneth Mason in 1912—both important Himalayan pioneers. Over the years several new routes have been made, including one on the South Face by John Hunt in 1935.

Three main summits dominate the great massif of Nun Kun. Nun is a beautiful icy wedge buttressed by tumbling *sérac* flows, while 2 miles away, across a high snow-plateau, rises rocky Kun. Pinnacle Peak (22,810ft/6,952m), close behind Kun and possibly climbed by the Workmans in 1906, is the highest of several satellites which include White Needle. First examined by Bruce and Arthur Neve early on, Nun has now been ascended several times. In 1977 it was climbed by an American guided party and descended on skis by Sylvain Saudan.

The highest peaks of the Zaskar Range rise from remote and empty country near the Sutlej river on the borders of Spiti. One of them, Shilla—whose originally computed height of 23,050ft (7,025m) is unlikely and is more probably only 21,325ft (6,500m)—was climbed solo by a native surveyor of the Survey of India,

Papsura, the legendary 'Peak of Evil', the third highest mountain in the Kulu-Lahul-Spiti Divide of the Punjab Himalaya. It was first climbed in 1967 by a British party, led by Bob Pettigrew via the wide couloir in centre of picture

in 1860—for some twenty years perhaps a world altitude record.

Kishtwar is an area explored by climbers only recently and it contains a jagged profusion of peaks, typically sharp, fluted and icy, only a few days' march from the road-head. Charles Clark has led several expeditions into Kishtwar, and the highest peak, Sickle Moon, was recently climbed from the north by an Indian team. It is an ideal area for small parties climbing alpine-style.

'On the edge of the habitable world', wrote Sanskrit sages of Lahul and Spiti, a desolate region which contrasts with the lush Beas valley of Kulu, famous for its orchards, through which it is approached from the south. Spiti, overlooking Tibet across the Sutlej, is Tibetan in its landscape and in the character of its few inhabitants. For long a closed area, it has been visited by few climbers. The Ratang Tower (20,705ft/6,311m), reached through the formidable Ratang gorge, is one of ten fine summits climbed in 1956 by Trevor Braham and Peter Holmes. Recently Indian climbers, too, have been active here.

Kulu and Lahul are, again, superb areas for small expeditions practising both alpine-style ascents and ski-mountaineering. Although Charles Bruce's guide Heinrich Führer climbed Solang Weisshorn (Hanuman Tibba—19,450ft/5,928m) and other summits in 1912, and Jimmy Roberts explored the region thirty years later, it was not until the 1950s, with other regions forbidden, that Pettigrew with the great Ladakhi 'sherpa' Wangyal began a decade of exploration and the climbing potential was truly realized. Since then several parties have been active each season, particularly in Kulu, the region of easiest access in all the Himalaya. Here jagged rock- or ice-peaks offer splendid routes for the 'tiger' and many easier goals for the less ambitious. Among the latter is the twin-summited Deo Tibba whose snow dome is visible from Simla 75 miles (120km) distant. Indrasan is a challenging peak of steep red granite long inviolate now climbed by at least four different routes. Sadly, Kulu's *golden age* has ended and, in Eric Byne's words: 'Tigers are left searching wistfully for unscratched rock'.

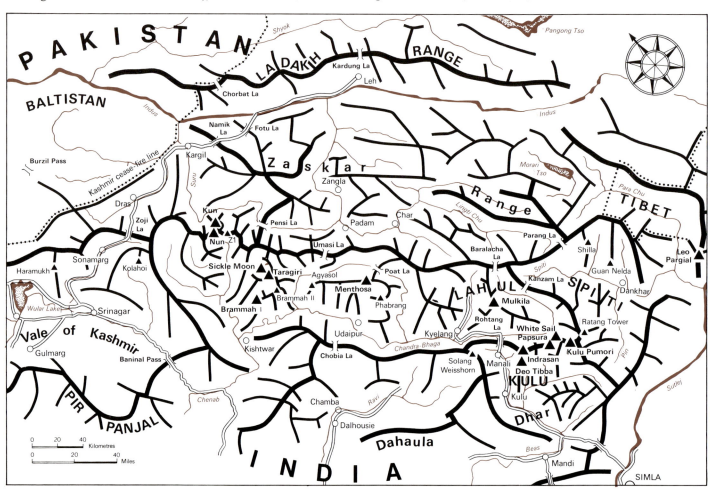

Situation: Republic of India—Kashmir and Himachal Pradesh

Some Important Peaks

Kashmir

(Height order, height in feet and metres, date of first ascent and party of first ascent)
162 Nun (23,410/7,135) 1953: Mme Claude Kogan, Pierre Vittoz
183 Kun (23,250/7,087) 1913: M. Piacenza's Italian expedition

Kishtwar

Sickle Moon (21,570/6,575) 1975: Tsering Norbu and Nima Dorje, Indian Border Police expedition
402 Tarangiri (21,047/6,415) 1977: British Kishtwar expedition
Brammah I (21,030/6,416) 1973: C. Bonington and N. Escourt

Kulu, Lahul, Spiti and Zaskar

273 Leo Pargial (22,210/6,770) 1933: Charles Warren and Pallis
347 Kulu Pumori (21,500/6,553) 1964: R. Pettigrew and Mohling

366 Mulkila (21,380/6,517) 1939: F. Kilb and L. Kremek
Papsura (21,165/6,451) 1967: G. Hill and C. Pritchard
387 White Sail—Dharmasura (21,148/6,446) 1941: J. O. M. Roberts
Menthosa (21,140/6,443) 1970: Lieutenant S. Rae and Captain R. Cape
473 Deo Tibba (20,410/6,221) 1952: Dr and Mrs Graaf and K. Berrill
474 Indrasan (20,410/6,221) 1962: Japanese expedition

Some Large Glaciers
The Bara Shigri on the Kulu-Spiti watershed is

some 16 miles (26km) long
The Candi ki Shigri System in Central Lahul is some 12 miles (19km) long, draining to the Chandra river
The Barmal Glacier, rising from Nun Kun, is some 12 miles (19km) long

Some Important Passes
Zoji La (11,578/3,529) this pass crosses the main Himalaya crest from Srinagar to the Upper Indus. Once the main caravan route to Central Asia via Leh, the Sasir Pass and the Karakorum Pass. Now crossed by a motor road.
Rohtang La (13,050/3,978) over the Pir Panjal crest, this is now crossed by a motor road linking Manali on the Beas river of Kulu with Chatru on the Chandra river of Lahul
Kanzam La (14,931/4,551) 20 miles further up the Chandra river crossing to the Spiti river
Baralacha La (16,200/4,938) 15 miles (24km) further on, at the head of the Chandra, this pass leads over the main crest into Zaskar

Guide-books and Bibliography
Several general 'expedition' books are useful:
Himalayan Circuit, by G. D. Khosla (Macmillan, 1956); *Kulu*, by P. Chetwode (John Murray, 1972); *Himalayan Venture*, by F. Kolb (Butterworth, 1959); *Himalayan Odyssey*, by Trevor Braham (George Allen & Unwin, 1974).

Otherwise numerous articles in both the *Alpine Journal* and the *Himalayan Journal*

Maps
The Japanese ITY 1:200,000 *kammkarte* map which covers Kashmir in five sheets is now virtually unobtainable.

Survey of India ½in and ¼in to the mile (1851 and 1921 Surveys) are now also difficult to obtain. The US AMS aerial survey maps, 1:250,000, do cover much of the area, but are of limited use.

The new Survey of India 1:50,000 maps are excellent but restricted to official use, although a fine new 'trekking map'—based on them—should be available late in 1978

Access
The north-west limit of the area covered is the Kashmir Ceasefire Line with Pakistan while the south-eastern limit is the Tibetan border. Thus certain areas are politically sensitive. Much of the area lies within the so-called 'Inner Line' and only recently has access beyond this been relaxed in certain places. However, areas do seem to be 'opened' or 'closed' at whim by the authorities.

From the International Airport at Delhi Srinagar may be reached, either by air, or by rail to Jammu and thence by road (bus). Kishtwar is approached by bus from Jammu (where there is also an airfield). Kulu is approached by rail to Chandigarh from where the Kulu valley is reached by road (bus). Perhaps a more reliable alternative is to travel by train to Pathankot and proceed by bus via Mandi, a local administrative centre, to Manali. Kulu can now also be reached by air.

Nun Kun, Zaskar, Leh and Ladakh can be reached by tortuous mountain road over the Zoji La and via Kargil. From Kulu there is a new road over the Rohtang La linking Manali to the Lahul valley

Nun, the highest of the two summits of Nun Kun in the Punjab Himalaya. This view is from the north, from the Snow Plateau, the 3-mile (5km) wide *cirque* **between Nun and Kun. The ascent route lies up the right-hand (west) ridge**

Garhwal

These are the mountains that cradle the infant Ganges. They stretch just over 180 miles (290km), from the Sujlej to the Nepalese border on the Kali river, and among them rise the highest summits in India. To mountaineers the region is known as Garhwal, while geographers refer to it as the Kumaun Himalaya—in theory Garhwal is the western section, while Kumaun lies east of the Alaknanda. Delhi is just 150 miles (240km) from the 10,000ft (3,050m) contour and mountaineers were able to penetrate the region early on in a stable political climate. In the 1920s and '30s there was more climbing activity here than in any other Himalayan range.

Once again three parallel mountain crests are in evidence and that of the Great Himalaya is flanked by the Dhaula Dhar to the south west and the Zaskar—along which runs the Tibetan frontier—to the north east. Each contains large peaks. Here, however, the Great Himalaya range is not unbroken, for, besides the two rivers at the region's extremities, three others cut southwards through the crest. The Sutlej, after rising in Lake Manasarowar in Tibet, flows parallel, north of the Zaskar, before turning abruptly south through all three crests on its way to the Indus. Thus the Zaskar is the divide between the Indus and Ganges.

Opposite right: **Changabang (left) and Kalanka from the Changabang Glacier. The first ascent line took the right skyline, gained from the tangled ice of Kalanka's South Face. The South East Face line lies below and to right of Changabang's summit**

Below: **Approaching Changabang from the Rhamani Valley. The formidable West Face (left) was climbed in 1976 by two Britons, Pete Boardman and Joe Tasker, in a remarkable lightweight assault**

Situation: Republic of India; far northern slopes in Tibet Autonomous Region of Chinese Peoples Republic

Some Important Peaks
31 Nanda Devi (25,645/7,817) 1936: Noël Odell and Bill Tilman
40 Kamet (25,447/7,756) 1931: Frank Smythe, Eric Shipton, R. L. Holdsworth and Lewa Sherpa
94 Abi Gamine (24,130/7,355) 1950: G. Chevalley, R. Dittert, A. Tissieres
121 Mana Peak (23,862/7,273) 1937: Frank Smythe and party
161 Badrinath (23,420/7,138) 1952: L. George and V. Russenberge
171 Trisul (23,360/7,120) 1907: Tom Longstaff, the brothers Brocherel and Karbir Burathoki—world's first 7,000 metre peak to be climbed
186 Dunagiri (Tolma Himal) (23,184/7,066) 1939: André Roch, F. Steuri, D. Zogg
234 Panchchuli (22,650/6,904) 1973: Mahendra Singh's Indian expedition
244 Changabang (22,520/6,864) 1974: C. Bonington, Balwant Sandhu, M. Boysen, D. Haston, D. Scott and Tashi Chewang Sherpa
333 Nilkanta (21,640/6,596) 1961? O. P. Sharma, Phruba, Lobsang and Lakpa Giyalbu Sherpa. Certainly 1974: A. P. Chamolis's Indian expedition
Shivling (21,467/6,543) 1974: Hukan Singh, Laxman Singh and four Sherpas (Indian Border Police expedition)
373 Nilgiri Parbat (21,240/6,474) 1937: Frank Smythe, Ondi Nurbu and Nurbu Bhotia

Major Passes
Mana Pass—Chirbitya La (18,400/5,608) a rocky glacier pass crossing the Zaskar crest at the head of the Saraswati branch of the Alaknanda river. An old trade-route into Tibet, it was the route of the first European crossing of the Himalaya, in 1624, by Portuguese Jesuit missionaries who used it regularly for fifteen years
Niti, or Kiunglang La (16,628/5,068) an old caravan-route across the Zaskar at the head of the Dhauli branch of the Alaknanda into Tibet. First European crossing in 1812 by the explorers Moorcroft and Hearsey, disguised as fakirs

Largest Glacier
The Gangotri Glacier, the sacred source of the Ganges, is some 16.5 miles (27km) long

Guide-books and Bibliography
Some useful references may be found in: *Kamet Conquered*, Frank Smythe (Gollancz, 1932); *This my Voyage*, Tom Longstaff (John Murray, 1950); *Nanda Devi*, Eric Shipton (Hodder & Stoughton, 1936); *The Valley of Flowers*, Frank Smythe (Hodder & Stoughton, 1938); *The Scottish Himalayan Expedition*, Bill Murray (Dent, 1951); *Himalayan Odyssey*, Trevor Braham (George Allen & Unwin, 1974); *Changabang*, Chris Bonington and others (Heinemann, 1975).

Also numerous articles in *Alpine Journal* and *Himalayan Journal*

Maps
The Japanese ITY 1:200,000 *kammkarte* is quite useful (three sheets) but now difficult to obtain.

The American AMS air survey 1:250,000 has limited use while the Survey of India ½in map is excellent but restricted

Access
Virtually the whole area was closed to foreigners from the Chinese invasion of 1962 until 1976, although latterly special exceptions were made for joint expeditions including Indian members. Official permits are required at the time of writing for both mountaineering and trekking.

From the international airport at Delhi, the foothills may be approached by road or rail to Hardwar or Rishikesh. Joshimath, on the Alaknanda, and Dharasu, on the Bhagirathi, are road-heads accessible from the south

Long known for its beauty, Garhwal has been compared to a scaled-up Switzerland. Although the climate north of the Great Himalaya is arid and the terrain Tibetan in character, that to the south is subject to the benign influence of the monsoon. Splendid forests of oak, cypress, deodar and rhododendron clothe the hillsides above charming seasonal villages and green terraced fields—always amid vistas of snow-clad peaks. Nomad shepherds tend flocks of sheep and goats, the former often used as pack animals, as yak are in the high north. Wildlife is abundant; bears still frequent the forests and tigers were once plentiful among the jungle foothills along the rim of the plains. Garhwal's flower-filled alpine meadows are famous. Longstaff writes of wading through flowers up to his waist in the Bhiundhar valley below Nilgiri Parbat, later immortalized as Frank Smythe's *Valley of Flowers*.

These mountains are the traditional abode of many of the Hindu deities and long pilgrim trails wind from the plains up the valleys of the Bhagirathi and the Alaknanda, the former to the source of the holy Ganges at the 'Cow's Mouth'—

the snout of the great Gangotri Glacier. Badrinath, the birthplace of Shiva, and a shrine of the greatest sanctity, lies on the sacred Alaknanda—the 'waters of Vishnu'. Towering close by is the isolated and sweeping snow-cone of Nilkanta, a beautiful peak sacred to pilgrims and, after its claimed first ascent in 1961, a centre of some controversy among mountaineers.

Nanda Devi (the 'Goddess Nanda') India's highest summit and once the highest peak in the British Empire—rises, a great white cone, from an all but inaccessible valley encircled by no less than nineteen peaks above 21,000ft (6,400m). As long ago as 1883, W. W. Graham and his two Swiss guides tried to force their way into this mysterious sanctuary through the wild gorge of the Rishi Ganga, and, in the ensuing fifty years, many other fine mountaineers have also tried and failed. Finally, in 1934, Eric Shipton, Bill Tilman and three Sherpas solved the problem, returning two years later with a small Anglo-American party to make the ascent of the highest summit yet climbed. The Poles climbed Nanda Devi East

(24,391ft/7,434m) in 1939, and in 1951 a French team boldly attempted to traverse the difficult 2-mile *arête* linking the two peaks. The lead climbers disappeared. In 1976 a large Japanese-Indian expedition, with support on both summits, succeeded. The same year a strong American expedition, led by Willi Unsoeld and Adams Carter—a member of the 1936 party—climbed the very difficult North Ridge by the west flank and in 1978 a British party is attempting the North Face. This imposing mountain has now been climbed several times and, by the usual route, the South Ridge, is considered one of the easiest of the great Himalayan peaks.

The first of the Sanctuary 'ring-wall' peaks to be climbed was Trisul—the 'Trident of Shiva'. It is an easy snow-climb from the north east, and was actually descended on skis—summit to snow-line—by Colonel Kumar's Indian expedition of 1976. The grand icy pyramid, Dunagiri, was finally ascended by its heavily corniced South-West Ridge, on which Graham (1883), Oliver (1933) and Shipton (1936) had already been high, but a notable ascent was that of the

South-East Spur, in 1975, by Joe Tasker and Dick Renshaw, in a single alpine-style push with ten bivouacs. It was a difficult and gruelling climb on rock and ice which they compared to Les Droites' North Face. Close by is incredible Changabang, described by Bill Murray as 'a vast eyetooth fang . . . its rock milk-white granite'. The first ascent, 'round the back' by the narrow, North East *arête*, proved technically straightforward, and three further lines have since been climbed.

In 1976 the Japanese used 8,000ft (2,438m) of fixed rope on the difficult South-West Ridge; Colin Read's team made an alpine ascent of the challenging ice of the South-East Face; while Pete Boardman and Tasker forced the exceptionally difficult 5,500ft (1,680m) West Face in twenty-five days, possibly the most truly outstanding lightweight Himalayan climb to date.

Several high summits surround Kamet. A conspicuous and attractive peak, it was attempted eight times before proving to be a fairly easy snow-climb by

Dawn over Nanda Devi, seen from the Changabang Glacier. On left is Nanda Devi East and in sunlight the North Face. The North Ridge, route of the '76 U.S. Expedition, divides light and shade right of the summit

the North-East Ridge. This was the first ever 25,000ft (7,620m) summit to be attained. Some 10 miles (16km) south is Niligiri Parbat, a graceful cone with a tangled icy brow, which Smythe considered his finest Himalayan ascent.

Third and largest of Garhwal's mountain groups are the peaks clustered round the Gangotri and its surrounding glaciers, where the Dhaula Dhar crest springs from the Great Himalaya. While only Chaukahamba I and II top 23,000ft (7,000m), dozens of fine peaks rise above 20,000ft (6,100m). Notable is Shivling, remarkably like the Matterhorn, but with an ice-clad summit and actually a portal of the Gangotri Glacier. It was eventually forced using contentious siege tactics, hundreds of pitons and 7,000ft (2,134m) of fixed rope.

Highest of a small knot of remote peaks to the south east, proud Panch Chuli was climbed by a strong Indian party after climbers from five nations had made nine attempts. It is in Garhwal especially that Indian climbers have won their spurs. Here are well over one hundred summits above 20,000ft (6,096m), typically gneiss or granite and—in the Kamet region to the north—there is an unbroken summer season from May to October, with no monsoon to speak of. Here there are opportunities enough for mountaineers of every ambition.

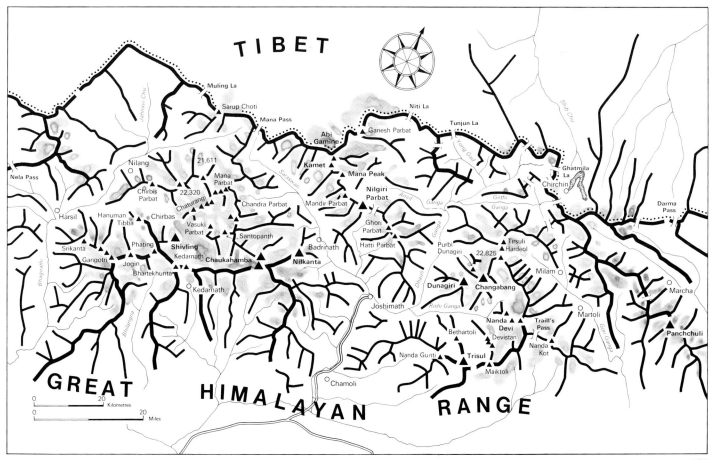

Nepal

That first sight of the Nepal Himalaya, from inside an aircraft approaching Kathmandu, is a traumatic moment in the life of any mountaineer. Too sharp to be clouds, the mountains float, ethereal, above the brown haze of the plains. To left and right, the line of great white massifs marches away into the distance, growing smaller and smaller until the eye can no longer distinguish earth from sky. Their scale, their extent and their apparent complete dissociation from the real world beneath are bewildering.

Ruled by the world's only Hindu monarch, Nepal is a small independent kingdom perched on the southern slopes of the central Himalaya and sandwiched precariously between those Asian giants, India and China (Tibet). Only 480 miles (772km) in length, with an average width a quarter of that, Nepal embraces the greatest concentration of the really high mountains in the world and is proudly aware of their economic value. Here are no less than eight of the world's fourteen '8,000 metre' (26,250ft) peaks: nine if you count Shisha Pangma (Gosainthan), just a couple of miles into Tibet. Some fifty summits topping 24,000ft (7,300m), and literally hundreds over 20,000ft (6,100m), rise within her borders.

The two main Himalayan crests cross the Kali river from Garhwal and run the length of the country, sometimes distinct and separate, often—especially towards the east—merged as one. The northern crest, the Zaskar Range of India, here known as the Tibetan Marginal Range, rarely rises above 23,000ft (7,000m) and often—but not always—marks the political frontier, in many places ill-defined! Inevitably, however, it forms the uplifted rim of the high and arid Tibetan Plateau. Typically, its structure is granite, while that of the southern crest is principally gneiss. As in India, the northern crest forms an important watershed, here between the eastward-flowing Tsangpo (later to become the Brahmaputra of Assam) and the roughly parallel Ganges. It is, however, breached in seven places by major rivers which, rising on the northern Tibetan slopes of the mountains, cut southwards to the Ganges. Many geographers suppose that the rivers were there before the mountain uplift commenced.

The mountains of the southern crest, segmented not only by these rivers, but also by important streams that rise in the transverse valleys between the crests, rise characteristically as huge isolated massifs. These are referred to as 'himals' and between them are found gorges as

deep as any in the world. The summits of Dhaulagiri I and Annapurna I are just 21 miles (34km) apart, while the Kali Gandaki flows between them—22,700ft (6,920m) beneath! Manaslu and Annapurna II tower only slightly less above the Marsyandi Khola.

Lying on the same latitude as Egypt or Florida, Nepal displays a wide climatic range, from the sub-tropical jungle of the Ganges plain, through the ice deserts

Below: **The Langtang Himal. View eastwards from the Tiru Danda in the Ganesh Himal foothills. The big peak is Dome Blanc (22,408ft/6,830m) on the east side of the Langtang Glacier, and to its right Langshisa Ri (20,649ft/6,294m) at the head of the Langtang glen can just be seen**

Right: **The beautiful peak of Ama Dablam (22,600ft/6,856m) and Lake Tshola Tsho, from the South Tshola Pass, Khumbu Himal**

Above: **Khumbu: the southern flank of Thamserku seen from the deep Dudh Kosi valley near Phakding**

around the high peaks, to the arid highland plateau of Tibet, and all in a distance of 80 miles (130km) or so. Lasting from June until the end of September, the monsoon dominates more than just the climate. Swollen rivers and leeches make travel difficult and unpleasant, and trade, agriculture and tourism must all bow to the rhythm of the rains. The monsoon comes earlier and stronger in the east than in the west. By contrast, winters are cold but relatively dry. Thus there are two distinct climbing seasons, that of the

pre-monsoon in April and May when the weather is not settled, but the days get longer and warmer, and that of the post-monsoon, in October and November, when daylight is shortening, wind and cold are increasing at altitude, but skies are generally clear and storms are rare. In recent years a 'slot' has been recognized late in the monsoon and several high peaks have been snatched during this period, among them Everest

itself. Trekking is possible at any time, except during the monsoon, and the winter months have much to recommend them.

Because of the monsoon, Nepal is basically green and fertile. Unlike emptier Himalayan regions to the west, small villages and hamlets are often scattered along the highland valleys and across their steep sides. Cultivation may extend up to about 8,000ft (2,440m), with rice paddies near the valley floor and terraces of millet, buckwheat, maize and barley extending up the hillsides.

Nepal Himalaya—Manaslu (26,760ft/8,156m), the world's tenth highest mountain, seen here from the Ganesh Himal to the east

yeti. Birdlife, however, is especially rich, and the beautiful golden pheasant, the national bird, is distinctive, as is the magnificent lammergeier vulture.

Lionel Terray called Nepal 'a world outside our time'. That was thirty years ago yet, particularly in rural areas, it remains true today. Communication relies on ancient footpaths, many of them important trade-routes still heavily used. Some, crossing the frontier into Tibet, have recently been reopened to local people after remaining closed for some years. Transport is on men's backs

otherwise deserted, while monastic communities keep alive the Tibetan Buddhist culture now destroyed north of the border. Characteristically, the ancient trade-routes to Tibet, and the trails through regions of Sherpa or Bhotiya settlement, are dotted with wayside chortens and stupas and with walls, stones and boulders inscribed with the sacred runes '*Om mani padme hum*'. Prayer flags flutter on the passes. It is difficult for the traveller in such situations not to share something of the local veneration of the high places.

Until, in 1948, the King overthrew the Ranas, the dynasty of hereditary prime ministers who had ruled since 1845, Nepal was a closed country. The great peaks had been triangulated from afar—Everest had been 'discovered' in 1852, and, although the Survey of India had been allowed to carry out basic mapping in the mid-twenties, British personnel had not been allowed to supervise the work. What little mountaineering there was had been on frontier peaks approached through Tibet or Sikkim, notably Everest and Kangchenjunga. After the second war Tibet was closed, and after Indian independence Sikkim too was forbidden. Thus the history of mountaineering in Nepal dates only to 1949.

Today tourism and Gurkha soldiers are Nepal's major 'industries'. Expeditions from all mountaineering nations operate every season in the Nepalese Himalaya: climbing is encouraged but strictly regulated and access is only allowed to peaks on the 'Permitted List'. Most of these have already been climbed and there are waiting lists for the most famous. Emphasis is more on new routes and, for some, lightweight tactics—no oxygen or Sherpas—rather than repeats of technically straightforward lines on major summits already reached several times before. However, many clandestine ascents of interesting peaks not on the 'Permitted List' have been made by small parties over the past twenty years and mountains officially classified as virgin may well not be so. Trekking was invented in Nepal by Colonel Jimmy Roberts, an ex-Gurkha officer and one of the big names in Nepalese mountain exploration, and it is now an important business. The landscape is ideally suited to this timeless mode of travel and it is a splendid experience besides being the only way of seeing this wonderful country—the true heart of the Himalaya.

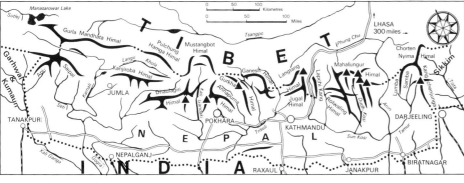

Here water buffalo provide milk and traction for the plough. Above village level luxuriant primeval forest holds sway and magnificent cedars, giant rhododendrons and bamboo thickets give way gradually to pine, larch, birch and bush rhododendron—the latter sometimes eventually forming a thick, stunted, ground cover. Alpine pastures, where sheep and yak are seasonally grazed, may extend to 15,000ft (4,570m). The high transverse valleys are dryer, a transitional zone between the lush southern slopes and the Tibetan semi-desert. One such area is Khumbu, and here some villages—inhabited throughout the year—are sited above 12,000ft (3,660m), and potatoes, an important staple crop, grown in small walled fields. Wild animals are seldom seen, although langur monkeys are common in the montane forests and various forms of mountain goat and sheep occasionally show themselves. This, too, is the habitat of the elusive

or, in the northern marches, on yaks: surprisingly horses are seldom seen in the hills. Nepal's population—some twelve million—contains dozens of distinctive ethnic groups, ranging from the Tibetan immigrant Bhotiya and Sherpa peoples, through the ancient Tibeto-Nepalese groups, such as the Tamangs, Gurungs and Newars, to the Indo-Nepalese Brahmans, Gurkhas and Thakurs. A 1952 census listed thirty separate languages and dialects, but English is something of a lingua franca and is taught in schools. Most travellers share the lasting impression of the Nepalese as a proud, happy and smiling people.

Nepal's culture is ancient and rich. Buddha himself was born here and both the Buddhist and Hindu religions—plus various obscure local sects—are observed in harmony and, sometimes it would seem, together. Gompas, or temples, grace many a mountain village and, indeed, many spectacular sites

West Nepal

These remote mountains of West Nepal are the least explored in the country and still offer great potential, though long and difficult approaches have only been partly ameliorated by the recent development of air services. As early as 1905 Tom Longstaff was in the region and attempted Gurla Mandhata (25,355ft/7,728m), an isolated glacier peak actually in Tibet, and on it survived an avalanche which swept him 3,000ft (914m). This Tibetan marginal crest stretches eastwards for over 160

miles (250km) and is studded with peaks of up to 22,400ft (6,830m). But, they are well separated from the main massifs to the south and are strictly 'out of bounds', so little is known of them.

The most westerly Nepalese Massif is the range of the icy chisel peaks, Api and Nampa which, together with other angular and impressive summits, rise from a long snowy crest which bears a steep 10,000ft (3,050m) southern flank. John Tyson and Bill Murray first explored the group in 1953. Api and

The fluted ridges of the Kanjiroba Massif seen from the north west, from the summit of Bhulu Lhasa. Kanjiroba II (north) is on the left and the higher Kanjiroba I (south) on the right, its highest point in the top right-hand corner of the picture; it was first climbed in 1970 by a Japanese expedition

Nampa—meaning respectively the 'Grandmother' and 'Holy Father'—were attempted several times and almost climbed before the final successful expeditions. A recent prize was Rokapi (Nampa South—22,443ft/6,841m high), climbed in 1977 by a two-man British party with twelve bivouacs.

Even less known is the complex Kanjiroba Massif, a series of great fluted ridges bearing jagged summits and guarded by deep gorges—one of which, the 20-mile (32km) Langu canyon to the north, is particularly fearsome. Very similar in shape to the Weisshorn, Kanjiroba I was first climbed from the south east, but Isherwood's 1976 party climbed it alpine-style from the south west. The easiest approaches are from the south and here several peaks on the Jagdula Lekh were climbed in 1953 and 1961, by parties led by Herbert Tichy and John Tyson. In 1964, Tyson's team also managed to reach Bhulu Lhasa (20,016ft/6,101m), in the Sisne group, from the north. In 1962 British ladies were active among the Kagmara Peaks and there climbed Lha Shamma (21,040ft/6,413m).

Dhaulagiri—the 'White Mountain'—

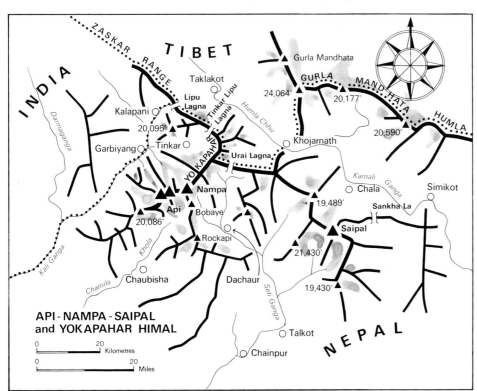

APID-NAMPA-SAIPAL
and YOKAPAHAR HIMAL

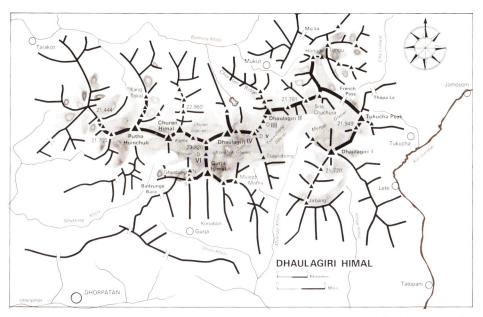

DHAULAGIRI HIMAL

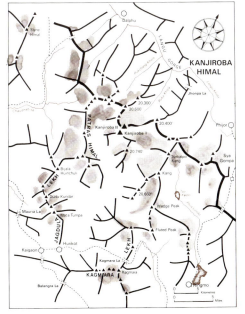

KANJIROBA HIMAL

Dhaulagiri II (25,429/7,751) 1971: A. Huber and Jangbu Sherpa, R. Fear and A. Wiessentiner (Austro-American expedition)
Dhaulagiri IV (25,135/7,661) 1975: S. Kawazu and E. Yusada (Japanese expedition)
93 Churen Himal (24,184/7,371) 1970: ascent disputed between Korean and Japanese expeditions
131 Putha Hiunchuli (23,774/7,246) 1954: Jimmy Roberts and Ang Nyima
Gurja Himal (or Dhaulashri) (23,600/7,193) 1969: T. Saeki and Lakpa Tenzing (Japanese expedition)
Tukucha (22,703/6,919) 1969: G. Hartmann's Swiss expedition

Most Important Passes
Jhonpa La (16,850/5,136) links the northern and eastern flanks of the Kanjiroba Himal
Jangla Bhanjyang (14,840/4,523) leads around the far western end of the Dhaula Himal
Sangda La (16,810/5,124) and Mu La (19,200/5,852) both lead around the north-eastern flank of the Dhaula Himal

Maps
'Kanjiroba Himal' 1:150,000 scale by John Tyson is published by the RGS.
'Dhaulagiri Himal and its Environs' 1:100,000 *kammkarte* is published by Yoshimi Yakushi, Japan

Access
The north-eastern flanks of Api and Nampa require access from India via the pilgrim-route on the Kali river. Otherwise there are convenient airstrips at Chainpur and Silgarhi on the Seti river. Jumla is only some 60 miles' (96km) march from the southern side of Kanjiroba, while Dhor Patan and Baglung give access to the south-west and south-east sides of the Dhaula Himal. Jomosom airstrip can be used to approach the north-eastern flank of Dhaulagiri.

It may well be better, however, to approach from Pokhara with its road link to Kathmandu and a larger airfield able to take bigger aircraft

The Yokapahar Himal from the Tinkar Lipu Pass. The chisel-shaped peak in the centre of the picture is Nampa (22,162ft/6,755m), with the eastern summit of Api to the far right. To the left are peaks NIII and NIV of the Yokapahar crest

attempt was successful, although the summit pair were, in fact, killed on the descent. Later that year the expedition returned and placed ten men safely on the summit.

[1]It is habitual to refer to the peaks of Dhaulagiri, in particular, and, to a lesser extent, other mountain groups, as—for instance—DI, DII, DV, DVI, etc.

Api and Nampa Group
165 Api (23,399/7,132) 1960: K. Hirabayashi and Gyltsen Norbu (Japanese expedition)
195 Saipal (23,100/7,040) 1963: a Japanese expedition
278 Nampa (22,162/6,755) 1972: F. Kimara and S. Takahashi (Japanese expedition)

Kanjiroba Himal
240 Kanjiroba I (south) (22,580/6,882) 1970: Osaka University (Japanese expedition)
350 Kanjiroba II (north) (22,510/6,861)

Dhaula Himal
9 Dhaulagiri I (26,810/8,172) 1960: Kurt Diemberger, P. Diener, E. Forrer, A. Schelbert, Nyima Dorji, Nawang Dorji (Swiss expedition)

is a crest some 30 miles (48km) long, from which rise a series of distinctive pyramid-shaped peaks, no less than fifteen topping '7,000 metres' (22,700ft). Complex glaciers, formidable ice-falls and a tangle of ridges make the actual topography confusing and at least one expedition has attempted the wrong mountain! DI[1], vast and aloof, has a reputation for difficulty and repulsed six expeditions before its summit was reached: it has since been climbed by Japanese (1970), American (1973) and Italian (1976) parties, and always from the North-East Col. In 1969 seven members of a strong American expedition were killed by an avalanche, while in 1976 the forbidding South Face turned back Messner's team. A similar aura of tragedy surrounds DIV on which fourteen climbers died before the eighth

187

Annapurna and Gurkha

One of the world's great mountain prospects is the sight, as the morning mists dissolve, of the glittering ice-hung southern ramparts of the Annapurna Himal rising 22,000ft (6,700m) above the mirrored lake and lush green fields of Pokhara. No less than eleven '7,000m' (23,000ft) summits and a score of other worthy tops adorn this massif but they are, more typically, impressive mountains rather than beautiful peaks. The notable exception is Machapuchare—the 'Fish's Tail'—a classic twin-headed 'Matterhorn' and one of the world's most beautiful mountains which stands isolated before the high crystal wall. Its summit is still virgin, for the lead climbers of Jimmy Robert's small 1957 expedition considered the final 150ft of delicate ice too dangerous to surmount. And, understandably perhaps, the mountain is now forbidden.

Annapurna I was the first '8,000m' (26,250ft) summit to be reached and the first big climb in Nepal. The epic story of that climb is well known. Another milestone in Himalayan mountaineering was the ascent, in 1970, of the most formidable 9,000ft (2,740m) South Face by a very strong British team led by Chris Bonington. Don Whillans and Dougal Haston reached the summit just seven days after a British Army party had repeated the French climb from the north side.

All the major peaks have now been climbed several times; AIV by seven

expeditions, for it is an easy summit passed closeby en route for remote AII. A recent tour de force was the 1975 ascent of AIV's extremely dangerous avalanche-raked South Face by Austrians Schubert and Bauman. During their single thirteen-day, alpine-style push, their companions concluded them dead and went home!

North of the Annapurna Himal, and cradling the headwaters of the Kali Gandaki, is Mustang, a strange area of desert country, a salient of Nepal into the Tibetan plateau. Mustang is still, at the time of writing, closed to foreigners, and its surrounding mountains are unexplored.

The Gurkha Himal runs, rather exceptionally, north to south, and its sou-

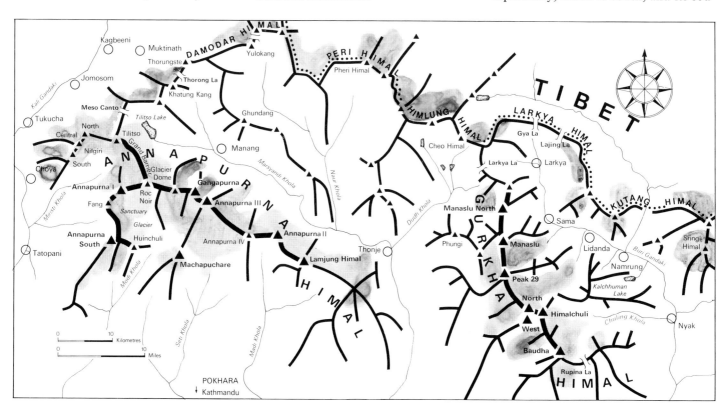

The icy ramparts of the Annapurna Himal wall, the northern horizon seen over the Phewa Tal lake near Pokhara: the lake lies at 2,600ft (792m) and Annapurna II, at the centre, is 26,041ft (7,937m) high. Left is Annapurna IV, and on the right Lamjung. Part of Annapurna III is seen on the extreme left

thern bastion, the great white fang of Himalchuli, reminiscent of the Dent Blanche, dominates the countryside from afar. While its East Face is impressive, its western flank is a complex of ice-fields and ridges holding two other summits. This was the site of the two ascents to date and, despite several attempts elsewhere, no other lines have

yet been climbed. Himalchuli was first attempted in 1953 by a Kenyan expedition led by Arthur Firmin, who died on the retreat, and the North-East Face is now to be attempted by a strong British party in the autumn of 1978.

Proud Manaslu, standing aloof to the north like an icy castle sustained by its curving buttresses, has so far only been climbed by five expeditions and has defeated many more. The summit rises from a large tilted ice-plateau to the north west and this has been reached from the east, the south and via the difficult West Ridge, besides by the original north-east line used again by a Japanese 'ladies only' team in 1974. It is said that one early Japanese reconnaissance expedition was de-bagged and sent packing by local villagers!

The ice-hung comb of Peak 29, seemingly insignificant between its two upstanding neighbours, has been climbed once, by the steep East Face. Tragically, the two lead climbers were killed on the descent and the peak has since remained stubbornly inviolate.

Annapurna Himal

13 Annapurna I (26,504/8,078) 1950: Maurice Herzog and Louis Lachenal (French expedition)
20 Annapurna II (20,041/7,937) 1960: Chris Bonington, Dicky Grant and Ang Nyima (British/Indian expedition)
62 Annapurna III (24,787/7,555) 1961: M. S. Kohli, Sonam Gyasto and Sonam Girmi (Indian expedition)
Annapurna South (23,805/7,256) 1964: S. Uyeo and Mingama Tsering (Japanese expedition)
163 Gangapurna (24,457/7,454) 1965: G. Hauser, L. Greissl, H. Kellensperger, E. Reismuller, Ang Temba and Phu Dorje (German expedition)
212 Machapuchare (22,958/6,997) 1957: Wilf Noyce and David Cox
Lamjung Himal (22,910/6,983) 1974: Dick Isherwood, John Scott, P. Neame, D. Chamberlain, M. Burgess (British expedition)

Gurkha Himal

10 Manaslu (26,760/8,156) 1956: T. Imanishi and Gyalzen Norbu (Japanese expedition)
27 Himalchuli (25,896/7,893) 1960: M. Harada and H. Tanabe (Japanese expedition)
29 Peak 29 (25,705/7,835) 1970: H. Watanabe and Lakpa Tsering (Japanese expedition)
159 Manaslu North (23,470/7,154) 1964: de Lint, Driessen, Schriebl, Nima Tenzing and Ila Tsering (Dutch expedition)
Baudha (21,890/6,672) 1970: Y. Kobayashi and K. Shibata (Japanese expedition)

Major Glaciers

The 'Sanctuary Glacier' below Annapurna's South Face is about 5 miles (8km) long
Chuling Glacier between Himalchuli and Baudha is some 8½ miles (14km) long

Important Passes

Thorong La (17,771/5,417) crossed by the old trade route linking the Marsyandi Valley and Manag to Mustang and Muktinath round the northern flank of the Annapurna massif
Larkya La (17,103/5,213) links the Buri Gandaki Valley to the upper Marsyandi Valley round the northern end of the Gurkha Himal

Maps

'Annapurna and Dhaulagiri Himal' trekking map, scale 1:250,000, published by Dr Harka Gurung (Kathmandu 1970) gives excellent general layout.
'Manaslu' scale 1:50,000, published by the Japanese Alpine Club is an excellent mountain map
A fine map of Himalchuli above the 13,00ft contour was published by Keio University Japan in 1964

Access

Pokhara, easily accessible by road and air from Kathmandu, is the important centre for the Annapurna Himal, although the north-east flank is better approached up the Marsyandi Khola from Dumre on the Kathmandu-Pokhara road.

The Gurkha Himal is approached from the west via the Marsyandi Khola and from the east up the Buri Gandaki, reached from the road-head at Trisuli Bazar.

There is an STOL airstrip at Jomoson, besides the airfields at Pokhara and Gurkha which can accommodate DC3s and similar sized planes

Seen from the Ganesh Himal, the eastern faces of the three great Gurkha peaks rear steeply above deep valleys. Left to right: Himalchuli, Peak 29 and Manaslu. The line of ascent on Himalchuli is on the far side, but currently attempts are being made on the steep North-East Face, in shadow to the right of the summit

Ganesh, Langtang and Jugal

Seen at dusk from the outskirts of Kathmandu, the alpenglow lingers on a series of icy crests visible over the hilltops to the north. These are the summits of the Ganesh, or 'Elephant', Himal. This is a compact and little known group of some nine large ice-peaks of truly daunting visage. Only in 1978 were they added, with qualification, to the 'permitted list'. Standing on the Tibetan frontier, Ganesh I is hidden from most angles and has been climbed twice, without apparent difficulty, from the Sangje Glacier above the rugged gorges of the Chilime Khola, first penetrated in 1949 by Tilman. Several expeditions in the fifties approached from the west and were uniformly unsuccessful. The conspicuous summits are Pabil, an horrendous, docked triangle of tangled ice, Lapsang Karbo, a savage wedge, and GV, with a long scalloped summit ridge ending in a huge eastern prow. Apart from GI and IV, the other seven major peaks are obviously difficult and still officially virgin. At the south-eastern extremity of the group, however, little Paldor (c19,450ft/5,928m), possibly climbed by Tilman, holds several elegant alpine ice-routes. At least one of the several fine peaks in the Kutang group, just north west of the Ganesh, has been

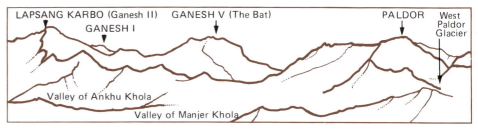

Above: **This is the south-eastern end of the Ganesh Himal seen from above the pass of Pasang Banjan on the Tiru Danda, looking due north**

Below: **Seen over the deep trench of the Trisuli River from the Ganesh Himal to the west, the Langtang peaks line the Nepal – Tibet border**

ascended, but these are close to the frontier in a now prohibited region.

Langtang is a desolate glen walled by large mountains and, being close to Kathmandu, makes a popular goal for trekkers and hardy tourists. Its inhabitants, like those of the Helambu region over the Gangja La, are Sherpas, while the Gosainkund lakes, where Shiva sleeps, are a place of Hindu pilgrimage. A group of attractive little peaks of around 19,000ft (5,790m), and ideal for alpine climbing, line the Helambu march. Overhanging the lower glen are huge rock walls falling from Langtang Lirung whose vast bulk dominates the

190

Trisuli valley, assuming completely different shapes from each direction. On the 'permitted list' since 1978 the mountain looks difficult and several tragic failures have given it a perhaps unwarranted reputation, for it is said to have been climbed, unofficially, solo! Vestal Gangchempo looks down on the middle glen, its beautiful fluted ice-*arêtes* fragile and inviolate: Tilman attempted the peak in 1949 and others have done so since, but it has recently been climbed surreptitiously, alpine-style. The head of the glen is wild country and a cluster of '7,000-metre' (22,970ft) peaks surround it, the two largest standing off in Tibet. Observed from a distance by early Everest expeditions, the approaches and actual location of Shisha Pangma were long a mystery. A massive mountain, its long crest falling as craggy ribs down its huge southern flanks, it was the last '8,000-metre' (26,250ft) peak to be climbed.

Lording it over the small and remote Jugal Himal is Dorje Lakpa II, a fierce ice-hung tooth which appears to offer no simple—or safe—line to its summit. The handsome pyramid of Dorje Lakpa I and shy Lonpo Gang, whose only ascent involved much steep ice-climbing, share a common crest with Langtang. While Jugal's major peaks are tantalizing but difficult prizes, many smaller peaks, especially in the north west of the area, offer challenging alpine-style climbing.

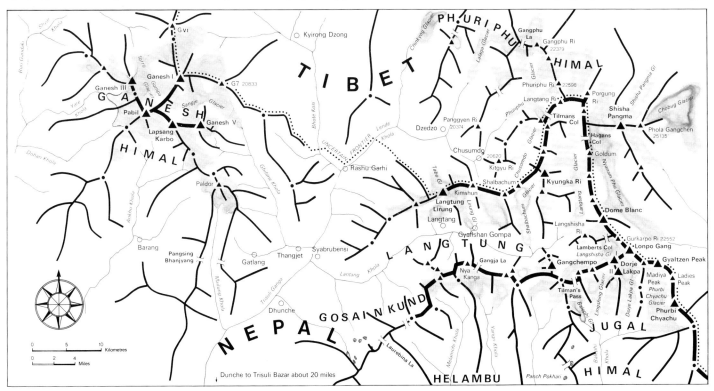

Ganesh Himal
86 Ganesh I (24,298/7,406) 1955: Raymond Lambert, Claude Kogan and E. Gauchat (Swiss expedition)
Lapsang Karbo (Ganesh II) (23,458/7,150)
164 Ganesh III (23,398/7,132)
176 Pabil (Ganesh IV) (23,300/7,102) 1978: 18 members of a Japanese/Nepali Expedition
Ganesh V (The Bat) (22,802/6,950)

Langtang Himal
16 Shisha Pangma (Gosainthan) (26,398/8,046) 1964: a ten-man Chinese party under the leadership of Hsu Ching
127 Langtang Lirung (Gangchen Ledrub) (23,769/7,245) 1978: a joint Japanese/Nepali expedition
533 Kyungka Ri (22,897/6,979) 1963: an Italian Alpine Club expedition
Dome Blanc (Kan Karmo) (22,408/6,830) 1955: Raymond Lambert's Swiss party
Gangchempo (Fluted Peak) (20,954/6,387) 1971: two Americans?

Jugal Himal
184 Lonpo Gang (Big White Peak) (23,238/7,083)

1962: a Japanese expedition
214 Dorje Lakpa I (22,930/6,989)
300 Gyaltzen Peak (21,998/6,705) 1955: Monica Jackson, Betty Stark and party
314 Phurbi Chyachu (21,844/6,658)
Dorje Lapka II (21,380/6,517)

Some Major Glaciers
Ganesh's Sangje Glacier is approximately 6.5 miles (10km) long
The Langtang Glacier is about 10.5 miles (17km) long, while the Nyanam Phu Glacier, over the frontier below Shisha Pangma, is some 12.5 miles (20km) in length
Both the Phurbi Chyachu and Dorje Lakpa Glaciers are approximately 7 miles (11km) long

Some Important Passes
In the Kutang area at the head of the Buri Gandaki ancient tracks cross both the Salbu La (16,537/5,040) and the Yamju Pass (Thaple La) (17,283/5,268) into Tibet.
Gangja La (16,805/5,122) is an important link, impassable to animals, between the villages of Helmu and Langtang
Hagans Col (c 20,000/6,000?) is a possible frontier crossing, over high glaciers, between the Langtang and Nyanam Phu Glaciers
'Tilman's Pass' (c 17,400/5,300) is a very useful

glacier pass between the Jugal and Langtang valleys. It is impassable to animals or laden porters without roped assistance.

Maps
The long-awaited Schneider (FNH) 1:50,000 scale map, 'Langtang and Jugal Himal', is still in preparation.
'Ganesh Himal 1:250,000' and 'Jugal Himal 1:125,000' are mountaineers' *Kammkartes*, privately published by John Cleare and Ian Howell (1977)

Access
None of these peaks were on the 'permitted list' until 1978 and those that are now included have certain qualifications attached.
The Ganesh is reached from the road-head at Trisuli Bazar up the Trisuli river or up the Buri Gandaki.
Langtang is reached from the Trisuli river or through Helmu and over the Ganjga La, while the Jugal is approached by road to Balephi and then up the Balephi Khola. Alternatively, from Panchkhol on the same road, the Indrawati river may be followed to the lakes at Panch Pokhari on Jugal's western-bounding ridge.
There are STOL airstrips at Thangjet and in Langtang near Gyallshan Gompa

Rolwaling and Khumbu West

Rolwaling's deep ice-crested trench cuts far into the knot of mountains that bounds Khumbu's western valleys. The first mountaineers to visit the area were Shipton's 1951 party and now, twenty-seven years later, Rolwaling is traversed every season by the more hardy trekkers bound for Khumbu by the 'back door'. In some 15 miles (24km) the valley climbs to over 14,000ft (4,270m) from where glacier tongues pour to its floor providing an icy pathway to the Tashi Lapcha and the fine peaks north and south.

The twin teeth of Gaurishankar, home of Shivar (or Shankar) and the Goddess Gauri, tower in savage isolation high above the entrance to Rolwaling. Considered one of the 'last great problems' of the Himalaya, it is one of the world's last unclimbed '7,000-metre' (22,970ft) summits. Raymond Lambert, leader of one of the unsuccessful attempts made in the 1950s declared that it was impossible above 18,000ft. But in 1964 Don Whillan's small British team discovered a route on the North-West Face and reached 22,000ft (6,700m) before avalanches forced a retreat. Until 1978 Gaurishankar remained forbidden and, as the northern flank is in Tibet, it will be interesting to see how future parties attempt this most intimidating mountain.

To the west of Rolwaling, a conspicuous rock-tower, rising actually on the frontier, terminates the intriguing Lapchi Kang group of Tibet. Closely resembling the Aiguille de Dru, and visible from Kathmandu where it is known as Jobo Bamare, the identity of this superb feature is confusing: Schneider labels it Chaduk Bhir. A tantalizing challenge anyway!

Menlungtse, too, would be a fine prize. A long-crested angular mountain of stark beauty rising 4 miles (6km) into Tibet, it was supposedly climbed in the '50s. Many of the fine peaks to the east were also climbed at that time and, rising to 22,000ft, their elevation above the high glacier plateaux that surround them makes them excellent objectives for small alpine parties.

South of the Tashi Lapcha lie the long crumpled snow-crests of the Bigphera group and the fine cone of Numbur which dominate the valleys to the south. Nearby Karyolung has repulsed several parties.

Once over the Tashi Lapcha, the trail descends into the Sherpa heartland, to Namche Bazar and the twin villages of Kunde and Khumjung, nestling beneath

the crags and jagged towers of Khumbui Yul La. This sacred mountain, visible from far down the Dudh Kosi, is the southern outlier of a chain of impressive little peaks which hardly ever exceed 20,000ft (6,100m) and lead, via rock spires and icy ridges in profusion, 16 miles (25km) northwards to the great amphitheatre at the head of the Ngozumpa Glacier—to Cho Oyu and Gyachung Kang.

Gyachung Kang is another large angular mountain and its flat crest and sharp ridges make its Nepalese flank appear most forbidding. Its ascent, however, by the North-West (frontier) Ridge proved remarkably straightforward. The gentle looking cone of Cho

Oyu is supposedly the easiest '8,000m' (26,250ft) peak, and technically this is probably true, although it was here that two expeditions met with disaster, Claude Kogan, the Swiss lady climber, being among those who died. Shipton's 1952 expedition established the route on the North-West Flank, having crossed the frontier at the Nangpa La to reach its foot, and Tichy's successful party was a lightweight one with only three leading climbers. For obvious reasons the mountain has now been 'off limits' for some years, but the tumbling ice of the South Face poses a fine future challenge. Its name, Cho Oyu, appears to mean 'Goddess of the Turquoise'.

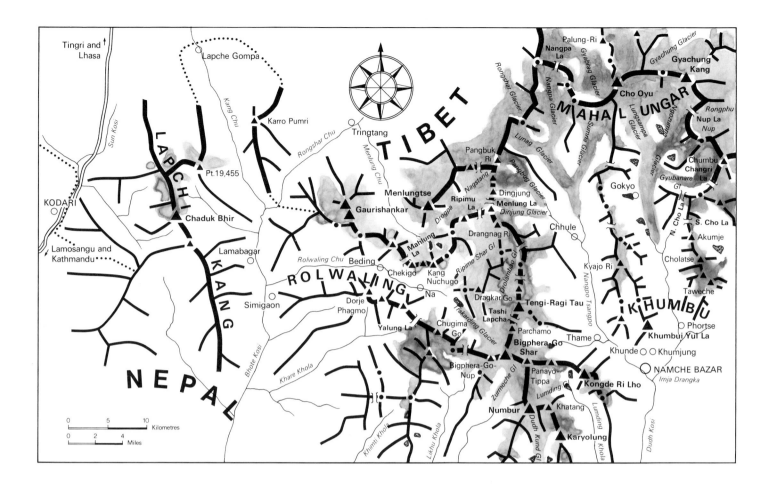

Above: **Gaurishankar dominates the countryside south and west of Rolwaling. This aerial picture was taken from the south**

Opposite above: **It is dawn at Gokyo Cho beside the great Ngozumpa Glacier and Cho Oyu is reflected in the still waters of the green lake**

Rolwaling Himal

141 Menlungtse (Jobo Garu) (23,560/7,181) a British party?
157 Gaurishankar (Jomo Tseringma) (23,440/7,146)
221 Numbur (22,817/6,955) 1963: K. Hirabayashi and Passang Putra (Japanese expedition)
Karyolung (*c* 21,360/6,511)
Bigphera-Go Shar (22,080/6,730)
Tengi-Ragi Tau (22,779/6,943)
Kongde Ri Lho (20,299/6,187)
Chaduk Bhir (Jobo Bamare) (19,465/5,933)

Khumbu West

11 Cho Oyo (26,750/8,153) 1954: Herbert Tichy, S. Jochler and Pasang Dara (Austrian expedition)
23 Gyachung Kang (25,910/7,897) 1964: Y. Kato, K. Sakaizawa and Pasang Phutar (Japanese expedition)
Khumbui Yul La (18,901/5,761)

Some Important Passes

Tashi Lapcha (18,865/5,750) a much used glacier pass connecting Rolwaling to Khumbu, subject to some stonefall danger
Mahlung La (18,425/5,616) an old glacier above Beding in Rolwaling, leading into Tibet
Kinjung La (Menlung La) (19,281/5,877) a high but straightforward glacier pass into Tibet
Yalung La (17,421/5,310) an alternative approach to Rolwaling from the south
Nangpa La (18,753/5,716) an old trade-route used by yak caravans over the glaciers between Khumbu and Tibet

Major Glaciers

In Rolwaling the Drolambao/Trakarding System is approximately 12 miles (19km) long.
In Khumbu both the Ngozumpa and Nangpa Glaciers are also some 12 miles (19km) long, while the Gyabrag (or Kyetrak) System, over the Nangpa La in Tibet, is about 13 miles (21km)

Access

Access to Rolwaling is by road to Lamosangu and thence, in some three days' walking, to Charikot above the Bhote Kosi which is followed to its junction with the Rolwaling Khola, a further five days or so.
Namche Bazar is usually reached in a further ten days' march via Those, Jumbesi and the Dudh Kosi valley. It can be approached over the Tashi Lapcha at the head of Rolwaling.
There are STOL airfields at Jiri, Phaphlu and Lukla, besides a VSTOL strip at Sangboche

Maps

The area is covered by the beautiful contoured 1:50,000 scale Schneider series (FNH)
The 'Lapchi Kang' and 'Rolwaling' sheets cover the Rolwaling valley and the 'Khumbu Himal' and 'Shorong Hinku' sheets cover the relevant Khumbu area. The Khumbu area is also covered by the 1961 RS 1:100,000 map—another fine production.
'Khumbu Mount Everest 1:100,000 Trekking map', by Rene de Milleville, published by Jore Ganesh Press, Kathmandu, is one of the best of its kind.
Although in Italian, Mario Fantin's booklet '*La lunga via che porta all' Everest*' contains topos covering the approach march to Khumbu as well as useful maps of Khumbu (scale 1:200,000) and Eastern Nepal (Kathmandu to the Arun) (scale 1:660,000)

193

Khumbu East and Makalu

The Tibetan flanks of the Mahalungar Himal were well known before the Second World War, but the first mountaineers into Khumbu itself were Charles Houston and Tilman, in 1950, and Shipton's party the following year.

Today the region is a National Park. The steep sharp peaks that stand in avenues along the valley flanks, the high open pastures and the neat villages and friendly Sherpa people have ensured Khumbu's place as the trekkers' mecca of the Himalaya. Wise visitors walk from Lamosangu, but most fly to Lukla and altitude sickness takes a heavy toll. Few reach Everest Base Camp, their ultimate goal. Luckily popular trails may be avoided.

Everest—whose Tibetan name Chomo Lungma means 'Goddess Mother of the Land'—is well documented elsewhere. Let it suffice to note that the huge East or Kangshung Face is still virgin and the beautiful West Ridge, the finest line on the mountain, has yet to be climbed—the brilliant 1963 American traverse of Everest avoided the true ridge by using the North-West Face. From the south, Everest is obscured by the high and serrated 4-mile (6km) crest of Lhotse (South Peak) and Nuptse (West Peak). North Peak, the ugly pyramid of Changtse (24,764ft/7,548m) lies in Tibet. Lhotse has been climbed twice from the Western Cwm, but so far attempts on the East Ridge and the so-called South Face—the true South Face is a forbidding 8,000ft (2,440m) rock wall—have failed. Nuptse was climbed by its fairly difficult South Face and its western summit was reached in 1977 by the attractive North-West Ridge, but there are at least two possible lines from the Western Cwm unclimbed.

Pumori means 'Daughter Peak', so named by Mallory in 1921 after his infant daughter, Clare. Its beautiful white cone has had several ascents by various ribs and ridges around the southern flanks, which are probably easier than they look. The first ascent was by the East Flank and North-East Ridge.

Three impressive mountains in particular dominate the route to Everest. Behind the famous monastery of Thyangboche rears a great wall of ice-streaked rock, topped by a curl of hanging ice between two white summits. This is Kangtega—'Saddle Peak'. Though probably impossible from Khumbu, members of Hillary's 'Schoolhouse Expedition' did climb the South Ridge from the east without too much difficulty. Neighbouring Thamserku

(21,680ft/6,608m), an intimidating pyramid of ice-flutings, gave the New Zealanders a rather harder climb on its South Ridge the following year. The magnificent chisel of Ama Dablam is the classic peak of Khumbu. Almost isolated, it is another impossible-looking 'Matterhorn peak'. A serious British attempt on the extremely difficult North Ridge, in 1959, met with disaster when the two powerful lead climbers disap-

The Everest massif is seen from Gokyo Ri, some 23 miles (37km) to the west. On the far left is Changtse – the 'North Peak' of Everest – then Chakri (20,240ft/6,169m) and then Everest itself above Pt. 5,865m (19,242ft) in the foreground. On the right the steep buttress of Lhotse's South Face is clearly visible. Also discernible are Everest's West Ridge and the South Face of Nuptse

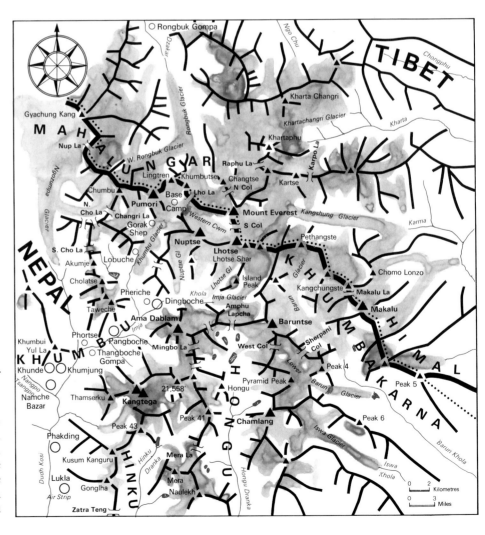

194

Major Peaks

1 Mount Everest (Sagarmatha, Chomolungma) (29,028/8,848) 1953: Edmund Hillary and Tenzing Norgay (British expedition)
4 Lohtse (27,890/8,501) 1956: Ernst Reiss and Fritz Luchsinger (Swiss expedition)
6 Makalu (27,790/8,470) 1955: Jean Couzy and Lionel Terray (French expedition)
26 Nuptse (25,850/7,879) 1961: Dennis Davis and Tashi Sherpa (British expedition)
105 Chamlang (24,183/7,371) 1962: S. Anma and Pasang Phutar (Japanese expedition)
135 Baruntse (23,688/7,220) 1954: G. Harrow, C. Todd, G. Lowe, W. Beaven (New Zealand expedition)
156 Pumori (23,442/7,145) 1962: G. Lenser, U. Hurlemann, H. Rutzel (Swiss-German expedition)
248 Ama Dablam (22,494/6,856) 1961: Mike Gill, Barry Bishop, Mike Ward, Wally Romanes (Anglo-American-New Zealand expedition)
265 Kangtega (22,340/6,809) 1963: Mike Gill, Tom Frost, D. Dornan, J. Wilson (American–New Zealand expedition)

Notable Glaciers

The Kangshung Glacier below the (Tibetan) East Flank of Everest is some 11 miles (17km) long, while the Khumbu Glacier is only 9½ miles (15km), measured to the base of the Lhotse Face in the Western Cwm.

The Barun Glacier is approximately 10 miles (16km) long

Important Passes

Mingbo La (19,084/5,817) a difficult glacier pass linking the head of Hongu valley to Tangboche region
Amphu Labtsa (18,963/5,780) the glacier pass linking the head of Hongu valley to Imja valley
Mera La (17,765/5,415) this easy glacier pass links Hinku valley to Hongu valley
Zatra Teng (16,217/4,943) an important trail this links Lukla to Hinku valley

Maps

The fine Schneider 1:50,000 sheet 'Khumbu Himal' covers the area as does the RGS 1:100,000 map 'The Mount Everest Region'.

A 1:25,000 scale contoured map 'Chomolongma- Mount Everest', is also produced by Schneider, published by Alpenverin, and covers the immediate Everest area

Access

Namche Bazar, the 'capital' of Khumbu, is reached in some thirteen days' march from Lamosangu, about three hours' drive along the 'Chinese Road' from Kathmandu (45 miles/72km).

The Hinku and Hongu valleys are approached from Lukla via the Zatra Teng pass and the Mera La.

Makalu and the Barun valley may be approached from the Upper Hongu via West Col (20,127/6,135) and Sherpani Col (20,045/6,110), from Dharan, up the Arun and Barun river valleys, or by a series of passes eastward of Jubing on the Dudh Kosi. Dharan is some 250 road miles (400km) from Kathmandu or may be reached by air via Biratnagar where there is an airfield. There are also STOL airstrips at Jiri, Phaphlu, Lukla and Tumlingtar, and a VSTOL strip at Sangboche

peared high on the mushroom-corniced, final *arête*. The South Ridge, climbed in winter by members of the scientific 'Silver Hut' expedition, proved not too difficult. Ama Dablam means 'Mother and her Necklace'.

Taweche is one of a trinity of savage ice-peaks guarding the foot of the Khumbu Glacier. The New Zealanders had been high on it in 1963, but soon afterwards the mountain was placed 'off limits'. Despite this, a team of Chamonix guides climbed it somewhat irresponsibly in 1974, by the East Flank, causing something of an international incident.

Undoubtedly Makalu is the most handsome of Nepal's '8,000 metre' (26,250ft) peaks, and, although it drains entirely to the Arun, it is generally considered to belong to Khumbu. A perfect pyramid with four sharp ridges, Makalu has been attempted by some sixteen expeditions to date, of which only five

Makalu, seen from the Base Camp of the 1954 Californian Expedition above the snout of the Barun Glacier. The shoulder on the right is the South-East Peak and the right skyline over it is the line of the long South-East Ridge route. The spur direct to it is the Czechoslovak 1976 line. The 1975 Yugoslav route takes the South Face directly below the summit, while the French West Pillar is the left skyline (1971)

have been successful. The French encountered little difficulty on the North Ridge during the first ascent and subsequently the Japanese have climbed the 2-mile long South-East Ridge (1970), repeated with variations by the Czechs in 1976. In 1971 the French climbed the formidable West Pillar, while a large Yugoslav expedition forced the 7,000ft (2,133m) South Face, most fearsome of all in 1975. There is potential on the West Face, already attempted by Americans in 1977 and, of course, on the fine looking East ridge rising from Tibet.

Eastern Himalaya, Sikkim and Bhutan

The summit crest of the great Kangchenjunga Massif forms the border between Nepal and the once independent—Indian-protected—state of Sikkim. Although many of the region's finest peaks rise within Nepal, and currently the only free access to the massif is from the Nepalese side, the 50 miles (80km) from Makalu to the Tamur river hold no important summits and it is convenient to consider the massif as part of Sikkim. As such it is the western end of the final stretch of the Himalaya.

Kangchenjunga and its massed satellites—'The Five Treasuries of the Great Snows'—float on the horizon, a series of interlocked triangles of shining light and shadow, only 46 miles (74km) north of the Indian hill station of Darjeeling. Until Nepal opened her frontiers in 1949, Kangchenjunga was the best known mountain in the Himalaya. Indeed, until 1849 it was thought to be the world's highest summit and in the ensuing century its vicinity was more frequented by travellers, scientists and mountaineers than any in the range.

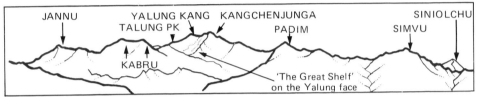

Douglas Freshfield, accompanied by the photographer Vittorio Sella, completed much valuable exploration when he circumnavigated the massif in 1899, and the first attempt to actually climb the mountain took place six years later. Led by the notorious Aleister Crowley, the enterprise was a fiasco and five lives were lost, but, remarkably, Crowley had selected a line on which the next attempt—fifty years later—was to succeed.

In the meantime, three major expeditions made determined attacks on the summit. In 1929 and 1931 the Bavarians under Paul Bauer fought their way through fearful cornices up the East Spur above the Zemu Glacier, but were unable to climb beyond 25,000ft (7,620m) to reach the North Ridge at its head. In 1930 G. O. Dyhrenfurth's International Expedition was defeated on the difficult North-West Face and Kangchenjunga gained a reputation for bad weather and terrible avalanches. However, close reconnaissances in 1953 and 1954 by John Kempe proved that a good line existed on the Yalung—or South-West—Face, and Charles Evans's smoothly run expedition the following year reached the summit without much difficulty. In 1977 Kangchenjunga was climbed once more by a powerful Indian expedition following Bauer's dif-

Siniolchu, one of the eastern outliers of Kanchenjunga, is one of the world's most beautiful mountains

This is the famous view of the Kangchenjunga Massif seen from Tiger Hill above Darjeeling: the summit of Kangchenjunga is some 46 miles (74km) distant. Jannu is seen on the far left and Siniolchu on the far right. The Great Shelf and the Sickle cliff on the Yalung Face of Kangchenjunga itself, features on the route of the first ascent, can clearly be seen just left of the summit

ficult route, and in '78 the Poles climbed the South Summits from the Yalung Glacier.

Several lesser tops and shoulders surround the main summit. The west top, Yalung Kang (27,625ft/8,420m) has been climbed from both the south west and the south while the shoulder of Kangbachan, a peak in its own right, was climbed via the rumpled ice of its North-West Face by both Poles and Yugoslavs in 1974.

Fiercest of Kangchenjunga's satellites is Jannu, a peak not unlike a huge Obergabelhorn when seen from the south west, but with two great shoulders below its rock-banded blade-like head. The ascent of its steep and narrow South Ridge was one of the hardest Himalayan climbs made up to that time, and one of the earliest to depend almost entirely on fixed ropes. The route was repeated in 1974 by a Japanese party, while the horrific North Face—5,000ft (1,524m) of extremely steep ice and rock—was forced, by the Japanese again, in 1976, only six months after a New Zealand

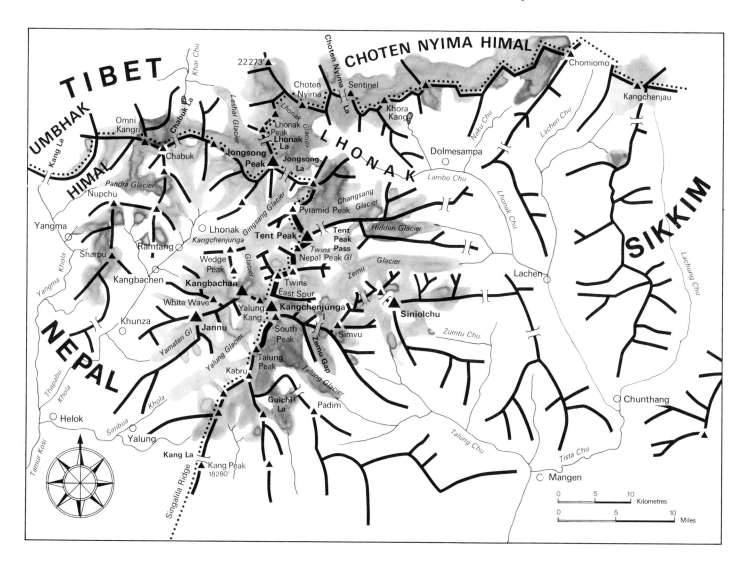

team had surmounted the face but re-treated from the final summit ridge.

On the Sikkim flanks of the massif rises Siniolchu, considered by many to be the world's most beautiful mountain. 'Its ridges are as sharp as a knife-edge, its flanks, though incredibly steep, mostly covered with ice and snow, are furrowed with the ice-flutings so typical of the Himalaya. The crest of the cornice-crowned summit stands up like a thorn!' So wrote Karl Wien who first reached its summit. The first post-monsoon ascent of a peak higher than 24,000ft (7,315m) was that of square-topped Kabru (24,002ft/7,316m) just south of Kang-chenjunga and conspicuous from Dar-jeeling. It had been attempted by W. W. Graham in 1883, while in 1907 Nor-wegians Rubenson and Aas reached within 100ft of the top. After their defeat on Kangchenjunga, the International Expedition climbed the graceful curled icefield of Jongsong Peak, Nepal Peak and others and activity continued throughout the thirties, with much sought-after Tent peak succumbing just before the outbreak of war. Since the war the Indians have discouraged foreign climbers in Sikkim while, in recent years, only Yalung Kang, Kangbachan and Jannu appeared on Nepal's 'permitted list'.

As Kangchenjunga forms the western boundary of Sikkim, so the crest south of Pauhunri (23,180ft) forms the eastern, while, beyond, a salient of Tibet extends through a gap in the Himalayan chain almost into India. Then the mountains rise again and a great wall of icy peaks arcs round the northern marches of Bhutan before becoming once more the Indo-Tibetan frontier and striking north east to the Himalaya's final sum-mits. From Sikkim eastwards the moun-tains are known as the Assam Himalaya.

Bhutan, the 'Land of the Peaceful Dragon' is a mountain kingdom the size of Switzerland. Many of its population of 750,000 are of Tibetan stock and their culture, strongly influenced by the Mahayana Bhuddist religion, is es-pecially rich. Peculiarities of the country are the *dzongs* or castles scattered through the valleys, and the national sport of archery. Strongly influenced by the monsoon, the landscape is lush and green, rhododendron-covered hillsides and forests of rare juniper rise to a fine range of mountains containing many '7,000 metre' (22,970ft) peaks and some enormous glaciers. Typically the main valleys run north to south and lateral communication is difficult.

Bhutan has always been a closed coun-try and has only been open to tourism, in a very selective and limited way, since 1974. Its mountains are little known and many are probably still unseen by Euro-peans. A notable exception is Chomo Lhari—'Goddess of the Holy Mountain'. Seen from Bhutan as a con-spicuous snow-cone, it rises preci-pitously from Tibet in a 10,000ft (3,050m) wall of ice and rock: its ascent from here, via the South-West Ridge, by a tiny party was a tour de force. Many of the finest peaks appear to lie in the remote Lunana region in the far north. Among them are Jejekangphu Kang with its three savage fangs, the immense cliff-girt ice-plateau of Chomo Lhari Kangri (*c*24,000ft/7,315m) and, on a spur northwards, Kunla Khari, prob-ably the highest peak of the Bhutan Himal, is listed by the Survey of India as holding four summits above 24,000ft.

East of Bhutan the northern forests of Assam are unadministered, the obscure McMahon Line is disputed, and the mountains are even less known. Just 50 miles (80km) from Bhutan stands the Kangdu Massif (23,258ft/7,089m) and the next important peak is the last. The

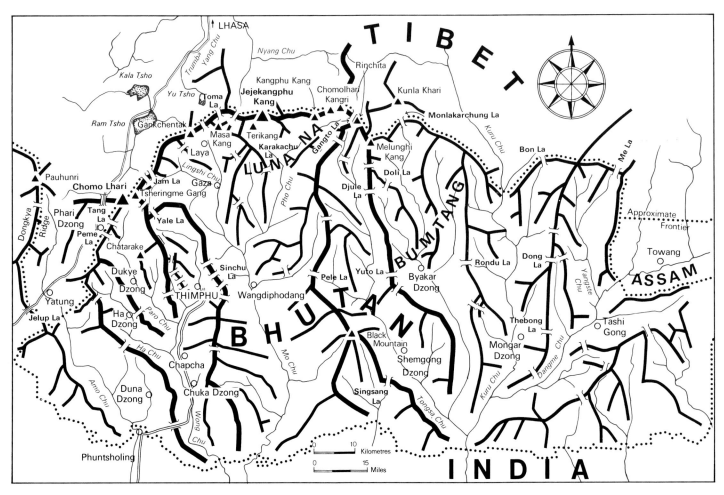

lovely icy pyramid of Namche Barwa stands just 450 miles (724km) from Kangchenjunga. Eighteen thousand feet below its summit, the gorges of the Tsangpo curl round its foot as the river doubles back on itself to become the Brahmaputra. It is a fitting final bastion to the greatest range on earth. Just 7 miles across the river Gyala Peri rises towards the mountains of China.

Above: **Gangchentak (c22,000ft/6,706m) rises on the Tibetan frontier above the headwaters of the Mo Chu in north-west Bhutan**

Top: **Chomolhari from the south: this view belies the tremendously impressive flank that falls northward into Tibet and was a landmark on the early prewar approach marches to Everest**

SIKKIM AND SINGALILA HIMAL
Situation: State of Sikkim; Kingdom of Nepal; Peoples Rupublic of China (Tibet Autonomous Region)

Important Peaks
3 Kangchenjunga I (28,208/8,595) 1955: George Band and Joe Brown (British expedition)
22 Kangbachan (25,925/7,902) 1974: five Polish climbers

47 Jannu (25,294/7,902) 1962: R. Paragot, P. Keller, R. Desmaison and Gyaltsen Mikchung (French expedition)
77 Jongsong Peak (24,518/7,473) 1930: E. Schneider, H. Hoerlin, Frank Smythe, G. Wood-Johnson (international expedition)
100 Tent Peak (24,089/7,342) 1939: E. Grob, L. Schmaderer and H. Paider (Swiss-German expedition)
189 Pauhunri (23,180/7,065) 1911: A. Kellas and Sonam Sherpa
238 Siniolchu (22,610/6,892) 1936: K. Wien and A. Gottner (German expedition)

Important Passes
Kang La (c16,800/5,100) crosses the crest from Nepal to Sikkim, south of the main mountain group`
Jongsong La (20,080/6,120) crosses the Nepal/Sikkim crest north of the main mountain group

Major Glaciers
The Zemu and Kangchenjunga Glacier Systems are each some 14 miles (22km) long

Access
The best approach is from Darjeeling, itself reached from Bagdogra Airport via Calcutta.
Darjeeling is reached by road and/or rail from Bagdogra which is accessible by air from the international airport at Calcutta. From Darjeeling a march of some fourteen days, either along the crest of the Singalila Ridge to the Kang La, or low down on its Nepalese flank, leads to the Yalung Glacier

Maps
The best is 'Sikkim-Himalaya', scale 1:150,000, published by the Swiss Foundation for Alpine Research, Zurich, 1952

Bibliography
Kangchenjunga—the Untrodden Peak, by Charles Evans (Hodder and Stoughton, 1956)

BHUTAN AND ASSAM
Situation: Kingdom of Bhutan; Republic of India; State of Assam; Tibet (Autonomous Region of Chinese Peoples Republic)

Some Notable Peaks
41 Namche Barwa (25,445/7,756)
63 Kunla Khari (Khula Kangri) (c24,784/7,554)
113 Chomolhari (23,997/7,314) 1937: F. Spenser Chapman and Pasang Dawa
Jejekangphu Kang (c 23,950/7,300)
153 Gyala Peri (23,458/7,150)

An Important Pass
Jelup La (14,390/4,386) the frontier crossing from Sikkim to Tibet, linking Gangtok to Lhasa; was a main trade-route over the Great Himalaya used in the twenties and thirties by Everest expeditions on their way to the north side of the mountain

Access
Phuntsholing, on the Bhutan frontier, is reach by road from Bagdogra airport and from here small vehicles can drive 112miles (180km) of mountain road to Thimphu, the capital, where there is also an airfield.
Currently access to Bhutan is by invitation, or in a strictly limited number of organized parties with a stipulated minimum spending requirement

The Mountaineer's Equipment

The modern mountaineer is no better and no bolder than his predecessor. The old adage that each generation climbs on the shoulders of the previous one and is thus able to reach a bit higher, is very true. There have always been men with determination, commitment and a yen for exploration—while skill is only a relative term. What has changed over the years, however, and never more swiftly than over the last two decades, has been the gear that has enabled both 'top' climbers as well as less ambitious mountain-lovers to pursue their recreation and to achieve their goals more easily, more comfortably and above all more safely than ever before.

Today's Himalayan climber, clad and equipped with the best that science and a booming 'outdoor industry' can provide, can only marvel at the men who, over a half century before, reached out to within a few rope-lengths of Everest's summit without oxygen and wearing Harris tweeds, layers of Shetland jumpers, military puttees and nailed boots.

The modern rock-climber with his highly sophisticated protection techniques, his jammed nuts and nylon ropes and wearing his harness, helmet and high-hysterisis rubber bootees, plays a game no more dangerous than football, if considerably more gymnastic, serious and specialized. As recently as 1951—when I first learnt to rock-climb—it was axiomatic that the leader did not fall. If he did, with his long unprotected run-outs and stiff yet frail hemp rope, he could expect to die. We wore tricouni-nailed boots or Woolworth plimsolls with socks pulled over them when the rock was wet. The best clothing was army-surplus. The equipment of earlier generations was even more primitive and I have often reflected if, perhaps, they were better men than we, for their achievements—in mountaineering's first century—were astonishing.

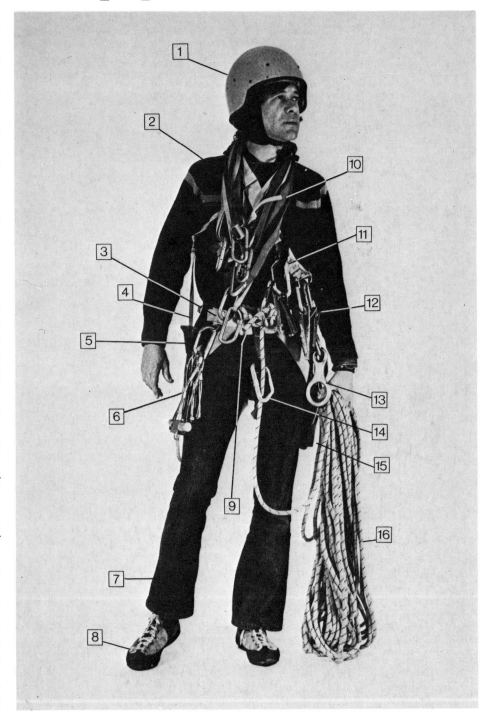

Comprehensive outfit for Rock-climbing
1 climbing helmet – as much to protect against stone fall as against the wearer falling !
2 loose – but not baggy—sweater
3 climbing harness – waist-and-hip-type comfortable to sit or hang in !
4 hammer sling
5 piton hammer in holster
6 selection of many different-sized nuts and chocks
7 free fitting jeans (or shorts often now – especially in USA)
8 smooth soled 'PA'-type climbing bootees known colloquially as 'magic boots', probably uncomfortable for normal feet !
9 rope knotted into climbing harness
10 selection of nylon tape slings and loops with karabiners already on ; easily whipped off over the head for instant use
11 a bandolier to carry equipment on known as a gear rack
12 pitons
13 figure 8 descendeur for rapelling
14 karabiner – in this case part of the harness system
15 'coins de bois' wooden wedges
16 150ft x 11mm kernmantel-type (i.e. sheathed) nylon or perlon climbing rope— *could* be 300ft of 9mm used double

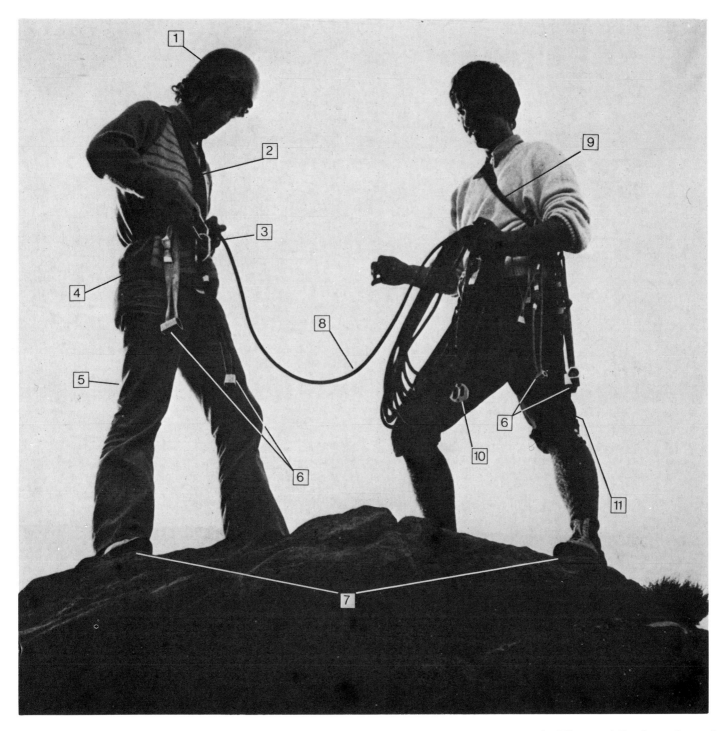

**Typical equipment used for
Rock-climbing on a British outcrop**
 1 crash helmet
 2 spare sling (tape)
 3 spare karabiners
 4 rope knotted round waist
 5 free-fitting jeans
 6 nuts and chocks of various sizes and
    shapes
 7 smooth-soled 'PA'-type rock-climbing
    bootees
 8 150ft x 11mm kernmantel-type
    climbing rope
 9 gear sling on which to hang gear
10 sticht belay plate
11 climbing breeches

A bewildering range and variety of equipment, clothing and gadgets is now available to those who frequent the wilderness and the mountains. Although much of it is not strictly necessary we are fortunate in this choice because it gives us more scope to practise our craft, at a time when the wilderness itself is growing smaller and politically more difficult of access every day. But we should always remember that gear is no substitute for hard-learned skill and wisdom.

There are basically four categories of mountain equipment and clothing: hill-walking, rock-climbing, alpine and big mountain. The specialized gear for each, like the skills required, are also applicable to the next category. The following pictures illustrate some of the gear that might be used in several typical situations.

The Mountaineer's Equipment

Typical alpine climbing outfit for alpine climbing

1. alpine rucksack with bivouac extension inside, has haul ring so can be hauled up on rope if necessary on a hard pitch. Rucksack contains down jacket, food, spare clothes, helmet, rope and perhaps a bivouac stove
2. woollen cap or balaclava
3. short dropped-pick ice axe
4. nylon windproof and showerproof cagoule – hooded
5. side straps for skis when ski-mountaineering or for fitting on more gear or extra side pockets if necessary
6. breeches or 'salopettes' of stretch fabric or wool
7. fabric snow-gaiters
8. holster on webbing belt – one on each side
9. 'climaxe' ice tool for difficult ice-climbing – probably an ice hammer on other hip
10. single alpine boots with stiffened cleated sole for difficult climbing

Modified alpine equipment used on a small Himalayan peak

1. short ice-axe for difficult climbing
2. gloves of matted wool
3. lots of pockets
4. crash helmet
5. long safety sling to axe for mixed climbing – a personal preference
6. nylon webbing belt supporting axe and hammer holsters
7. spare karabiner
8. crampons with non-freezing straps
9. snow goggles
10. plenty of glacier cream smeared on face against sunburn
11. shirt sleeves – it's hot!
12. alpine rucksack on back containing windproofs, spare clothes – down jacket, etc.
13. one-piece bib-and-brace 'salopettes' in stretch fabric – more practical, more weatherproof and more comfortable than breeches
14. fabric overboots over double mountain boots

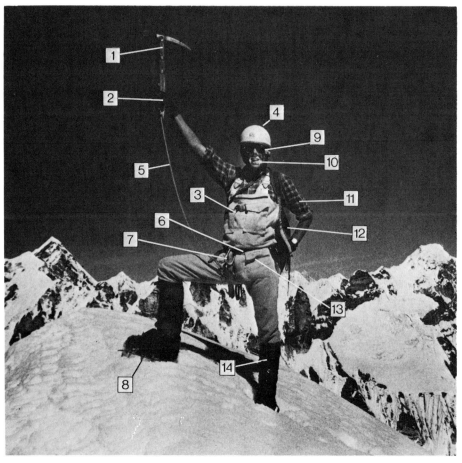

An alpine bivouac on a small ledge with a typical collection of gear for a major rock route on a big snowy mountain – probably about 10–12,000ft (3,048 – 3,658m), in Europe or a bit lower in USA. Variations on the theme could apply to 25,000ft (7,620m) in Himalaya or, unlikely but occasionally, to 3,000ft (914m) in Britain! ALL FIRMLY TIED ON – likewise the two climbers!

1 wind and showerproof parka – *almost* waterproof. Large hood
2 camera
3 small pad of closed-cell foam for comfortable sitting/sleeping!
4 'pied d'elephant' waist-length lightweight sleeping bag
5 peg hammer – with short pick it can be used on ice
6 north wall hammer i.e. hammer axe
7 crampons – for snowy descent
8 hammer
9 piton
10 spare climbing gear hung out of way where it can't be lost or dropped
11 belay round flake
12 chock in crack
13 climbing helmet
14 snow goggles
15 balaclava
16 down or fibrefill padded jacket
17 matted-wool mittens
18 food
19 gas stove
20 light pot for brewing hot drink
21 spare rope 150ft x 9mm
22 rucksack with bivi extension pulled out and the whole pulled over legs and up to waist

Equipment used on Everest SW Face
1 pack frame, multi-purpose, to carry large awkward loads and also oxygen bottles
2 climbing harness waist-and-hip-only-type
3 'terrordactyl' ice hammer in holster
4 one-piece windproof suit with hood over down jacket and pants over fibre-pile suit
5 silk balaclava and aviator's flying cap to hold oxygen mask
6 one-piece goggles against glare and spindrift
7 oxygen mask
8 pipe leading to regulator valve and on to bottles in pack
9 fibre-filled mittens over pile mittens over silk gloves
10 zipped doubleskin neoprene overboots – *over* double mountain boots

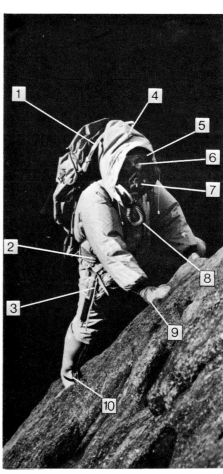

Glossary

Abseil see **Rappell**

A Cheval Method of climbing a narrow ridge or *arête* with one leg either side – astride as on horse-back

Aid Climbing Artificial climbing: progress using gadgets such as pitons, expansion bolts, bat-hooks, or nuts for direct-aid on ground where free climbing is not possible. In theory, given the effort and rock of any quality, no climb is impossible using aid tactics

Aiguille French for 'needle': used in the Alps, particularly the Mont Blanc Range, and now elsewhere to describe a sharp-pointed mountain – usually a rock peak

Alpine-style To climb relying on speed of movement and economy of materials, as opposed to 'Himalayan tactics' whereby an expedition lays siege to its objective with a chain of well-stocked camps and an abundance of equipment. There is an increasing tendency for small parties to climb even major Himalayan objectives alpine-style

Arête A narrow or knife-edged ridge or rock feature; may be vertical or horizontal

Ascender Mechanical device for climbing a fixed rope – see also Jumar and Prusiking

Belay An attachment, or point of attachment, to the rock or ice for security purposes

Bergschrund 'schrund or rimaye: the crevasse between an ice or *névé* slope and the glacier or further slope beneath, which is moving in a different direction or angle. Often a serious obstacle at the bottom of a rock-wall or ice-slope

Bolt Expansion bolt: a nail-like fitting used as a piton but requiring a hole to be drilled in the rock in which it is inserted. There are various methods of expanding the end or locking the bolt into the hole. Used with discretion by a first-class climber to overcome a blank section of rock or to provide essential belays or protection, bolts can make possible routes where otherwise there would be none – but their use is considered by many to be unethical

Bong A large piton made of metal folded at an angle and originating in California

Bridging A climbing move where the body, usually the legs in a wide stride, acts as a bridge between holds which may only be usable by the opposition pressure of the 'bridge'

Chockstone A stone, boulder or pebble, jammed in a crack or chimney. Artificial chocks in metal or plastic now used for protection. See Nuts

Col A dip, or saddle, in a ridge, usually between two peaks; a pass

Cornice An overhanging curl of snow or snow-ice usually along one side of a ridge crest or plateau edge and formed by wind action. May overhang for many feet

Couloir A gully, usually a snow or ice gully, on a big mountain

Crampon A steel frame closely fitting the sole of the climbing boot with – nowadays – 10 downward-pointing spikes and 2 forward-pointing spikes (lobster points) about 2in long. Used for ice-climbing or moving over verglassed rock

Crux The most difficult or crucial move, pitch or section of a climb

Cwm A *cirque* or corrie: Welsh word describing a small hanging valley, holding – or once holding – a glacier. Sometimes the blind head of a valley

Descendeur A metal (usually alloy) friction device, used for rappelling – the best is shaped like a figure 8; much favoured by British climbers

Dièdre A dihedral: a vertical rock feature, two walls set at an angle like an open book, often with some form of crack up the angle

Exposure That psychological factor, to which height above the ground, distance from safety and steepness of the rock all contribute, which makes a given move on rock or ice more difficult than the same move would be at ground level

Free Climbing Climbing without artificial aids using only the natural holds on the rock for progress. On ice, using only the accepted techniques of crampons and ice axe or hammers, but not pitons, for progress

Friction Climbing On smooth rock, which is not too steep, progress may be made even if there are no holds by using only the friction of the boot soles, friction of the palms of the hands and cunning distribution of weight. At its greatest development on the big walls of Yosemite and elsewhere it is a highly skilled and delicate precision technique

Girdle A traverse, particularly the horizontal traverse from side to side of a cliff

Glissade A technique of sliding down steep slopes of hardish snow on the boot-soles, a sort of 'poor man's skiing'

Grades There are several different grading systems used to describe the difficulty of a climb, and these are often confusing and conflicting. On big mountains the best system is the French 'Vallot' system, used also by the British. A big mountaineering route is given an adjectival overall grade such as 'Assez Difficile' (AD) through 'Difficile' (D), 'Très Difficile' (TD) to 'Extrêmement Difficile' (ED) which takes into account the length, seriousness and objective dangers of the climb. The hardest individual pitches are then given a numerical classification, I to VI, which describes their technical difficulty in normal conditions. Thus the Eigerwand is graded ED with several pitches of V, while the easy way, the West Flank, is graded 'Peu Difficile' (PD). Artificial (Aid) pitches are graded A1 to A4. There has been much recent discussion concerning the possible introduction of a seventh grade into the Alpine Grading System, and indeed in 1977 a new rock-climb in the Wilder Kaiser region was given

a Grade VII rating. The British use three domestic systems: the traditional adjectival one of Moderate (M), Difficult (D), Very Difficult (VD), Severe (S), Very Severe (VS) and Extremely Severe (ES) with subdivisions of 'Easy', 'Mild' and 'Hard', and a numerical system I to VI (with usually a, b and c subdivisions) reserved for outcrops, in which V approximates to VS (Very Severe) and to continental VI. Very confusing! The Aid grades are similar, A1 to A4. On Scottish ice a further numerical system is used which bears no relationship to any other system. For instance Grade I is an uncomplicated snow-climb with no ice-pitches but maybe cornice difficulties at the top, while Grade V, although no harder technically than Grade IV, covers a long sustained route of the greatest difficulty, a really serious undertaking requiring not only a powerful party but also favourable conditions
In the U.S.A. there are further systems, perhaps the best known being the Californian Decimal System. For an Englishman this is fairly complex, but once mastered is at least logical if often superfluous. Thus Class 3 is easy ground, 'scrambling' not requiring a rope, Class 4 might need a rope while Class 5 requires a rope and protection. Class 5 is subdivided into 5.1 to 5.10 and further; 5.8 being approximately British VS. If, therefore, one solos a pitch of a technical difficulty of 5.7, it reverts to 3rd Class! A further 'grade' of I–VI covers the length and seriousness of a climb; Grade I could be a single pitch 'problem' of 5.10 difficulty and Grade V an extremely hard route requiring two days. Grade VI is reserved for very serious multi-day climbs only. The Australians have a logical and sensible system using cardinal numbers – their hardest climbs are currently running at grade 21!

Grass Piton Extra long piton or stake which can be driven into grass tufts or earth to provide some sort of security

Hand-jam A hold formed by jamming the hand or fist in a crack, often by just tensing the muscles. Usually feels reassuringly safe if used properly. Other parts of the body may also be jammed – finger, arm, foot etc

Harness Besides offering a method of attachment to the rope, a climber's harness can also absorb much of the shock in the event of a fall. There is a great variety of harnesses, usually made of nylon webbing; the 'Swami Belt' is a simple waist harness. There are also chest-harnesses, sit-harnesses and specialized whole-torso harnesses

Hexentric A form of nut shaped like an eccentric hexagon, developed by Yvon Chouinard in the U.S

Ice Screw A modern form of ice piton threaded for easy retrieval – may be corkscrew form or tubular

Inselberg A peculiar rock formation: an isolated rock spire or fang rising steeply from the

surrounding flat country

Iron Ironmongery, hardware: American slang term describing pitons, karabiners and other metal gadgets used by climbers

Jug Handle (Jug hold, jug): a perfect hand-hold

Jumar A Swiss metal clamp which, when clipped onto a rope, will slide up it but not downwards. Two are used for climbing a hanging rope

Karabiner 'Krab' – a snap-link with a spring-loaded gate usually made of light alloy and used for a wide variety of attachment purposes

Karabiner Brake Several karabiners linked in such a way as to provide considerable friction to a rope running through them and used, particularly in the U.S., as a rappel device

Kloof South African term: a gully or steeply descending river gorge

Névé The upper snow or snow-ice slopes from which a glacier is born

Nut A small artificial chockstone, originally an engineer's nut, but nowadays a specially designed metal or plastic chock or wedge, which is cunningly inserted into a crack in such a way that it cannot be pulled out in the direction of any likely loading. Used now instead of pitons. The use of nuts for protection has revolutionized free climbing

PA Originally a highly specialized lightweight canvas and rubber climbing bootee with a smooth hard rubber sole designed by French guide and equipment manufacturer, Pierre Allain. Nowadays used to describe any of the many similar 'magic boots' on the market

Peel A peel-off, a fall off

Pendule A horizontal move made by swinging on the rope like a pendulum

Pin Piton, peg, nail. A steel blade, in various forms, shapes and sizes, which is hammered into a crack either for security or as an aid to progress. Nowadays considered unethical if nuts can be used instead

Pitch Section of a climb, usually of 60–150ft (20–50m), between ledges or belay points. A 'lead' – the distance a leader will climb before stopping to bring up his second man

Prusiking Method of ascending a fixed rope, slow and strenuous. Originally employed two prusik knots, friction hitches, which would be slid up the rope but which would jam under strain. Nowadays various mechanical prusiking devices are replacing the sliding knots – see Ascender and Jumar

Rappel Abseil. Roping-down, a means of descent by sliding down a rope under the control of the friction of the rope passing either round the body or through a friction device of some kind. See Descendeur, Karabiner Brake

Rimaye (Fr) a bergschrund

Rognon literally a 'kidney': a rock island in a glacier or ice-field.

Roof A horizontal overhang

Running Belay Protection: a point of attachment to the rock or ice, usually using a rock-spike, a nut or a piton, on which the climbing rope runs freely through a karabiner. There may be several 'runners' at

in a gully. Always awkward and tedious to ascend, but 'scree running' can provide a speedy and exhilarating method of descending loose small-stone scree-slopes

Sérac An ice-cliff

Sky-hook A simple gadget shaped like a picture-rail hook and

originating in California; used in aid climbing. Hooked onto a rock crystal or slight flaw in the rock surface it will support the weight of a climber

Sling A loop of ropes or nylon tape: it has a multitude of uses, but particularly for running belays

Stack An isolated pinnacle, usually rising from the sea or foreshore

Stance A belay ledge on which a climber can adopt the best position to hold a fall by the leader above him or the second man below him – or the position itself

Swami Belt A length of nylon tape wound round and round the waist to

which the climbing rope is knotted

Tension Using tension from the rope to remain in balance, particularly when moving in a horizontally trending direction

Terrordactyl A form of advanced ice-climbing tool

Three-point Contact moving only one hand or foot at a time so that the climber is on three holds at any one moment

Traverse A series of side-ways moves – a horizontal section of climbing

Tyrolean Traverse A traverse made by climbing along a rope fixed

at both ends. Originally used in the Tyrol where an otherwise inaccessible pinnacle was lassooed from the summit of an adjacent pinnacle.

Verglas Thin film of ice covering rock: it makes climbing difficult and dangerous and often necessitates rock-climbing in crampons

Zardsky Sack A lightweight bag or small pole-less tent used for bivouacs on small ledges or elsewhere during long and difficult climbs. A bivouac sack

Zawn An old Cornish word adopted by sea-cliff climbers, and describing a sea-filled gully or chimney, a common feature peculiar to sea cliffs

Bibliography

Ahluwalia, Major H. P. S. *Faces of Everest*, Vikas Publishing House, New Delhi 1978 (History of the mountain)

Bell, J. H. B. *A Progress in Mountaineering*, Oliver & Boyd 1950

Benuzzi, Felice *No Picnic on Mt. Kenya*, William Kimber 1952

Blackshaw, Alan *Mountaineering, from Hill Walking to Alpine Climbing*, Penguin 1970 (the definitive how-to-do-it book)

Boardman, Peter *The Shining Mountain*, Hodder & Stoughton 1978 (Changabang's West Wall, alpine-style)

Bonington, Chris *I Chose to Climb*, Gollancz 1966

Bonington, Chris *The Next Horizon*, Gollancz 1973

Bonington, Chris *Everest, the Hard Way*, Hodder & Stoughton 1976

Brown, Joe *The Hard Years*, Gollancz 1967

Clark, Ronald W. *Men, Myths and Mountains*, Weidenfeld & Nicholson 1977

Clark, R. W. and Pyatt, E. *Mountaineering in Britain*, Phoenix House 1957

Cleare, John *Mountains*, Macmillan 1975

Cleare, John and Collomb, Robin *Sea-cliff Climbing in Britain*, Constable 1973

Cleare, John and Smythe, Tony *Rock Climbers in Action in Snowdonia*, Secker & Warburg 1966

Diemberger, Kurt *Summits and Secrets*, Allen & Unwin 1971

Gray, Dennis *Rope Boy*, Gollancz 1970

Harrer, H. *The White Spider*, Hart-Davis 1959, 1976 (Story of the Eiger)

Haston, Dougal *In High Places*, Cassell 1972

Jones, Chris Climbing in North America, American Alpine Club 1976

Longstaff, Tom *This My Voyage*, John Murray 1950

MacInnes, Hamish *Climb to the Lost World*, Hodder & Stoughton 1974

Mason, Kenneth *Abode of Snow*, Rupert Hart-Davis 1955 (Definitive history of mountaineering in the Himalaya)

Messner, Reinhold *The Challenge, Two Men Alone at 8000m*, Kaye & Ward 1977

Noyce, W., and McMorrin, I. *World Atlas of Mountaineering*, Nelson 1969

Patey, Tom *One Man's Mountains*, Gollancz 1971

Pearse, R. O. *Barrier of Spears, Drama of the Drakensberg*, Howard Timmins, South Africa 1973

Ricker, John F *Yuraq Janka, A Guide to the Peruvian Andes (Part I)*, Alpine Club of Canada/American Alpine Club 1977

Rowell, Galen *The Vertical World of Yosemite*, Wilderness Press, Berkley, California 1974

Rowell, Gallen *In the Throne Room of the Mountain Gods*, George Allen & Unwin 1977

Scott, Doug *Big Wall Climbing*, Kaye & Ward 1974

Shipton, Eric *That Untravelled world*, Hodder & Stoughton 1969

Whillans, Don *Portrait of a Mountaineer*, Heinemann 1971

Wilson, Ken *Classic Rocks*, Hart Davis Macgibbon 1978 (80 of the finest climbs in Britain described by distinguished mountaineers)

Wilson, Ken (editor) *The Games Climbers Play*, Diadem Books 1978 (anthology of some of the best mountaineering articles of the last 20 years)

The particularly important thing about the following books is their pictures:

Clar, Ronald W. *The Splendid Hills*, Phoenix House 1948 (Life & photographs of Vittorio Sella, the first great mountain photographer)

Hagen, Toni *Nepal*, Kummerly & Fry 1961

Garris & Hasler *A Land Apart*, Reed 1972 (New Zealand Alps)

Hornbein, Tom *Everest, The West Ridge*, Sierra Club 1966

Moravetz, Bruno *Das Grosse Buch Der Berge* 1978

Rebuffat, Gaston *Mont Blanc to Everest*, Thames & Hudson 1956

Shirakawa, Yoshikazu *The Alps* (text by Max A. Wyss), Thames & Hudson 1973

Shirakawa, Yoshikazu *Himalayas*, Harry N. Abrams 1976 (concise edition 1977)

Photographic Acknowledgements

All photographs are by John Cleare except the following:

H. Adams Carter, 130-1, 133, 134-5; Marian Baka, 154-5; Paul Baner, 196; Mike Banks, 162; Des and Jen Barlett, 138; Fred Beckey, 122, 124, 181; David Bennet, 87, 88; Donald Bennet, 137; Ray Brooks, 127; Hamish Brown, 54, 60, 70, 132b, 181; John R. Brownlie, 143; B. Closs, 56, 57, 58-9; Rob Collister, 176; Ed Cooper, 94, 102-3, 104-5, 107, 110, 114-15, 116, 185; Derek Fordham, 86-7; Alfred Gregory, 132r, 160t; John Grindley, 82tb; George Lehner, 156b; Hamish MacInnes, 128-9; Janusz Onysziewicz, 150, 151, 158; Bob Pettigrew, 177; Galen A. Rowell, 126, 144, 146, 160b, 161b, 179; Doug Scott, 90, 152, 156t, 180, 182-3; Wm Sirs, 195; John Spezia, 141; Peter Steele, 161t; Ian Sykes, 142la; John Tyson, 186, 187; Tom Weir, 61, 148-9; Jurgen Winkler, 172-3, 174.

Index

Figures in italics refer to illustrations

Index

Index

228.